The President of the United States

CONTEMPORARY POLITICAL STUDIES

Series Editor: John Benyon, *Director, Centre for the Study of Public Order, University of Leicester*

A series which provides authoritative, yet concise introductory accounts of key topics in contemporary political studies.

CONTEMPORARY POLITICAL STUDIES

The President of the United States

DAVID MERVIN

HARVESTER WHEATSHEAF

New York   London   Toronto   Sydney   Tokyo   Singapore

First published 1993 by
Harvester Wheatsheaf
Campus 400, Maylands Avenue,
Hemel Hempstead,
Hertfordshire, HP2 7EZ
A division of Simon & Schuster International Group

Typeset in 10/12 pt Times
by Inforum, Rowlands Castle, Hants

Printed and bound in Great Britain by
Biddles Ltd, Guildford and King's Lynn

British Library Cataloguing in Publication Data

A catalogue record for this book is available from the
British Library

ISBN 0–7450–1212–4 (hbk)
ISBN 0–7450–1213–2 (pbk)

---

1 2 3 4 5 97 96 95 94 93

To Jack and Harriet

Contents

Acknowledgements

I am most grateful to John Benyon, the editor of this series and my former student (an essay is still outstanding!), for encouraging me to write this book and for his many helpful suggestions. I am also indebted to Professor Wyn Grant, Chairman of the Department of Politics and International Studies at the University of Warwick, who provided invaluable advice.

There is no one to whom I owe more than Dr Kathleen McConnell Mervin. As always, her careful scrutiny of the manuscript led to many clarifications and improvements and her counsel, support and forbearance were essential to the completion of this project.

David Mervin
University of Warwick

Introduction

The President of the United States sometimes appears to be an all-powerful leader who completely dominates the political system, whereas on other occasions he has the appearance of a helpless giant, burdened with many responsibilities, but prevented from meeting them by a range of formidable restraints. In this book I will attempt to show how this has come about before considering how some notable incumbents have dealt with the challenges of the office.

The first three chapters provide some essential historical background. It will become apparent from Chapter 1 that the dual character of the American presidency is firmly rooted in the past. When drawing up the Constitution the Founding Fathers went out of their way to construct an executive that would be powerful, yet not too powerful. In other words, they wanted to provide a constitutional framework that was sufficiently strong to overcome the difficulties that had been experienced under the Articles of Confederation, but not so strong as to threaten the hard-won liberties of the citizenry.

The devising of a written instrument was only a first step in constitution-making and much would depend on how that instrument was put into effect and how it developed in the future. Chapter 2 accordingly concentrates on a group of four early presidents – George Washington, Thomas Jefferson, Andrew Jackson and Abraham Lincoln – all noted for having had a major influence on the development of the office. No man contributed more to the founding of the United States than Washington. The assumption that he would be the first president had guided those who framed the Constitution and in office his charisma, dignity and restraint coupled with his determination to claim executive primacy in foreign affairs was essential to the successful establishment and the future development of the presidency.

Thomas Jefferson was a strong, assertive President who worked through his party allies in Congress to gain control of the legislative process and set important precedents for the future. However, after Jefferson, the office of president went into something of a decline at the expense of the legislature, a tendency that was halted and reversed by Andrew Jackson's uncompromisingly energetic leadership. In the 1860s the Civil War and the threat to the Union which that conflict involved subjected Abraham Lincoln's presidency and the Constitution itself to the severest of tests. Lincoln's actions in successfully meeting that challenge were to have momentous consequences for the future of the office he held.

After Lincoln, Congress regained a position of ascendancy over the presidency which it broadly held on to for the remainder of the nineteenth century. All this was to change in 1901 when Theodore Roosevelt entered the White House and the modern presidency began to take shape. Many scholars date the beginning of the modern presidency from 1933 and the accession of Franklin Roosevelt whereas others have suggested, and I will argue in Chapter 3, that this is to oversimplify. This is not to deny the importance of 1933 as turning point, but rather to maintain that much of the groundwork built on by Franklin Roosevelt had been laid by his cousin Theodore and Woodrow Wilson.

Few presidents have more boldly asserted the powers of the office than Theodore Roosevelt. He insisted that the president had a special responsibility for the welfare of the people and was obliged to take a lead both in domestic affairs and in the making of foreign policy. The first Roosevelt, however, was a man of action rather than an intellectual whereas Woodrow Wilson, who shared many of the same views, provided a doctrinal justification for the emergence of the modern presidency. In his writings and speeches long before he became President, Wilson stated at length the case for making the presidency the 'vital center of action' in the political system.

None of this detracts from the contribution to the development of the presidency made by Franklin Roosevelt. Wilson had been followed by a succession of 'traditional' presidents, but with FDR the 'modern' presidency became a permanent fixture. The scope of the office was massively enlarged and presidential power was exercised with a skill unmatched before or since. For all that, Roosevelt enjoyed more than his share of good fortune and his conduct of the presidency was not without blemishes. Moreover, his presidential style was not, as some have seemed to argue, appropriate for all seasons and for all incumbents.

My consideration of the presidency in its present form begins in Chapter 4 with a discussion of the many restraints that stand in the way of chief executives meeting their responsibilities, most notably in the making of domestic policy. They must cope with an anti-authority political culture and an awesomely powerful legislature which, in recent decades, has become increasingly individualistic. In addition, the federal administration and the national judiciary often act as obstacles to presidents seeking to exercise their authority.

In Chapter 5 foreign policy is the principal focus of attention. If presidents are often reduced to impotence in domestic affairs their chances of getting their way in foreign policy are rather better, even though here too they are obliged to share power with the legislative branch. Thus the Senate must ratify treaties, Congress possesses the constitutional right to declare war and the legislature can use its power of the purse as a restraint on executive action. Nevertheless, despite these limitations the president in modern times is the dominant partner in the making of foreign policy. The persistence of an 'age of crisis' since World War II and the responsibilities of the president as commander in chief have allowed him to evade congressional attempts to curtail his freedom of action in international affairs.

Chapters 6, 7, and 8 provide mini case studies of three of the more important presidents of the last fifty years. Early evaluations of President Eisenhower's two terms of office in the 1950s were generally highly critical, but since the 1970s his incumbency has been seen in a different light. Revisionists have argued that, far from being a genial nonentity as many had assumed, Eisenhower was a leader of great subtlety and skill who met the mood of the times while, to an unusual degree, consistently retaining the confidence of the American people. Eisenhower revisionism has not only corrected the historical record, it has also made important contributions to our understanding of the presidency. It is now recognized that the Franklin Roosevelt model of presidential power is not the only viable one and that Eisenhower's approach had many strengths, some of which his successors would have done well to emulate.

One who falls into the latter category is Lyndon Johnson, the subject of Chapter 7. Unlike Eisenhower's quiet leadership from behind the scenes Johnson led noisily and aggressively from the front, a style that served him well initially, but eventually helped to bring about his downfall. In the early years of his presidency Johnson drew on his experience and his remarkable understanding of the American political system to put in place a wide range of domestic programmes. He then fatally turned his attention to the situation in South East Asia, with consequences disastrous for him personally and for the office he held.

The presidency of Ronald Reagan is scrutinized in Chapter 8. The discussion begins with a consideration of what criteria should be used in evaluating presidents. After spelling out some possible criteria and setting Reagan's performance against these yardsticks I argue that, leaving aside our personal political preferences and contrary to popular assumptions, Reagan was rather more successful in office than most who have sat in the White House in recent decades. Despite many shortcomings, some policy disasters and his failure to achieve his objectives in full, Reagan was *relatively* successful in moving the United States in the directions he had chosen.

In my concluding chapter I bring the discussion up to date by considering President Bush's incumbency. This enables me to draw out some of the themes touched on in earlier chapters. Furthermore, Bush's experience in office neatly exemplifies the dual character of the presidency referred to at the beginning of this introduction. In early October 1990 the President was humiliatingly rebuffed by Congress as he tried to meet his economic policy responsibilities whereas, five months later, as the war in the Gulf came to its conclusion the President's command of the political system appeared to be complete. However, in 1992, an election year, Bush's foreign policy success dwindled in significance while his alleged failure at home became a principal election issue.

1

Inventing the Presidency

The American presidency was created at the Constitutional Convention that met in Philadelphia in the summer of 1787 and that famous exercise in constitution-making will be the centrepiece of the analysis in this chapter. Before coming to those events, however, it is necessary to consider briefly the background to the Convention and the circumstances that led to its being called. The emergence of the former British colonies as a separate nation dates from 1776 with the signing of the Declaration of Independence. Five years later, as the war with Britain drew to its conclusion, the Articles of Confederation, the 'first' Constitution of the United States, came into effect.

The Articles of Confederation

The Articles provided for a 'perpetual union' and established a 'league of friendship' among the former colonies, now transformed into states. Within this union the states were to retain their 'sovereignty, freedom and independence' and the national government was to have only limited powers. The instrument of national government, according to the Articles, was to be Congress, a unicameral assembly standing alone with no provision made for separate executive or judicial branches. While representation in Congress was to be, to some extent, proportional, each state was to have one vote. All important legislation would require the assent of at least nine of the thirteen states and any amendment to the Articles would need confirmation by the legislatures of all the states.

Certain powers were conferred on Congress under the Articles including authority to direct the nation's armed forces; to regulate 'the trade and managing all affairs with the Indians'; to send and receive ambassadors; to enter into treaties; to declare peace and war and to establish a 'Committee of the States', consisting of one delegate from each state, to direct the affairs of the union when Congress was not sitting.

Crucially, Congress was not granted power of direct rule over the citizenry; the national assembly was to rule Americans only indirectly through the states. Thus the central government could not impose taxes directly on the people and although there was to be a common treasury for general purposes, financed by the states, Congress had no means of compelling the states to make their statutory contributions. Similarly, Congress, while authorized to ask the states to raise and equip armed forces was incapable of enforcing such demands. In short, the Articles provided for a weak limited union, with central institutions not adequate to the needs of a viable, nation state.

Loosely binding arrangements had been sufficient during the war when the rigours of a common struggle held the states together, but with the cessation of hostilities the principal incentive for interstate cooperation was removed. In these new circumstances Congress was unable to address effectively the severe problems of both domestic and foreign policy that the new nation faced. For instance, to fight the war the government had taken out massive loans at home and abroad, but was now unable to obtain from the states the revenue needed to repay these public debts.

American political and social elites in the 1780s were greatly alarmed by condition of the country. They were concerned that the government of the United States as it was then constituted was not only incapable of honouring its debts, it was also unable to offer adequate protection to the rights of property; nor could it establish the conditions necessary for economic development or provide for the defence of the country against the depredations of foreign powers. One leading politician, James Madison, writing to the Governor of Virginia, said, 'Our situation is becoming every day more critical. No money comes into the federal treasury, no respect is paid to the federal authority; and people of reflection unanimously agree that the existing confederacy is tottering to its foundation.'[1]

In the *Federalist Number 15*, Alexander Hamilton wrote of the shameful inability of the United States in the 1780s to meet its obligations and defend its interests,

> We may indeed with propriety be said to have reached almost the last stage of national humiliation. There is scarcely anything that can wound the pride or degrade the character of an independent nation which we do not experience . . . Do we owe debts to foreigners and to our own citizens contracted in a time of imminent peril for the preservation of our political existence? Have we valuable territories and important posts in the possession of a foreign power [Britain] which, by express stipulations, ought long since to have been surrendered? These are still retained to the prejudice of our interests, not less than of our rights. Are we in a condition to resent or repel the aggression? We have neither troops, nor treasury, nor government.[2]

A concern for property was clearly an important part of the motivation of many political leaders at the time. As they saw it, the weakness of the central government *vis-à-vis* the states was detrimental to the rights of property owners for state governments were now often dominated by their legislatures, bodies which harboured radical democrats and were excessively influenced by debtor farmers and other elements hostile to the interests of those who owned property.

The worst fears of those concerned with the sanctity of property rights were aroused by the Shays Rebellion of 1786–7, an armed revolt by farmers in western Massachusetts who were seeking relief from debts and mortgage foreclosures. Shays, a former revolutionary war officer, now a destitute farmer, led a band of 1,200 who physically prevented judges from conducting foreclosure hearings. The rebellion was swiftly put down, but the almost hysterical reaction to it among the American elite gave powerful impetus to the demands of those who sought constitutional change.

Shortly after the uprising, Congress agreed to call a national constitutional convention, 'for the sole and express purpose of revising the Articles of Confederation. . . [in order to] render the federal constitution adequate to the exigencies of government and the preservation of the Union'.[3]

Reluctantly, George Washington agreed to attend and explained the situation of crisis that had arisen in a letter to Thomas Jefferson,

> That something is necessary, none will deny; for the situation of the general government, if it can be called a government, is shaken to its

foundation, and liable to be overturned at every blast. In a word it is at an end; and, unless a remedy is soon applied, anarchy and confusion will inevitably ensue.[4]

Even if, as is often suggested, Washington and others were being unduly alarmist, there is litle doubt that in the late 1780s the fledgling United States was at a turning point. To say the least, the Articles of Confederation had proved inadequate and without some strengthening of the institutions of national government economic development would have been held back, the country's chronic vulnerability to imperialist powers would have continued and dismemberment, in the long term, would have been a real possibility. At stake were not only the rights of property owners, but also the preservation of a hard-won freedom and the continuance of the United States itself.

The Constitutional Convention

The fifty-five delegates who gathered in Philadelphia in the summer of 1787 included some of the great names in American history. The chairman of the proceedings was George Washington, the hero of the Revolution and destined to be the first president of the United States. The internationally renowned, if aged, Benjamin Franklin was included in the Pennsylvania delegation. Also present was James Madison, a future president, and one of the authors of *The Federalist Papers*. Another of the authors, Alexander Hamilton, then aged only 32, was also a member. In the Convention itself Hamilton was not one of the most influential delegates, but within a short while he would be a major figure, first in the struggle for ratification and then as Secretary of the Treasury in Washington's administration. James Wilson and Gouverneur Morris, both of Pennsylvania, were especially influential and important members. Other notable participants included Edmund Randolph and George Mason, both from Virginia, Elbridge Gerry of Massachusetts, Roger Sherman of Connecticut and Luther Martin of Maryland. Prominent absentees included Patrick Henry, Thomas Jefferson and John Adams.

The average age of the delegates was 43 and a number were in their thirties. Thirty-one were college graduates and thirty were lawyers, while 'also present were thirteen commercial or business men, ten planters, several high ranking army officers and three physicians.'[5] In other words, those who drew up the US Constitution were, not surprisingly, members of the elite; a few were plutocrats whereas the remainder, almost to a man, were either substantial farmers, businessmen or members of the professional classes. It was also hardly surprising that at the Convention such men proved to be conservative in their thinking, sceptical of the merits of democracy in its purer forms and particularly anxious to provide for the protection of the rights of property.

It does not follow, as some have alleged, that the Founding Fathers were counter-revolutionaries, bent on subverting the democratic ideals expressed in the Declaration of Independence.[6] In general, the Fathers were conservatives, but not reactionaries. The records of the debates in the Convention show conclusively that virtually all delegates were committed to government by the people in some form. Thus James Madison, conceivably the most influential delegate present, although much concerned with the dangers of democratic excess insisted that at least one branch of the national legislature should be popularly elected. He also made it clear that, ideally, he would prefer the president to be elected by the people at large.

James Wilson, another notably influential delegate, went even further in urging that both branches of the legislature and the executive should be directly elected by the people. Even Alexander Hamilton, commonly regarded as one of the most conservative of delegates, was to be found arguing that it was 'essential to the democratic rights of the people, that [the first branch of government] be directly elected by the people' Indeed, Hamilton favoured an assembly elected by all free male citizens and inhabitants – a remarkably radical arrangement given that it did not include a property qualification and conceded the suffrage even to those who were not yet citizens.[7] In Britain, in the late eighteenth century, such sentiments would have been regarded as deeply subversive.

Latter-day critics of the Convention have made much of apparently antidemocratic comments attributed to Roger Sherman of Connecticut and Elbridge Gerry of Massachusetts. In discussing how the first branch of the legislature should be elected Sherman appeared to oppose popular elections, saying that the people 'should have as little to do as may be about the Government. They want information and are constantly liable to be misled.' Three weeks later, however, Sherman spoke like a radical democrat extolling the virtues of annual elections and insisting that legislators should stay close to their constituents:

> Mr Sherman preferred annual elections, but would be content with biennnial. He thought the representatives ought to return home and mix with the people. By remaining at the seat of Govt. they would acquire the habits of the place which might differ from those of their Constituents.[8]

Meanwhile Gerry, on 31 May 1787 said, 'The evils we experience flow from the excess of democracy. The people do not want virtue; but are the dupes of pretended patriots.' Yet a week later the same delegate made it clear that he nevertheless favoured one popularly elected legislative branch with the other selected on some other basis:

> [Gerry] was not disposed to run into extremes. He was as much principled as ever agst. aristocracy and monarchy. It was necessary on the one hand that the people should appoint one branch of the Govt. in order to inspire them with the necessary confidence. But he wished the election on the other to be so modified as to secure more effectually a just preference of merit.[9]

Like most of their colleagues, Sherman and Gerry were, in American terms, moderate conservatives.[10] They accepted the need for basing government on the consent of the governed, but they were realistic enough to recognize the dangers of democratic excess. Their position was well represented by George Mason when he said, 'I am for preserving inviolably the democratic branch – True, we have found inconviencies from pure democracies; but if we mean to preserve peace and real freedom, they must necessarily become a component part of a national government.'[11]

Such men rejected Thomas Paine's idealistic notions of government by unicameral, annually elected, popular assemblies checked only by a bill of rights. Instead they adopted a sensible middle position:

> On certain fundamentals [the Founding Fathers] generally agreed; that government derived its just powers from the consent of the people, but that society must be protected from the tyranny of the majority; that the people at large must have a voice in their govern-

ment, but that checks and balances must be provided to keep any one group from dominating power; that a stronger central authority was essential, but that all power was subject to abuse.[12]

Fortunately for the future of the United States, the delegates to the Convention did not share the bizarre view expressed later by one of their most famous critics, J. Allen Smith, who insisted that only two forms of government were possible: that of the many or the few,

> There is, in fact, no middle ground. We must either recognize the many as supreme, with no checks upon their authority except such as are implied in their own intelligence, sense of justice and fair play, or we must accept the view that the ultimate authority is in the hands of the few.[13]

It was precisely the middle ground that the Founding Fathers were trying to reach. They understood that while democracy in its purer forms might be possible in city states or town meetings, such arrangements were not realistic in a nation spanning an enormous territory and encompassing a wide variety of interests. This did not mean that the principle of self government had to be abandoned; rather, it was necessary to strike a new and more appropriate balance between representation and effective government, between the rights of individuals and the needs of the community at large.

In short, the main purpose of the Philadelphia Convention in 1787 was the construction of a new constitutional balance, one that would allow for central institutions which were sufficiently strong for the good government of the nation and yet not so strong as to threaten the hard-won liberties of American citizens.

The Virginia and New Jersey plans

The two plans presented initially to the Convention – the Virginia plan and the New Jersey plan – represented two schools of thought regarding the form of the new constitutional balance. The Virgina plan, which set the terms of the debate, provided for a potentially all-powerful national government. There would have been a bicameral national legislature, and equality of state representation in Congress as existed under the Articles would have been abandoned completely. Members of the first branch of the legislature would be elected by the people, whereas the second branch would be elected by the first. The national legislature would have the enormously important power to veto state laws and would also choose both the national judiciary and a national executive.

Not surprisingly, many delegates were much alarmed by the implications of the Virginia plan and the New Jersey plan was presented as an alternative. Rather than jettisoning the Articles and devising a new constitution, as the Virginia plan had effectively done, it was proposed that the Convention adhere to its original terms of reference requiring that the Articles be only 'revised, corrected and enlarged'. The existing unicameral legislature with one vote per state was to be preserved, but with its powers moderately enhanced. It would be allowed to raise revenue independently through import duties, stamp taxes and postage, to regulate trade between the states and to collect taxes directly from the people when states failed to provide agreed financial requisitions. Under this plan acts of Congress and treaties would become the 'supreme law of the respective states' and there would be a plural national executive elected by the legislature.

If either one or the other had been implemented in full it is evident that the subsequent history of the United States would have been profoundly different. Neither the separation of powers nor federalism would have survived under the Virignia plan; the judiciary, the executive and the legislature would have been effectively welded into one and the states would have become subservient to a forbiddingly powerful national government. Under the New Jersey scheme the states would have remained relatively much stronger *vis-à-vis* the centre and the executive branch would not have assumed a position of predominance in the national government.

The advocates of both plans were agreed on the need to strengthen the national government at the centre, yet they disagreed substantially on the extent of that strengthening. A national executive in some form was deemed essential, but how it should be constructed, the powers that should be assigned to it and the checks that should be placed upon it were to be the subject of intense debate.

The Presidency emerges

The prescription for a national chief executive that eventually emerged after weeks of deliberation in Philadelphia was, like the

Constitution itself, no one delegate's ideal arrangement. It was an office constructed out of a series of compromises, engineered by realists who did not lack strong convictions, but who saw the need for negotiation and were willing to settle for the best that could be achieved in the circumstances. Nevertheless, it was those who laid great stress on the need for a genuinely strong 'well mounted' national government with a potentially formidable executive at its core who came the closest to realizing their ambitions.[14]

The shape of the American presidency was determined in a series of debates that addressed questions such as: Should there be a single or plural executive? How should the executive be selected? How long should the executive's term be and would he be eligible for reappointment? How would he be removed in the case of misconduct? What sort of veto on legislative acts was the president to possess? What specific powers were to be allocated to the chief executive?

A single or plural executive?

Initially, some delegates were attracted to the idea of a plural executive, but the majority came to accept, relatively quickly, the view expressed by James Wilson of Pennsylvania that the energy and responsibility required at the centre of the national government was attainable only with a single executive. On the other hand, Edmund Randolph of Virginia found the prospect of 'unity in the Executive magistracy', extremely alarming regarding it as 'the foetus of monarchy'. In pressing his point Randolph insisted that the people would be most unhappy with an office bearing any resemblance to a monarchy. Another member of the Virginia delegation, George Mason, expressed similar views; he had no doubts as to the need for a powerful executive, but feared that if strong executive powers were placed in the hands of one man the government would tend to degenerate into monarchy, an arrangement 'so contrary to the genius of the people that they will reject even the appearance of it'.[15] In responding to these fears Wilson claimed that rather than being a 'foetus of monarchy', unity in the executive would be a safeguard against tyranny. He saw no evidence that public opinion was opposed to a single executive and argued that while the thirteen states agreed on little else they all had governments headed by a single executive. A plural executive, moreover, was a recipe for disaster that would lead to animosity and division at the heart of the national government.[16]

When the Convention voted without dissent on 17 July in favour of a resolution 'that the Natl. Executive consist of a single person' Wilson had clearly won the argument, but the anxieties that had been expressed had not disappeared.[17] They were to be reflected in the many checks that were placed on the executive and were to re-surface in the struggles over ratification.

The method of selection

Having disposed of the question of whether there would be single or a plural executive the Convention found it infinitely more difficult to agree on how the executive would be selected; indeed, according to Wilson the question was 'the most difficult of all on which we have had to decide.' For some weeks it appeared that the matter had been settled with the responsibility for choosing the executive placed with the national legislature. This was part of both the Virginia and the New Jersey plans and the weight of opinion behind the idea was reflected in a number of votes in Philadelphia, including unanimous approval on 17 July.[18]

But opposition to this arrangement was repeatedly voiced by some of the most influential delegates in the Convention: James Wilson, James Madison and Gouverneur Morris who argued for a national executive elected by the people at large. As noted above, Wilson appeared to have an unlimited faith in the ability of the people to choose their own political leaders and with regard to the national executive, 'in theory he was for an election by the people; Experience, particularly in N.York and Massts, shewed that an elec-tion of the first magistrate by the people at large, was both a conven-ient & successful mode.' In arriving at the same conclusion, James Madison said that he regarded the separation of powers as a 'funda-mental principle of free Govt.' and this would be violated by an ar-rangement that made the appointment of the executive dependent on the legislature. Election by the legislative branch would also lead to intrigue and Madison 'was disposed for these reasons to refer the appointment to some other Source. The people at large was in his opinion the fittest in itself.'[19]

More surprisingly perhaps, Morris, commonly regarded as an aristocrat and a conservative, spoke vigorously in support of popular election of the national executive. As he saw it, a president, elected by and open to impeachment by the legislature, would be a 'mere creature' of that body and any such election would be 'the work of intrigue, of cabal, and of faction: it will be like the election of a pope by a conclave of cardinals'. Like Madison, Morris was deeply sceptical of legislatures in general and this partly explains his reluctance to entrust the responsibility for choosing a president to the national legislature. He also entertained serious reservations about giving votes to those without property, but, ultimately, Morris proved to be another moderate who believed that the people at large should choose their own national executive – the electorate for him being preferably restricted to freeholders, which he optimistically estimated as 90 per cent of the population.[20]

Wilson, Madison and Morris were hardly radicals – in fact they were leaders of the nationalist, or federalist, group in the Convention who were anxious to see the states and their allegedly pernicious legislatures put in their place. They sought to make the central government sufficiently strong to meet its responsibilities and believed that the best way to achieve this was to provide for a popularly elected national executive. However, the idea of turning the United States into one vast national constituency for the purpose of electing a president was not acceptable to other prominent delegates such as Mason, Charles Pinckney, Gerry and Sherman.

The responses of this latter group cannot be reasonably dismissed as no more than reactionary noises. George Mason, for instance, made caustic reference to election of a national executive by the people as being comparable to a 'trial of colours to a blind man'. But Mason was by no means antidemocratic as such. He had argued strongly for popular election of the first branch of the legislature and refused to sign the Constitution at the end in part because it did not include a bill of rights. However, when confronted with the notion of a popularly elected national executive Mason sensibly argued that the 'extent' of the country made it impossible for the people to assess adequately the character and qualifications of contending candidates.[21] Offensive though such reservations may be to later generations of radical democrats, Mason was surely right to question whether the people could properly evaluate national candidates, given the vast distances involved and the primitive state of communications in the late eighteenth century.

Pinckney and Gerry also objected to a popular election of the national executive because the people *en masse* were liable to manipulation and exploitation by unscrupulous elements. Pinckney worried about the people being 'led by a few active and designing men'. While Gerry used almost identical language when he said, 'The people are uninformed and will be misled by a few designing men.' A week later Gerry provided an example of who these 'designing men' might be: 'a popular election', he said,

> 'is radically vicious. The ignorance of the people would put it in the power of some one set of men dispersed through the Union & acting in Concert to delude them into any appointment. He observed that such a Society of men existed in the Order of the Cincinatti. They were respectable, United and influencial [*sic*]. They will in fact elect the chief Magistrate in every instance, if the election be referred to the people.'[22]

Those opposed to a national, popular election also desired to maintain the integrity of the states and to prevent the smaller states from being overwhelmed by their larger counterparts. Hugh Williamson of North Carolina noted that 'The principal objection agst. an election by the people seemed to be, the disadvantage under which it would place the smaller States.' Meanwhile Sherman said that if the national executive was elected by the people they, 'would generally vote for some man in their own State and the largest State will have the best chance for the appointment'. Similarly, Oliver Ellsworth said, 'The Citizens of the largest States would invariably prefer the Candidate within the State; and the largest States wd. invariably have the man.' Finally, Charles Pinckney pointed out that 'The most populous States by combining in favor of the same individual will be able to carry their points.'[23]

As the Convention moved towards its conclusion various unresolved matters including the method of choosing the executive were referred to a committee on 'remaining matters'. This committee abandoned appointment of the national executive by the legislature, but declined to go the whole way in the other direction by making the choice dependent on election by the people at large.

Instead the committee picked up the compromise suggestion floated earlier by some delegates that the executive be selected by electors appointed by the states:

Each State shall appoint in such a manner as its Legislature may direct, a number of electors equal to the whole number of Senators and members of the House of Representatives to which the State may be entitled in the Legislature. The Electors shall meet in their respective States, and vote by ballot for two persons. . . . The Person having the greatest number of votes shall be the President, if such a number be a majority of that of the electors.[24]

The wording was slightly amended before incorporation in the Constitution and changed further by Amendment XII in 1804.[25]

It is reasonable to conclude that after much agonizing the Founding Fathers finally arrived at a sensible solution in this matter of choosing a national executive. In the long term, appointment of the executive by the legislature would have been wholly destructive of the separation of powers principle. Likewise, to turn the country into one massive national constituency for the purpose of presidential elections would have been ultimately fatal to the idea of federalism. It was infinitely more wise for the constitution-makers to adopt a middle position, an arrangement that allowed, in the long run, for both the people and the states to be represented in the process for choosing a president.

Length of tenure

Questions concerning the length of the executive's term of office were also resolved by compromise after long negotiation. For some time the agreed policy of the Convention was a single executive, elected by the legislature for a seven-year term and not eligible for re-election. As we have seen, the nationalists were bent on the establishment of a strong executive. 'Energy' in the executive was, according to Gouverneur Morris, indispensable to the success of a large, self-governing republic. Removing the dependency on election by the legislature was important to that end, but Morris, like Hamilton, favoured the permanent appointment of an executive, subject to 'good behavior'. This proposal horrified the likes of George Mason who, once again, raised the spectre of a revived monarchy; he 'considered an Executive during good behavior as a softer name only for an Executive for life. And that the next step would be an easy step to hereditary Monarchy.'[26]

Madison was no less opposed to monarchy but feared it might enter by the back door if the new executive was insufficiently strong in relation to the legislature:

Experience had proved a tendency in our governments to throw all power into the legislative vortex. The Executives of the States are in general little more than Cyphers: the legislatures omnipotent. If no effective check be devised for restraining the instability & encroachments of the latter, a revolution of some kind or other would be inevitable.[27]

Even though he certainly did not favour election of a president for life, Madison wanted to ensure that a proper balance was struck; otherwise revolution would follow and republican government would founder.

Election of a president for life had little chance of general acceptance given the anti-monarchical sentiments of many delegates, nevertheless the nationalists regained the initiative when provision was made for an executive appointed for a four-year term with no limits on re-election. This they considered to be a vast improvement on an executive elected by the legislature for a seven-year term and not eligible for re-election.

Removal in the case of misconduct – impeachment

The division at Philadelphia between nationalists, determined to institute a strong, 'high toned' central government, and those unwilling to see the integrity of the states undermined, reappeared in the discussions about the arrangements for impeaching and convicting the national executive. The Virginia plan included provision for the removal of a national executive found guilty of 'malpractice or neglect of duty', but had not specified a procedure. The New Jersey alternative, on the other hand, included a procedure which, typically, called for the direct involvement of the states in the process. The national executive would be removable following impeachment and conviction, 'by Congress on Application of a Majority of the executives of the several States'.[28]

Not surprisingly, this was not acceptable to ardent nationalists such as Gouverneur Morris, Charles Pinckney and Rufus King of Massachusetts who spoke against including any mechanism for impeaching the national executive. As always, Morris, keen to ensure that the executive was a sufficient check on the legislature, argued that such a restraint would be unacceptably imperilled by the threat of impeachment. The latter, according to Morris, 'will hold [the national executive] in such dependence that he will be no

check on the Legislature, will not be a firm guardian of the people
and of the public interest'.[29]

Rufus King indicated that he would have preferred a national
executive appointed subject to 'good behavior', but as this was not
to be there was no case for an impeachment procedure; in any
case, 'under no circumstances ought he to be impeachable by the
Legislature. This would be destructive of his independence and of
the principles of the Constitution. He relied on the vigor of the
Executive as a great security for the public liberties.'[30] But the
nationalist camp was divided on the issue of impeachment, with
Wilson, Franklin and Madison agreeing that some such procedure
was necessary. The case for was stated with typical eloquence by
Madison, who

> thought it indispensable that some provision should be made for
> defending the Community agst. the incapacity, negligence or perfidy
> of the chief Magistrate. The limitation of his period of service, was
> not a sufficient security. He might lose his capacity after his appoint-
> ment. He might pervert his administration into a scheme of pecula-
> tion or oppression. He might betray his trust to foreign powers.'[31]

In the face of this opposition, Morris conceded that he had been
influenced by the debate and accepted the need for impeachment
in some circumstances. This may be seen to have paved the way for
yet another compromise. According to the procedure finally
agreed, the states would not particpate directly in the impeachment process as the proponents of the New Jersey plan had hoped.
On the other hand, the need for a two-thirds majority in the Senate
to convict provided a degree of insurance against irresponsible use
of the machinery and undue dependence by the executive on the
legislature.

The veto

The question of the power of the executive was also central to
discussions on the veto. The nationalist manifesto – the Virginia
plan – had included an arrangement whereby the executive in
conjunction with some members of the judiciary would constitute a
council of revision able to veto bills passed by the national legislature. The alternative New Jersey plan, sponsored mostly by delegates from the smaller states, included no such provision.

Enthusiastic nationalists like James Wilson and Alexander Hamilton wanted to equip the president with an absolute, unqualified negative, or, failing that, Wilson suggested a veto exercised jointly by the executive and the judiciary. Some delegates were predictably appalled by these suggestions. Sherman, for example,

> was agst. enabling any one man to stop the will of the whole. No one man could be found so far above all the rest in wisdom. He thought we ought to avail ourselves of his wisdom in revising the laws, but not permit him to overrule the decided and cool opinions of the legislature.

Similarly, Gunning Bedford from Delaware was opposed to any check at all on the legislature beyond that provided by bicameralism: 'The Representatives of the People were the best judges of what was for their interest, and ought to be under no external controul whatever. The two branches would produce a sufficient controul [sic] within the Legislature itself.'[32]

It was not only delegates from small states like Connecticut and Delaware who were troubled by the idea of an unlimited executive veto. The moderate Benjamin Franklin drew on the experience of his own state in noting that in Pennsylvania an absolute veto in the hands of the governor had weighted the scales of power too heavily in favour of the executive. The veto had been deployed to extort funds from the legislature and had created a situation where 'No good law whatever could be passed without a private bargain with [the governor]. . . . This was a mischievous sort of check.' In supporting Franklin, George Mason inveighed against making the executive altogether too powerful and warned again of the danger of degenerating into some form of monarchy. 'We are Mr Chairman going very far in this business. We are not indeed constituting a British Government, but a more dangerous monarchy, an elective one.'[33]

The proposal for an absolute, unqualified veto was quickly and overwhelmingly defeated and eventually the idea of including a judicial element in the arrangements was also discarded. At an early stage Elbridge Gerry had offered a resolution that the Convention had accepted providing for an executive veto subject to being overturned by a two-thirds majority vote in both houses of Congress. Later, nationalists like Madison, Wilson, Morris and

Washington, worried by the alleged iniquities of legislatures, fought a rearguard action to increase the two-thirds majorities to three-quarters, a manoeuvre that succeeded for a while, but in the end the constitution-makers reverted to two-thirds majorities.

Once again the Convention had gone down the middle between two extreme positions, rejecting both no veto at all and an unqualified executive negative on legislation. As before, differences of emphasis and interest were resolved by compromise. Nevertheless, the advocates of a strong executive had had the better of the argument; by agreeing to a veto, not easily overturned, the Founding Fathers had included in the president's armoury a potentially formidable weapon and placed a major check on the power of the legislature.

To summarize this discussion of the emergence of the presidency so far: first, the Convention had agreed that there should be a single rather than a plural executive; second, competing proposals for direct popular election of the president, or for allowing the legislature to make the choice, had been rejected in favour of a system of indirect election that included a degree of both popular and state involvement in the process; third, it had been agreed that the president would serve a four-year term and would be permitted to seek re-election; fourth, he would be subject to impeachment; fifth, he would be armed with a veto, not an absolute unlimited veto, but one subject to reversal by two-thirds majorities in the legislature.

Having outlined the structure of the new office the Founding Fathers now moved to add substance to it by allocating specific powers to the executive.

Executive powers

The constitution-makers in Philadelphia in 1787 produced a balanced form of government, one which avoided the extremes of autocratic tyranny on the one hand and democratic impotence on the other. Although generally a militant nationalist, Gouverneur Morris neatly expressed the general intention of the Convention in fashioning an executive when he said 'It is [the] most difficult of all rightly to balance the Executive. Make him too weak: the Legislature will usurp his powers. Make him too strong: he will usurp on the Legislature.'[34] To make the executive sufficiently strong, it was necessary to endow the president's office with specific powers, powers that would belong to him as of constitutional right. On the other hand, it was necessary to guard against executive tyranny. There would therefore be no handing out of blank cheques and almost all of the president's powers would be shared with Congress. The principal powers accorded the president by the Constitutional Convention were: (1) the executive power; (2) the capacity to influence the judiciary; (3) a share in the legislative power; (4) the power to conduct foreign policy.

The executive power

The Convention had little difficulty in agreeing the wording of the first sentence of Article II of the Constitution, 'The executive Power shall be vested in a President of the United States of America.' Similarly, the various draft constitutions put forward at Philadelphia – the Virginia plan, the New Jersey plan, the Pinckney plan and the Hamilton plan – all included provisions foreshadowing the wording that was to appear in Article II, Section 3, requiring the president to 'take Care that the Laws be faithfully executed'. However, 'executive power' was never precisely defined and in an age when legislation was a rarity the constitution-makers could not have foreseen the contemporary situation when the passing of laws that the president is responsible for executing has become an everyday occurrence.

At a late stage, and with only brief discussion, it was agreed that presidential nominations to federal offices would be subject to Senate approval. This decision, with major consequences for the future, was taken notwithstanding the objections of Charles Pinckney and James Wilson who took the Hamiltonian view that federal appointments should be the sole prerogative of the executive. Wilson, for instance,

> objected to the mode of appointing, as blending a branch of the Legislature with the Executive. Good laws are of no effect without a good Executive; and there can be no good Executive without a responsible appointment of officers to execute. Responsibility is in a manner destroyed by such an agency of the Senate.[35]

Some modern students of administration would sympathize with Wilson's misgivings, for it is evident that divided responsibility in appointments, in conjunction with congressional control of the purse strings, has obstructed the development of a properly accountable federal administration.

Some of Wilson's colleagues, however, were not concerned with administrative niceties: they wished to limit the power of the executive by involving the legislature in the appointment process. This was another compromise between nationalists wishing to maximize executive power and those determined to check that power. Nevertheless, by vesting the executive power in the president, giving him responsibility for executing the laws and for appointing federal officials the Founding Fathers prepared the ground for the eventual appearance of a vast federal bureaucracy with the president, theoretically at least, at its head as chief executive.

Influencing the judiciary

The constitutional right of presidents to appoint federal judges subject to confirmation by the Senate has proved to be a weapon of great consequence in the right hands. As the Reagan administration demonstrated, the careful selection of appointees to the Supreme Court and to the lower levels of the federal judiciary allows the president to influence judicial action, and thereby public policy, not only while he is in the White House, but long after he has left office.[36]

In a strange reversal of what might have been expected, the Virginia plan allowed for the appointment of federal judges by the national legislature while the New Jersey plan gave that responsibility to the executive. When discussions on this matter got underway the nationalist, or Federalist, majority appeared divided. Predictably, Wilson was adamantly opposed to the appointment of judges being left to the legislature, but John Rutledge of South Carolina was no less opposed to leaving it to the executive, '[We cannot] grant so great a power to any single person. The people will think we are leaning too much towards Monarchy.' On the other hand, Madison, while opposed to allowing the legislature as a whole to appoint judges, was, at first, inclined to give this power to the Senate alone. This idea gained ground for a while and was agreed to at one stage without a dissenting vote.[37]

During these early discussions Hamilton, although contributing little to the debate, did suggest that judges should be appointed by the executive subject to confirmation by the Senate. When the matter was taken up again a month later, Nathaniel Gorham of Massachusetts revived Hamilton's suggestion, saying that this had been the procedure followed by his state for the past 140 years.[38]

This plan was not attractive to delegates from the small states and others nervous about making the president too powerful. Thus Luther Martin and Roger Sherman, supported by Mason, Randolph and Bedford, insisted that judicial appointments be left with the Senate. When a vote was taken on 18 July the Convention appeared to be deadlocked, with four states voting in favour of Gorham's position and four voting against.[39] A few days later Madison joined the ranks of those committed to appointment by the executive subject to approval by the Senate; in arguing the case for this arrangement, Madison noted that this was a compromise similar to others that had been agreed.[40] He argued that 'The principle of compromise which had prevailed in other instances required in this that their [sic] shd. be a concurrence of two authorities, in one of which the people, in the other the states, should be represented.'[41] At this point the Hamilton/Gorham/Madison view did not prevail, but it did so when the committee on 'remaining matters' attended to the question shortly before the Convention ended. This committee duly recommended what appears in the Constitution – the appointment of federal judges by the national executive, subject to the advice and consent of the Senate. Quietly, in other words, and almost as an afterthought, the Convention took a decision that would eventually have momentous consequences.

A share in the legislative power

The Founding Fathers did not anticipate that the president would eventually become the chief legislator, one of the most important roles of all for a modern president. Indeed, there was hardly any discussion at all of the legislative function, and what discussion did take place appeared to place the responsibility for formulating and passing bills exclusively in the hands of Congress, with the executive role confined to the veto.

Two parts of the Constitution that subsequently contributed much to the expansion of the president's legislative power were included without discussion by the Convention at large. Neither

the Virginia plan nor its New Jersey counterpart made any reference to the executive's making 'state of the Union' addresses to
Congress, nor did they envisage him recommending measures to
the national legislature. The plan presented by Charles Pinckney,
however, did include such proposals – '[The President] shall from
time to [time] give information to the Legislature of the state of
the Union & recommend to their consideration the measures he
may think necessary.'[42]

The Pinckney plan was considered by the Committee of Detail
established at the end of July 1787 to formulate a constitution
based on the resolutions so far agreed by the Convention. In fact,
the report of this committee included wording extremely close to
Pinckney's: '[The President] shall, from time to time, give information to the Legislature, of the state of the Union: he may recommend to their consideration such measures as he shall judge
necessary, and expedient.'[43] With the exception of one or two
miniscule changes this is the wording finally included in the
Constitution.

Pinckney was himself a nationalist and the Committee of Detail
was made up almost exclusively of like-minded men – Wilson,
Rutledge, Nathaniel Gorham of Massachusetts and Randolph. The
only representative of the smaller states on the Committee was
Ellsworth of Connecticut. By slipping into the Constitution the
sense of Pinckney's phraseology, the members of this committee
contributed more than they ever realized to the nationalist cause.
In the long run, these apparently innocuous words contributed
greatly to the emergence of the modern presidency, and provided
constitutional justification for the president's becoming chief
legislator.

The power to conduct foreign policy

It has generally been agreed that while Congress has a role to play,
the president is principally responsible for the conduct of American foreign policy.[44] Legalistically, there are two parts of the Constitution that do most to justify that pre-eminence: the commander
in chief clause and the clause concerned with treaty-making.

In the commander in chief clause, the hand of Charles Pinckney
is once again to be seen and, as with the legislative power, another
step with profoundly significant long-term consequences was taken

with little discussion in the Convention at large. There was no explicit mention of these matters in the Virginia plan although the New Jersey alternative, assuming a plural executive, gave that branch the right, 'to direct all military operations', with the caveat that none of those making up the executive should personally command troops. Alexander Hamilton, in his 'sketch' of a constitution, also included among the national executive's responsibilities 'the direction of war when authorized or begun'. The first appearance of the words 'commander in chief', however, occur in the Pinckney plan considered by the Committee of Detail.[45] The wording was included by the committee in its report and it eventually passed into the Constitution.

At least since the administration of Abraham Lincoln the president's role as commander in chief has been interpreted as permitting him to commit the United States to military action in defence of the 'public safety' or, in modern terminology, the national security, without waiting for a declaration of war by Congress.[46] 'As commander in chief the president exercises a vast array of "war powers" . . . [allowing him to] deploy American forces anywhere in the world and, as has happened many times in American history, order them into action against a foreign foe without a declaration of war by Congress.'[47] It is, of course, the case that members of Congress, citing the legislature's right to declare war, have often fulminated against such interpretations and the actions that have followed but, generally, to little effect.

If the war power is, in constitutional terms, divided between the president and Congress with the former paramount, much the same can be said of the procedures for agreeing treaties with foreign powers. With the exception of Hamilton's 'sketch' the various draft plans before the Covention in its early stages made no reference to treaties. Hamilton, however, gave to the executive the power of making treaties subject to the 'advice and approbation' of the Senate. This proposal was not picked up by the Committee of Detail who in their report on 6 August proposed that 'The Senate of the United States shall have power to make treaties.'[48]

The nationalists did not allow the matter to rest there and when the question was returned to on 23 August Madison 'observed that the Senate represented the States alone, and that for this as well as other obvious reasons it was proper that the President should be an agent in Treaties.' Gouverneur Morris went even further in suggesting that he was not convinced that treaties should be referred to the Senate at all.[49]

When the question of treaties was considered by the committee on 'remaining matters' it returned to Hamilton's proposal in suggesting that 'The President by and with the advice and Consent of the Senate, shall have the power to make treaties.' Late attempts were made to add the House to the advice and consent procedure and to leave with the Senate the sole right to make peace treaties, but these interesting suggestions were fended off.

Elbridge Gerry and John Rutledge did succeed in tacking on the requirement that Senate consent to treaties would need two-thirds majorities. This last provision was an essential part of yet another compromise reconciling different interests in the Convention. No doubt the nationalists were pleased that the principal responsibility for treaties would lie with the president, whereas others could draw consolation from the fact that the Senate, fortified by the two-thirds rule, was to have a major role.

Conclusions

There can surely be little doubt that the United States was in a state of crisis in the later 1780s. In the previous decade Thomas Paine and other radical democrats had played an important part in fostering a revolutionary consciousness and in encouraging the colonists to throw off the shackles of imperialism. But once that apocalyptic stage had passed some hard-headed consideration of the realities of effective self-government was required. Shortly after the Revolutionary War ended it became clear that the ambitions of this new nation could not be satisfied by the Articles of Confederation, as that constitution left too much power with the states at the expense of viable political institutions at the centre. Without fundamental constitutional change economic development would be impeded, and foreign adversaries would continue unchecked; in the long term, moreover, there was a real possibility that the country would disintegrate. As Nathaniel Gorham pessimistically remarked in the Convention, 'Can it be supposed that this vast country . . . will 150 years hence remain one nation?'[50]

The majority of the Founding Fathers recognized that if the ultimate disaster of disintegration was to be avoided there had to be an energetic, vigorous national government with a suitably strong executive branch at its core. In the past, republicanism had been synonomous with a suspicion of executives and the conviction that the voice of the people was to be found in the legislature. This doctrine was well stated by Roger Sherman who 'considered the Executive magistracy as nothing more than an institution for carrying the will of the Legislature into effect . . . [for the legislature] was the depository of the supreme will of the Society.'[51] However, this stress on the supremacy of the legislature had now become an outdated minority viewpoint. The majority of political leaders were now of the view that satisfactory political institutions required a properly instituted executive branch able to provide the energy at the centre that good government demanded.

The need for energy in government that so obsessed federalists like Washington, Hamilton and Madison has been dismissed by one critic as no more than 'code for the protection of property', but this is to oversimplify.[52] As I have argued, a concern for the rights of property loomed large in the thinking of the Founding Fathers, yet that was only part of their motivation. Furthermore the argument for a reasonably strong, 'well mounted' central government stood on its own merits in a vast and infinitely diverse, new country. As Gouverneur Morris, another federalist, aptly put it:

> It has been a maxim in political Science that Republican Government is not adapted to a large extent of Country, because the energy of the Executive Magistracy can not reach the extreme parts of it. Our Country is an extensive one. We must either renounce the blessings of the Union, or provide an Executive with sufficient vigor to pervade every part of it:[53]

These were eminently sensible sentiments that even today retain their validity. As modern constitution-makers in the European Community and elsewhere are only too well aware, constructing a democratic order for the government of a large territorial area poses special problems. More specifically, an unwillingness to confer sufficient energy, or strength, on the institutions at the centre may indeed mean that the advantages of union have to be forgone.

The arguments of those who have chosen to regard the Founding Fathers as reactionary conservatives are ultimately unconvincing. The debates show that, virtually to a man, they were committed to republicanism, to democracy in some form, to the belief that government should be based on consent. The relatively progressive attitudes, for the late eighteenth century, of the majority of these men are reflected in their consistent rejection of proposals to place property limitations on voting or office holding. Even those like Hamilton, Gerry and Sherman, so often believed to have harboured anti-democratic sentiments, sometimes reveal rather different views – they were by no means hostile to democracy as such, but feared the consequences of democratic excess.

Two hundred years later who can reasonably doubt that the democratic impulse, if left completely unchecked, can lead to demagoguery, to the tyranny of the majority, or to irresponsible government prejudicial to the common good? Furthermore, unbalanced political institutions may be unable to address, and deal with, the problems that face the nation, thereby creating situations which can lead to the destruction of democracy itself. This was no doubt what Madison had in mind when he suggested that the omnipotence of legislatures and the weakness of executives in the states had led to difficulties that threatened to bring about revolution and ultimately, perhaps, the reintroduction of monarchy.

Madison is often credited with authorship of the Virginia plan, but that is difficult to reconcile with many of his comments in the Convention, particularly his insistence that the separation of powers was an essential principle of free government. However, it is possible that he and the other Virginians presented their scheme as an opening bargaining position from which they expected to be moved during negotiations. Nevertheless, whoever compiled it and whatever the strategy that lay behind it, the plan did enable those who sponsored it to seize the initiative, and, at the end, it was clear that the Founding Fathers had gone a long way towards meeting the requirements of the Virginia plan.

In other words, at the Constitutional Convention the running was clearly made by the nationalists, those who later become known as Federalists. To a large extent they got their way and realized their intention to provide for a vigorous and effective executive branch. On the other hand, by no means did they get their way entirely. They were repeatedly obliged to compromise and to concede a range of restraints and checks on the power of the president. These concessions were nevertheless insufficient to satisfy some delegates, worried that the presidency had been made too powerful.

George Mason, for instance, one of three members who declined to sign the Constitution, did so because of such concerns. In the Convention Mason attempted to limit the expansion of executive power, expressing, several times, his fear that the new office that was being created might degenerate into monarchy. This fear of a monarchy reappearing was shared by others including Randolph, Franklin, Rutledge, Gerry, Sherman, Luther Martin and Hugh Williamson of North Carolina.[54] The same concern surfaced in the ratification debates and was extensively dealt with by Alexander Hamilton in the *Federalist Number 69*.

Hamilton heaped scorn on those who suggested that the powers of the president were to be equated with those of George III. Unlike the latter, an hereditary prince, the president was to be elected for four years; the King enjoyed an absolute veto over acts of Parliament, whereas the president's veto was a qualified one. The president like the monarch was commander in chief of the armed forces, but the King's position was made infinitely more powerful by his possession of the right to declare war and to raise armed forces on his own authority. The president was to share the power of making treaties with the legislature whereas George III was the *sole possessor* of the treaty-making power.

Similarly, the American chief executive was to share with Congress the power to appoint federal officers, whereas British national government officials were appointed by the Crown. A president could confer no honours or titles, but the monarch could make noblemen out of commoners. The president

> can prescribe no rules concerning the commerce or currency of the nation; [the King] is in several respects the arbiter of commerce and in this capacity can establish markets and fairs, can regulate weights and measures, can lay embargoes for a limited time, can coin money, can authorize or prohibit the circulation of foreign coin.

Moreover, the monarch was the head of the national church in contrast to the president who had 'no particle of spiritual jurisdiction'.[55]

Hamilton's analysis was well-founded. The presidency as invented in Philadelphia was far removed from the British monarchy. In the United States, unlike the situation in Britain, executive power was to be hedged about with innumerable restraints that even yet make life extraordinarily difficult for those who occupy the White House. Today, of course, the contrast is not between monarch and president but between prime minister and president, for the former has, in practice, assumed most of the constitutional powers of the Crown.

It is not correct to interpret what happened at Philadelphia as some sort of coup by plutocrats and their lackeys obsessively bent on defending property rights. Nor can it be reasonably seen as a counter-revolution that overturned the ideals incorporated in the Declaration of Independence. The constitution-makers were undoubtedly members of the elite and they were interested in preserving the rights of property. Their purpose is best understood, as Ralph Ketcham has suggested, as a striving to reconcile the Aristotelian ideal of government devoted to pursuing the public good, with the emphasis of John Locke requiring that government should be based on the consent of the governed.[56]

Those who drew up the Constitution were hardly 'demi gods' as Jefferson suggested, possibly tongue-in-cheek. Nevertheless the debates in the Convention were, as Richard Hofstadter said, 'carried on at an intellectual level that is rare in politics, and . . . the Constitution itself is one of the world's masterpieces of practical statecraft'.[57] By any standard, the Founding Fathers constituted a remarkable gathering. Fortunately few of them were in any sense ideologues; most of them were hard-headed, practical men who, while not lacking in ideas or convictions, recognized that successful constitution-making demanded a willingness to compromise. Most of them also had that essential understanding that workable democratic systems require a balance between representation on the one hand and the need for effective government on the other.

Notes

1. Richard Pious, *The American Presidency*, Basic Books, New York, 1979, p. 19.

2. Clinton Rossiter (ed.), *The Federalist Papers*, The New American Library, New York, 1961, p. 106.
3. Winton Solberg (ed.), *The Federal Convention and the Formation of the Union of the American States*, Bobbs Merrill, Indianapolis, 1958, p. 64.
4. Max Farrand (ed.), *The Records of the Federal Convention of 1787* (revised edition), 4 volumes, Yale University Press, New Haven, 1937, vol. III, p. 31.
5. Solberg, *op. cit.*, p. 387.
6. See, for example, John F. Manley and Kenneth M. Dolbeare (eds), *The Case Against the Constitution*, M. E. Sharpe, New York, 1987, *passim.*
7. Farrand, *op. cit.*, vol. I, p. 69, p. 364; vol. III, p. 619.
8. *ibid.*, vol. I, p. 48 and p. 362.
9. *ibid.*, vol. I p. 48 and p. 132.
10. Clinton Rossiter, *Conservatism in America*, Vintage Books, New York, 1962, p. 127.
11. Farrand, *op. cit.*, vol. I, p. 364.
12. George B. Tindall and David E. Shi, *America* (brief 2nd edition), W. W. Norton, New York, 1989, p. 164.
13. Manley and Dolbeare, *op. cit.*, p. 16.
14. Clinton Rossiter, *The American Presidency*, Harcourt Brace, New York, 1956, p. 76.
15. Farrand, *op. cit.*, vol. I, p. 66, p. 88 and p. 113.
16. *ibid.*, p. 66 and p. 96.
17. *ibid.*, vol. II, p. 29.
18. *ibid.*, p. 501 and p. 32.
19. *ibid.*, vol. I, p. 68 and vol. II, p. 56.
20. *ibid.*, vol. II, p. 29 and pp. 202–3.
21. *ibid.*, p. 31.
22. *ibid.*, p. 30, p. 57, and p. 114.
23. *ibid.*, p. 113, p. 29, p. 111 and p. 30.
24. *ibid.*, pp. 497–8.
25. In a number of states it was soon agreed that presidential electors would be popularly elected. In 1796, for example, electors in eight out of sixteen states were chosen by popular vote, a practice that became largely nationwide by the 1820s; South Carolina, however, did not abandon the appointment of electors by the state legislature until 1864. By 1840 every state with the exception of South Carolina had adopted the arrangement whereby the total electoral vote in the state went to the candidate with the highest popular vote. Since 1892 this has been the practice in all states. See William Nisbet Chambers, *Political Parties in a New Nation*, Oxford University Press, Oxford, 1963, p. 127 and Rossiter, *The American Presidency, op. cit.*, p. 186.
26. Farrand, *op. cit.*, vol. II, p. 35.
27. *ibid.*
28. *ibid.*, vol. III, p. 614.
29. *ibid.*, vol. II, p. 53.

30. *ibid.*, p. 67.
31. *ibid.*, pp. 65–6.
32. *ibid.*, vol. I, p. 99 and p. 101.
33. *ibid.*, p. 99 and p. 101.
34. *ibid.*, vol. II, p. 105.
35. *ibid.*, pp. 538–9.
36. See David O'Brien, 'The Reagan Judges: His Most Enduring Legacy?' in Charles O. Jones (ed.), *The Reagan Legacy*, Chatham House, New Jersey, 1988.
37. Farrand, *op. cit.*, vol. I, p. 119 and p. 233.
38. *ibid.*, p. 128 and p. 44.
39. *ibid.*
40. No doubt Madison particularly had in mind the Connecticut Compromise, which was concerned with the basis of representation in the legislature and the federal principle. The federalist majority had wanted proportional representation in both houses whereas those especially concerned with the rights of the states had favoured equality of state representation in both branches of the legislature. This division came close wrecking the Convention altogether, but had been resolved by the Connecticut Compromise which provided for proportional representation in the House and equality for the states in the Senate. This agreement has been widely seen as the rock upon which the whole Constitution was built. See for example Carl Van Doren, *The Great Rehearsal*, The Viking Press, New York, 1948, Ch. 7.
41. Farrand, *op. cit.*, vol. II, p. 80.
42. *ibid.*, vol. III, p. 599. See also vol. II, p. 157 n15.
43. *ibid.*, vol. II, p. 185.
44. Rossiter, *The American Presidency*, *op. cit.*, p. 26.
45. Farrand, *op. cit.*, vol. I, p. 244, p. 292 and p. 158.
46. Arthur Schlesinger Jnr, *The Imperial Presidency*, André Deutsch, London, 1974, pp. 61–3.
47. Jack Plano and Milton Greenberg, *The American Political Dictionary* (6th edition) Holt, Rinehart and Winston, New York, 1982, p.206.
48. Farrand, *op. cit.*, vol. I. p. 292 and vol. II, p. 183.
49. *ibid.*, p. 392.
50. Farrand, *op. cit.*, vol. II, p. 221.
51. *ibid.*, vol. I, p. 65.
52. John Manley, 'Class and Pluralism in America' in Manley and Dolbeare, *op. cit.*, p. 109.
53. Farrand, *op. cit.*, vol. II, p. 52.
54. *ibid.*, vol. IV, p. 182.
55. Rossiter (ed.), *op. cit.*, pp. 415–23.
56. Ralph Ketcham 'Concepts of Presidential Leadership, Citizenship and Good Government . . .' in Herman Wellenreuther (ed.), *German and American Constitutional Thought*, Berg, New York, 1990.
57. *The American Political Tradition*, Vintage Books, New York, 1948, p. 15.

2

The Development of the Presidency

The presidency as we see it today is the product of more than 200 years of institutional development. That development has, however, been uneven. Some occupants of the White House have come and gone without having any positive effect on the office and there have been periods when the presidency has gone into decline. A few incumbents have enlarged and extended the office significantly and it is this latter group that is of especial interest. This chapter therefore will briefly review the contributions to institutional development of George Washington, Thomas Jefferson, Andrew Jackson and Abraham Lincoln.

George Washington, 1789–97

George Washington's role in launching the presidency was immense. Even though, as chairman of the proceedings, he said little in the Constitutional Convention itself his mere attendance was a matter of consequence. In the words of Douglas Freeman, Washington's 'largest contribution was not that of his counsel but that of his presence'.[1] Subsequently, as the first President of the United States from 1789 to 1797 Washington was vitally instrumental in placing the new constitutional framework on a sound footing and in determining the future shape of the presidency.

In considering the unique importance of Washington's role it should be remembered that in the last quarter of the eighteenth century he was, by far, the most admired and respected man in America. First and foremost he was the hero of the Revolution, the man who had commanded the victorious Continental Army. But, in addition, Washington's modesty and reserve, his dignity, his gravitas and his transparent lack of political ambition all combined to give him a reputation as the most virtuous and most laudable of national leaders.

With great reluctance Washington went as a delegate to the Constitutional Convention where, by a unanimous vote, his colleagues agreed that he should be the chairman of their proceedings. In the crafting of the Constitution Washington's considerable influence fell on the side of those most anxious to provide for an energetic and effective national government. Furthermore, in designing the presidency it was widely assumed that Washington himself would be the first incumbent and this gave essential reassurance to those fearful of making the office too powerful. As one delegate, Pierce Butler of South Carolina, later observed:

> [The President's] powers are full great and greater than I was disposed to make them . . . they would [not] have been so great had not many members cast their eyes towards General Washington as President; and shaped the Ideas of the Powers to be given to a President, by their opinions of his Virtue.[2]

The drawing up of the Constitution was, however, only a first step towards resolving the crisis of legitimacy that this new nation had been passing through since the Revolution; a period when the old order and the values upon which it was based had disappeared, but had not yet been replaced by a viable alternative.[3] The question now at issue was whether the new constitutional framework with the presidency at its centre would be formally ratified, and accepted as authoritative by the American people. The fact that this period of crisis was successfully negotiated owed much to Washington's charisma, to his almost god-like status among his fellow citizens.

After his unanimous election to the presidency by the Electoral College Washington moved carefully, conscious of the importance of the precedents he was setting and respectful of the spirit and the letter of the Constitution. In his early dealings with Congress he deferred to the constitutional prerogatives of the legislature. As he saw it, on rare occasions he might make broad suggestions to

Congress, but otherwise he did not intend to be involved in the detail of the legislative process at all:

> With measures of general legislation he would make himself acquainted, and he might form a personal opinion, but he would not voice this otherwise than in confidence to trusted friends. The initiative, the choice, the form, the scope and the prompt enactment or deliberate postponement of legislation were for the determination of Congress, unhindered by the Executive. The President's power over lawmaking, as he saw it, was confined to his veto.[4]

In line with his restrictive interpretation of his legislative role, Washington generally refrained from making policy recommendations to Congress and used his veto on only two occasions throughout his two terms in office. However, although Washington held himself personally aloof from the legislative process, he did not extend that same restriction to the heads of executive departments.[5]

Washington's Secretary of the Treasury, Alexander Hamilton, accordingly responded enthusiastically to congressional requests for initiatives in the fields of public finance and economic development and even sought to go one step further by requesting that he be allowed to present his proposals on the floor of the House of Representatives. Fortunately for the future of that vital principle of the Constitution, the separation of powers, the House rejected Hamilton's request.[6] Approval of Hamilton's audacious suggestion would have made possible the emergence of the Secretary of the Treasury as prime minister, with the President as a quasi-monarch. Parliamentary government, in other words, might have entered the United States by the back door.

If Washington carefully kept out of the legislative process in domestic matters, he had no doubt as to the constitutional primacy of the president in the making of foreign policy. From the beginning, he assumed a 'positive direction of foreign affairs, the control of which [he believed] was vested in him by the Constitution'.[7] Members of the legislature, however, soon proved unwilling to grant total supremacy to the president in these matters, thus beginning a protracted constitutional struggle that goes on to this day.

The reluctance of the Senate to concede control of foreign policy surfaced in August 1789. The President appeared in the chamber, accompanied by his Secretary of War, intent on obtaining swift approval of arrangements designed to facilitate the formulation of a treaty with the Creek Indians. To Washington's obvious displeasure, the Senate declined to agree his proposals on the nod, insisting that they be referred to a committee before they gave their 'advice and consent'. Senator William Maclay, a leading player in this drama, drew sinister conclusions from Washington's behaviour: 'I can not now be mistaken. The president wishes to tread on the necks of the Senate . . . [he wants] to bear down our deliberations with his personal authority and presence. Form only will be left to us. This will not do with Americans.'[8]

Washington got the approval he sought a few days later, but scarred by his initial rebuff he now decided that written messages rather than personal appearances were the appropriate means for communicating such proposals to the Senate. In other words, in future the president would keep his distance in treaty-making; no doubt this was just as well, for further personal humiliations on the floor of Congress would have ultimately undermined the authority of the chief executive in the making of foreign policy.

The determination of Washington to assert the powers of his office in matters concerned with international relations arose again in 1793 when war began between Britain and France. Advised by Hamilton, Washington took it upon himself to issue a proclamation of neutrality. By this means foreign policy was made unilaterally by the President and put into effect by executive pronouncement. This action horrified Thomas Jefferson and James Madison, both of whom argued that if Congress had the constitutional right to declare war it must also possess the right to say when the country would not go to war. Madison denounced the proclamation as a 'most unfortunate error', that appeared 'to violate . . . the Constitution by making the Executive Magistrate the organ of the disposition, the duty and the interest of the nation in relation to war and peace'.[9]

The Madisonian view was vigorously rebutted by Hamilton who, as always, sought to maximize the power of the executive. He interpreted the opening words of Article II of the Constitution, namely, 'the executive Power shall be vested in a President', in a manner that gave the president authority, with very few limits, in the making of foreign policy. In Hamilton's opinion the executive power was constrained only by that specified in the constitution –

in the case of foreign affairs by the clauses involving the Senate in appointments and treaties and the legislature's right to declare war. Other than these exceptions, Hamilton claimed, 'the executive power of the United States is completely lodged in the President'.[10] This stunningly wide-sweeping reading of the Constitution that, in effect, made the president overwhelmingly predominant is even now unacceptable to some members of Congress.

Washington set another precedent of great importance when he voluntarily retired after two terms in office. The Constitutional Convention had considered proposals to include in the Constitution a clause limiting the eligibility of presidents for re-election, but these had been set aside, in part because of the expectation that the eminently trustworthy Washington would be the first president.[11] When Washington left office of his own free will after two terms, he helped to make possible an orderly, non-violent presidential succession, a matter of some importance in a nation still only precariously established.[12]

Furthermore, the two-term precedent that Washington originated eventually became so entrenched in constitutional practice that none of his successors prior to Franklin Roosevelt dared violate it. Roosevelt claimed that special circumstances justified his breaking with tradition in 1940, but the passage of the 22nd Amendment ensured that what had for long been a constitutional convention now became a permament constitutional reality. Whatever its form there can be no doubt that the two-term tradition begun by Washington has been an important limitation on the power of the president throughout most of American history.

Thomas Jefferson, 1801–9

Washington's rejection of pleas that he seek a third term arose from personal convenience rather than principle, but Thomas Jefferson, in response to similar overtures in 1807, helped to institutionalize what was to become a tradition by grounding his refusal in republican principles. He argued that without some form of check on re-election the presidency would become an 'office for life, and history shows how easily that degenerates into an inheritance'.[13]

In office, Jefferson's republican instincts lay behind his efforts to depomp the presidency. Washington had travelled in an elaborate coach escorted by uniformed outriders, but Jefferson rode about the capital on a horse accompanied by one servant.[14] In addition, Jefferson abandoned Washington's custom of making personal addresses to Congress, a practice that to good republicans smacked too much of speeches from the throne. Jefferson sent his recommendations to Congress in writing where they were read out by a clerk, a procedure that continued until 1913 when Woodrow Wilson reinstituted personal, presidential addresses.

Jefferson's most important contribution to the development of the presidency, however, lay in his assumption of the role of party leader which he then used to gain control of the machinery of government. Parties had been anathemas to George Washington who believed them to be destructive of the national interest, but he was trying to hold back an irresistible tide and after his departure the parties that had begun to emerge during his administration acquired a much more substantial form.

Those who came to be known as the Federalists, such as Hamilton and Washington's successor, John Adams, favoured a strong national government. In foreign policy they were inclined to be pro-British, they were sceptical of democratic excess and their opponents suspected them of hankering after the introduction of a monarchy. By contrast, Jefferson's Democratic-Republicans were concerned to preserve the position of the states; they took the claims of popular government more seriously and their sympathies in the struggle between Britain and France lay primarily with the latter. At the heart of the inter-party division, however, lay different conceptions of executive power. The Federalists emphasized the need for a strong presidency unhindered by excessive congressional restraint, whereas the Democratic-Republicans stressed the importance of the national legislature and the dangers of an over-powerful executive.[15]

With Jefferson in the White House the differences between the parties often seemed to be 'more a matter of tone or temperament than of hard substance', and, in some respects, he deviated little from Federalist conceptions of executive power.[16] By any standard, Jefferson's was a strong assertive presidency and his accomplishments as chief legislator have been equated with those of Woodrow Wilson. Despite his ostensible attachment to literal interpretations of the Constitution, Jefferson threw his weight behind the Louisiana Purchase; his administration enforced a highly controversial embargo on foreign trade in an effort to preserve American neutrality between Britain and France, and, aided by Albert Galliatin, his Secretary of the Treasury, Jefferson, 'exercised as much control of domestic policy as Hamilton had during the Washington administration'.[17]

Jefferson's assertion of presidential power was largely personal rather than institutional and his contribution to the development of the office was, at best, mixed. In line with Democratic-Republican orthodoxy he was elaborately deferential to the national legislature declaring that, 'nothing shall be wanting on my part to inform, as far as in my power, the legislative judgement, nor to carry that judgement into faithful execution.'[18] However, by working closely with congressional party leaders and by use of the caucus, over which he occasionally himself presided, Jefferson was remarkably successful in dominating Congress and in obtaining the legislative outcomes he desired. These were short-term, personal triumphs, however, gained at the expense of the independence of the presidency in the long run.

By relying so extensively on the extra-constitutional machinery of party Jefferson made it possible for congressional leaders in the future to gain control of that machinery and to control thereby the executive branch.[19] According to Clinton Rossiter, while Jefferson himself was unquestionably an 'effective leader', 'if we let our gaze halt at any year between 1809 and 1829, we must conclude that Jefferson damaged the office severely by compromising its independence.'[20]

The three presidents who followed Jefferson – James Madison, James Monroe and John Quincy Adams – lacked his remarkable talents. Furthermore, Madison and Monroe suffered from the system then in use of nominating presidential candidates through congressional caucuses, an arrangement that made chief executives beholden to the legislature. The election of Adams in 1824, meanwhile, was decided by the House of Representatives following the failure of any one of four candidates to obtain a majority in the Electoral College. These developments in the two decades after Jefferson did much to facilitate the dominance of the legislature and even placed in jeopardy the separation of powers.

Fortunately for the survival of that most important constitutional principle, Andrew Jackson was elected President in 1828.

Andrew Jackson, 1829–37

Andrew Jackson 'was second only to Washington in terms of influence on the Presidency'.[21] The future of the office itself had been clouded with uncertainty when he first entered the White House. Washington and Jefferson had been high profile, strong presidents responsible for establishing and extending the powers of the executive, but more recently incumbents had operated in the shadow of the legislature. It was Jackson's greatest achievement to reverse these trends and to 'remake' the presidency, giving it a new force and strength and securing its future place in American history.[22]

Jackson's first election in 1828 needs to be seen in the context of changes that had been taking place in the United States in the forty years since the ratification of the Constitution. There had been a threefold population increase and eleven new states had entered the Union, mainly from recently settled areas in the South and West. By 1826 adult white male suffrage had been effectively established in twenty-one of the twenty-four states. Two years later the appointment of presidential electors by state legislatures had been replaced by popular elections in all but two states, whereas voting turnout leapt from an estimated 9 per cent of adult white males in 1820 to 57.6 per cent in 1828.[23]

Prior to Jackson's election, the presidency had been monopolized by Eastern seaboard-based elites; all previous incumbents came from Virginia or Massachusetts and had been either Vice President or Secretary of State before becoming president. By contrast Jackson's background was that of an 'outsider'; born in South Carolina and long resident in Tennessee, he was a half-educated, self-made man. He had served only briefly in Congress and such national fame as he enjoyed derived primarily from his exploits as commander of the American troops that had defeated the British outside New Orleans in 1815. In an era when demands for economic and political equality had gathered momentum Jackson was a godsend to party managers; he could be presented both as a military hero, and as a man of the people.

General Jackson's populist credentials were given added credibility by the circumstances of his defeat in 1824. In the presidential election of that year he had won more Electoral College votes than any other candidate as well as a larger share of the popular vote. However, his failure to obtain an absolute majority in the Electoral College had thrown the contest into the House of Representatives from where John Quincy Adams, the candidate of the Eastern establishment, had emerged as the victor. Adams' subsequent appointment of Henry Clay, the Speaker of the House, as Secretary of State appeared to confirm the existence of a 'corrupt bargain' and paved the way for Jackson's success in 1828 as the victim of these alleged machinations. The status of 'Old Hickory' as the candidate of the common man was partly bogus. He was a wealthy plantation owner and had played no part in the movement towards democratic reform; he was, nevertheless, the first president who could claim to have been popularly elected.

Jackson was also the first president to be the leader of a party in a recognizably modern form. Since Jefferson's departure the embryonic, largely elite parties of that earlier era had more or less disappeared. By 1820 the Federalist Party no longer existed and within a few years the Democratic-Republican Party had degenerated into a collection of factions. However, in 1828, a number of political leaders coalesced around Jackson in a group that was to grow into the Democratic Party, 'the first organized party of modern democracy'.[24] The level of organization utilized by the Jacksonians was unprecedented; a network of committees of correspondence was established throughout the country, literature was distributed, the support of newspapers acquired and a wide variety of meetings and social gatherings arranged which were then, 'provided with orators primed on the imperfections of the Administration, the iniquities of the bargain, and the virtues of General Jackson'.[25]

The emergence of a party with a national organization extending into the grass roots was further boosted by the introduction of arrangements providing for the selection of presidential candidates by conventions rather than congressional caucuses. The Democrats instituted such procedures in 1832 and their opponents, now known as Whigs, followed suit in 1836. Local organizations sent delegates to state conventions which in turn appointed delegates to national conventions, the principal purpose of which was the selection of a presidential candidate. This was a change of great significance. First, the survival of that vastly important constitutional principle, the separation of powers, was ensured by breaking the link for nomination purposes between Congress and president. Second, conventions at every political level provided an essential basis of party organization and gave the man in the executive mansion a stable body of nation-wide popular support.

Thus fortified, Jackson in office was a dynamic and commanding presence. From the beginning he made it clear that he had no intention of being anything but the master of his own Cabinet and did not hesitate to remove members who baulked at his leadership. Within the national government at large, Jackson aggressively asserted the power of the executive, unwilling at any time to concede an inch to either Congress or the Supreme Court. This was demonstrated in his message vetoing the bill that would have re-chartered the Second Bank of the United States. Congress was castigated for authorizing arrangements that benefited the privileged at the expense of the common people, whereas the Supreme Court's claim to a monopoly of constitutional interpretation was dismissed out of hand with Jackson effectively maintaining:

> that the executive was not only an autonomous part of the government but that it was also the most important part, and it occupied this position because it alone was responsive to the wishes of a majority of the voters. Implicit, if not explicit, in Jackson's statement was his conviction that the Justices of the Supreme Court spoke only for themselves, that the members of Congress reflected the interests of factions and that he alone represented the people.[26]

This was a stunningly modern interpretation of the president's role that has been invoked by many of Jackson's successors.

The veto of the bank bill also set a precedent of considerable importance. Previously, the power of veto had been used on a total of nine occasions in forty years and normally bills were vetoed only on constitutional grounds. By contrast, Jackson vetoed twelve bills in his two terms in office, used the 'pocket veto' for the first time and made it clear in his bank veto message that he believed a president was entitled to veto any bill that he deemed to be injurious to the nation.[27] The legislative power is usually thought of in positive terms, as the capacity to initiate action, to cause bills to pass, but Jackson demonstrated the formidable possibilities of the president's negative power to veto legislative proposals.

Not surprisingly, Jackson's aggressive leadership alarmed Whigs dedicated to maintaining the primacy of the legislature and ever alert to the danger of executive tyranny. However, while Jackson was utterly dedicated to preserving the integrity of his office within the national government, he was not seeking to extend the reach of that government as such. He was, rather, a Jeffersonian anxious to limit the growth of governmental power; a primitive liberal dedicated to the virtues of *laissez-faire* and a 'strict constructionist' anxious to uphold states' rights: 'He repeatedly warned against attempts to increase the power of the national government at the expense of the states and insisted that the Federal authority should never transcend the limits imposed on it by the Constitution.'[28]

His commitment to states' rights did not prevent Jackson from taking a hard line with those who seemed to threaten the sanctity of the Union. South Carolina 'nullifiers' led by John. C. Calhoun appeared to be doing just that in their dispute with the national government over the tariff. The President rejected out of hand Calhoun's argument that states were entitled to nullify federal statutes that they believed to be unconstitutional. He saw this doctrine as a grave threat to the foundations of the federal union that had to be firmly resisted at all costs. When South Carolina adopted an ordinance nullifying federal tariff legislation and threatened to secede if any attempt was made to collect the disputed duties, Jackson made it clear that he would use physical force if necessary to preserve the Union.

Robert Dahl has likened the American presidency to a house that has grown substantially larger over the years. Originally it was a relatively small structure, but it had since been much extended by subsequent generations: 'Confronted by some new need, a President adds on a new room, a new wing; what began as a modest dwelling has become a mansion.'[29] When we consider the precedents set by Jackson's vigorous leadership and his uncompromising responses to challenges to his authority it is difficult to see that any nineteenth-century president contributed more to the building of Dahl's 'mansion'.

In making this major contribution, Jackson was, in some instances, the beneficiary of changes achieved by others rather than the moving force behind those developments. He had had no part in the various democratic reforms leading to the vast increase in popular, political participation. Similarly, the construction of a

Democratic Party organization was due to the efforts of skilled political operators like Martin Van Buren rather than to anything contributed by Jackson. Nevertheless, even if others made it possible, Jackson was the first president who could claim to have been elected by the people and was the first to be the leader of a modern political party.

Once in office, Jackson brilliantly exploited these sources of strength. He repeatedly confounded his opponents in Congress by appealing over their heads to their constituents in a way that no chief executive had ever done before, a tactic that was to become routine for those who aspired to be strong presidents in the future.[30] It should be noted, however, that Jackson rarely made speeches; he appealed to the people through messages to Congress and proclamations.[31] Jackson also broke with precedent by insisting that he as President and not Congress spoke for the people at large; a fact which, he argued, in common with many of his successors, justified the executive branch's claim to primacy in the national political system.

Unlike twentieth-century counterparts Jackson did not seek to be chief legislator. On the other hand his willingness to use the veto ensured that, in the future, chief executives would have available to them a valuable weapon, allowing them to exercise a negative power of great consequence in the legislative process. Finally, Jackson's clash with Calhoun and the South Carolina nullifiers foreshadowed the bloody and bitter struggle between North and South of thirty years later. In this earlier crisis Jackson was the first president obliged to face up to the possible use of force in defence of the Union; by making it clear that he was prepared to do that if necessary Jackson set the precedent later followed by Lincoln.[32]

Abraham Lincoln, 1861–5

Abraham Lincoln has a deserved reputation as one of the great presidents of the United States. He has been seen as an heroic figure who guided his country through its most desperate crisis while profoundly influencing the institutional development of the presidency. None of this seemed likely when Lincoln was first elected. A largely self-educated 'prairie lawyer' from Illinois, he had, for some years, been a state legislator; he had served one term as a Whig member of the US House of Representatives and had fought a famous, if unsuccessful, campaign for a seat in the US Senate. As a compromise candidate of the Republican party in the 1860 presidential election, Lincoln won barely 40 per cent of the popular vote and many commentators expected him to be a weak, ineffective chief executive certain to be overwhelmed by the crisis then facing the United States.

At issue in that crisis was a matter of unparalleled importance, the disintegration of the Union over the question of slavery. The new president was not himself an abolitionist. He did not seek, at this stage, to abolish slavery in those states where it already existed, but was totally opposed to its extension elsewhere in the nation. Nevertheless, Lincoln's election was interpreted in the South as a declaration of war against slavery as an institution.[33] Within weeks of the election South Carolina seceded, swiftly followed by six other Southern states. Lincoln proved equal to the challenge, boldly asserting the power of his office to deal with an extraordinary situation and in so doing not only restoring the Union, but also setting precedents of enormous consequence for the future of the presidency.

Lincoln's substantial extensions of the boundaries of executive power and his place in history were entirely dependent upon the existence of a dire national emergency and without that crisis he might well have passed into history as a passive, unadventurous and not especially competent president.[34] In office, for instance, he was to show no signs of aspiring to the role of chief legislator in the manner of a modern president. As a member of Congress in the 1840s he had said, 'Were I President, I should desire the legislation of the country to rest with Congress, uninfluenced in its origin or progress, and undisturbed by the veto.' Shortly before he entered the White House Lincoln reaffirmed this Whiggish view. He referred to the 'indirect means' whereby presidents could influence the legislative process before saying,

> my political education strongly inclines me against a very free use of any of these means by the executive to control the legislation of the country. As a rule, I think it better that Congress should originate as well as perfect its measures without external bias.[35]

In accordance with these sentiments President Lincoln displayed little interest in the legislative process and he rarely made use of the veto. Students of the presidency have also commented adversely on his record as an administrator and criticized his failure to exercise adequate control over his cabinet.[36] In several key areas of executive leadership, in other words, Lincoln's performance was not outstanding.

Comments by Lincoln earlier in his career suggested to his many contemporary critics that he would also be excessively cautious in exercising his powers in a war in defence of the union. Following President Polk's invasion of Mexico, and notwithstanding the constitutional support for this action eventually provided by a congressional declaration of war, Lincoln attacked presidential war-making:

> Allow the President to invade a neighboring nation, whenever *he* shall deem it necessary to repel an invasion . . . and you allow him to make war at his pleasure. Study to see if you can fix *any limit* to his power in this respect. . . . If, today, he should choose to say he thinks it necessary to invade Canada, to prevent the British from invading us, how could you stop him? You may say to him, 'I see no probability of the British invading us,' but he will say to you, 'Be silent; I see it, if you don't.'[37]

As a Whig congressman, Lincoln had found such justifications for presidents committing the country to war to be wholly unacceptable, but in the White House, faced by an armed rebellion, his position changed diametrically.

From the beginning of his presidency, Lincoln flatly denied the right of states to secede, insisted that the preservation of the Union was his paramount responsibility and claimed the right to do whatever was necessary to further that end. After his first inauguration, he delayed the convening of Congress and appeared to set aside the Constitution while he took a series of bold steps that, he believed, were required by military necessity. He called up state militias, imposed a naval blockade on the rebellious Southern states, massively increased the size of the army and spent large amounts of public money without congressional approval, sanctioned the arbitrary arrest of persons suspected of treasonable activity and, most stunningly of all, suspended *habeas corpus*. Provision for suspension in special circumstances was included in the Constitution, but under Article I which details the powers of Congress.

In justification of these and other arbitrary actions taken during the press of civil war, Lincoln cited his 'war power', which he derived from three sources – his oath of office, the clause in the Constitution that required him to execute federal laws and his designation as commander in chief. At his inauguration Lincoln had sworn on the Bible to 'preserve, protect and defend the Constitution of the United States'. As he understood it, this oath conferred upon him the obligation to defend the Union, 'the duty of preserving by every indispensable means, that government – that nation of which the Constitution was the organic law'.[38]

In drawing on his constitutional responsibility to 'take Care that the Laws be faithfully executed', Lincoln argued that the rebellion in the Southern states meant that federal laws were not being executed in a large area of the country. This made necessary emergency measures to deal with the situation including in particular the suspension of *habeas corpus*. In reference to the latter, the President, in a memorable passage, said to Congress, 'Are all the laws but one to go unexecuted, and the government itself go to pieces, lest that one be violated.'[39]

The most important source of Lincoln's war power, however, was that clause of the Constitution that makes the president, 'the Commander in Chief of the Army and Navy of the United States, and of the Militia of the several States, when called into the service of the United States'. The Founding Fathers, according to Alexander Hamilton in *Federalist Number 69*, had had in mind a narrow definition of this clause: 'it would amount to nothing more than the supreme command and direction of the military and naval forces.'[40]

President Lincoln placed a much wider construction on the clause. As he saw it, it required the president to decide when the public safety was threatened from without or within and to act accordingly. For instance, he believed that it allowed him to take actions such as issuing a proclamation emancipating the slaves, which he admitted had no 'constitutional or legal justification excepting as a military measure'. He claimed also that in such an emergency he could 'do things on military grounds which cannot constitutionally be done by Congress', and said, 'as commander in chief . . . I suppose I have a right to take any measure which may best subdue the enemy.'[41]

Not surprisingly, Lincoln's claim to do whatever he deemed necessary in emergency situations was deeply troubling to many of his contemporaries and led to charges of dictatorship. In the long run he was vindicated, but not without devastating consequences for the balance of powers in the American Constitution. The power of the president, in the circumstances of war, rebellion or the threat of such, was substantially inflated and that of Congress accordingly diminished. From Lincoln onwards presidents have been liable to claim that their constitutional 'war power' allows them to decide when the national security is threatened and to take such measures to meet that crisis as they see fit whatever Congress, the media or anyone else might say.

An authority on these matters, Arthur Schlesinger Jnr emphasizes, in defence of Lincoln's actions, that, 'it cannot be forgotten that [his] assertion of the war power took place in the context of domestic rebellion and under the color of a most desperate national emergency.'[42] On the other hand, Schlesinger would have us believe that such justifications are not relevant in the cases of 'imperial' presidents like Lyndon Johnson and Richard Nixon.[43] This line of argument seems rather doubtful. Lincoln is the only president who has had to cope with civil war, but many of his successors have had to deal with 'desperate' national emergencies or situations where the 'public safety', or the national security, has been at risk.

In the 1860s, extraordinary measures by the chief executive could be justified on the grounds of invasion or rebellion; the enemy could be said to be at the gate, or, worse still (in the circumstances of civil war), inside it. Given the existence of a dire emergency so it could be argued, the commander in chief must be allowed to do what is necessary to save the nation. In the modern, interdependent, technological age, however, the position of the gate has changed. The United States no longer enjoys the protection afforded in the past by vast distances and presidents may perceive threats to the nation's vital interests thousands of miles from its borders. These threats, they may argue, constitute national emergencies no less 'desperate' than those faced by Lincoln.

By accepting the latter's right to draw on his war power and to exercise wide-ranging, arbitrary powers in certain circumstances an ominous precedent had been established: 'The danger of allowing a President like Lincoln to act without regard to constitutional restraints in a great crisis is that lesser men may take Lincoln as precedent in lesser causes.'[44]

To suggest that the emergency faced by Lincoln was different from the wartime situations encountered by his successors is to reduce the argument to constitutional niceties. If Lincoln's right to act as he did is accepted, it is difficult to deny the claims of Lyndon Johnson in Vietnam, Richard Nixon in Cambodia or Ronald Reagan in Central America to take the steps they believed were necessary to the nation's security. We may not agree, of course, that the security of the nation was genuinely at risk, but that is another matter. More recently, not everyone approved of the US response to Iraq's invasion of Kuwait, but George Bush might have cited the example of Lincoln in defence of his policy. The American intervention, among other things, was concerned with countering a threat to the supply of oil; the nation's vital interests, in other words, were threatened in a distant part of the globe. Buttressed by historical precedent, Bush appeared to be bent on military action, without congressional approval if that should have proved necessary.

Notes

1. Douglas Southall Freeman, *George Washington: A Biography*, Charles Scribner's Sons, New York, 1954, vol. 6, p. 112.
2. Max Farrand (ed.), *The Records of the Federal Convention of 1787* (revised edition), Yale University Press, New Haven, 1937, vol. 3, p. 302.
3. Seymour Martin Lipset, *The First New Nation*, Basic Books, New York, 1963, p. 16.
4. Freeman, *op. cit.*, p. 221.
5. *ibid.*, p. 303.
6. Clinton Rossiter, *Alexander Hamilton and the Constitution*, Harcourt, Brace and World, New York, 1964, pp. 74–5.
7. Freeman, *op. cit.*, p. 205.
8. *The Journal of William Maclay*, Fredereich Ungar, New York, 1965 (first published 1890), p. 128.
9. As quoted in Rossiter, *op. cit.*, p. 85.
10. *ibid.*, p. 214.
11. Clinton Rossiter, *The American Presidency*, Harcourt Brace and World, New York, 1956, p. 229.
12. Lipset, *op. cit.*, p. 21.
13. Edward S. Corwin, *The President: Office and Powers*, New York University Press, New York, 1957, p. 332.
14. Sidney Milkis and Michael Nelson, *The American Presidency: Origins and Development*, Congressional Quarterly Press, Washington DC, 1990, p. 103.

15. *ibid.*, p. 101.
16. Carl Degler, *Out of Our Past*, Harper and Row, New York, 1970, p. 92
17. Milkis and Nelson, *op. cit.*, p. 102.
18. Corwin, *op. cit.*, p. 18.
19. Milkis and Nelson, *op. cit.*, p. 105.
20. *The American Presidency, op. cit.*, p. 95.
21. *ibid.*, p. 98.
22. Corwin, *op. cit.*, p. 19–20.
23. Joel Silbey, Allan Bogue and William Flanigan (eds), *The History of American Electoral Behavior*, Princeton University Press, Princeton, 1978, p. 175.
24. Merrill Peterson, *The Jefferson Image in the American Mind*, Oxford University Press, New York, 1962, p. 69.
25. Marquis James, *Andrew Jackson*, Grosset and Dunlap, New York, 1937, p. 145.
26. Harold Syrett, *Andrew Jackson*, Greenwood Press, Westport, Conn., 1953, p. 29.
27. Milkis and Nelson, *op. cit.*, p. 122. If the president holds a bill for ten days without signing it while Congress is in session, it automatically becomes law. If, however, the president declines to sign a bill and Congress shortly adjourns, the bill falls and the president is deemed to have exercised a 'pocket veto'.
28. Syrett, *op. cit.*, p. 38.
29. Robert Dahl, *Pluralist Democracy in the United States*, Rand McNally, Chicago, 1967, p. 90.
30. Corwin, *op. cit.*, p. 21.
31. Jeffrey Tulis, *The Rhetorical Presidency*, Princeton University Press, Princeton, 1987, pp. 73–4.
32. Milkis and Nelson, *op. cit.*, p. 119.
33. Benjamin Thomas, *Abraham Lincoln: A Biography*, Alfred Knopf, New York, 1952, p. 228.
34. On Lincoln's competence see J.G. Randall, *Constitutional Problems Under Lincoln* (revised edition), Peter Smith, Gloucester, Mass., 1963, p. xxv. On emergencies and the expansion of executive power see Rossiter, *The American Presidency, op. cit.*, p. 86.
35. Corwin, *op. cit.*, p. 324.
36. Rossiter, *The American Presidency, op. cit.*, p. 144: Corwin, *op. cit.*, p. 24: Marcus Cunliffe, *American Presidents and the Presidency*, Fontana/Collins, London, 1972, p. 94.
37. Lincoln to Herndon as quoted in Arthur Schlesinger Jnr, 'Congress and the Making of American Foreign Policy' in Rexford Tugwell and Thomas Cronin (eds), *The Presidency Reappraised*, Praeger, New York, 1974, p. 87.
38. Arthur Schlesinger Jnr, *The Imperial Presidency*, André Deutsch, London, 1974, p. 61.
39. Randall, *op. cit.*, p. 122.
40. Clinton Rossiter edition, New American Library, New York, 1961, p. 418.

41. Schlesinger, *The Imperial Presidency*, *op. cit.*, p. 63.
42. *ibid.*, p. 65.
43. *ibid.*, Ch. 7.
44. Hugh Gallagher, 'Presidents, Congress and the Legislative Functions' in Tugwell and Cronin, *op. cit.*, p. 223.

3

The Modern Presidency Emerges

The special circumstances created by a dire emergency made it possible for Abraham Lincoln to assume a position of primacy in the direction of the federal government, but once that crisis had passed, determined congressional reassertion shifted the balance of powers back towards the legislature. By the 1870s, leading members of Congress were apt to treat the president with something close to disdain. As one source put it:

> The most eminent Senators – Sumner, Conkling, Sherman, Edmunds, Carpenter, Frelinghuysen, Simon Cameron, Anthony, Logan – would have received as a personal affront a private message from the White House expressing a desire that they should adopt any course in the discharge of their legislative duties that they did not approve of. If they visited the White House it was to give, not to receive advice. . . . Each of these stars kept his own orbit and shone in his sphere within which he tolerated no intrusion from the President or from anybody else.[1]

A few presidents in the last quarter of the nineteenth century – notably Rutherford Hayes and Grover Cleveland – endeavoured to restore some degree of presidential authority, but, in general, the office lacked weight for most of this period. Thus Woodrow Wilson, in 1884, at that point a graduate student at Johns Hopkins University, could plausibly say, 'The business of the President occasionally great, is usually not much above routine. Most of the time it is *mere* administration, mere obedience of directions from the masters of policy, the Standing Committees [of Congress].'[2]

All of this was to change dramatically in 1901 when Theodore Roosevelt swept into the White House and, with the enormous gusto for which he was already famous, set about laying the foundations of the modern presidency.

Theodore Roosevelt, 1901–9

Above all else the first Roosevelt was intent on being a strong president, one who deferred neither to Congress nor to anyone else and who made the maximum use of the powers available to him. As he noted towards the end of his second term:

> I have used every ounce of power there was in the office [of president] and I have not cared a rap for the criticisms of those who spoke of 'my usurpation of power'. . . . I believe that the efficiency of this Government depends upon it possessing a strong central executive.'[3]

Roosevelt's extraordinarily expansive view of presidential power and responsibility required the chief executive to act as the 'steward of the people', striving to protect and pursue the people's interests rather than contenting 'himself with the negative merit of keeping his talents undamaged in a napkin'. He regarded with contempt strict constructionists such as President James Buchanan who took a 'narrowly legalistic view' of their responsibilities, deferring to Congress and refusing to act without specific constitutional authorization:

> My belief was that it was not only [the President's] right but his duty to do anything that the needs of the nation demanded unless such action was forbidden by the Constitution or by the laws. Under this interpretation of executive power I did and caused to be done many things not previously done by the President and the heads of the departments. I did not usurp power, but I did greatly broaden the use of executive power.[4]

The President's response to the anthracite coal strike of 1902 was illustrative of his 'stewardship' theory. As Roosevelt saw it, the public welfare demanded that he use whatever powers he possessed to avert, in his words, 'the terrible nature of the catastrophe impending, a winter fuel famine'.[5] To meet this crisis Roosevelt used executive branch officials to try to bring about a settlement. He met with employers and union leaders and, finally, threatened to send in the army to 'dispossess the operators and run the mines as a receiver'.[6] Such action would have been blatantly unconstitutional and Roosevelt was saved from himself by the ending of the strike. Nevertheless by his vigorous intervention he had set a precedent of great importance. According to George Mowry:

> By both his actions and his threats Roosevelt had moved the government away from its traditional position of isolation from such economic struggles. The government by precedent if not by law, had become a third force and partner in major labor disputes.[7]

Roosevelt had no doubt that his obligation to take care of the public welfare required him to take the lead in the legislative process. As he said later:

> In theory the executive has nothing to do with legislation. In practice, as things now are, the Executive is or ought to be peculiarly representative of the people as a whole. . . . Therefore a good Executive under present conditions of American life must take a very active interest in getting the right kind of legislation in addition to performing his Executive duties with an eye single to the public welfare.[8]

In securing the passage of an impressive amount of legislation Roosevelt contributed to another innovation of great moment, the emergence of the rhetorical presidency. Hitherto it had been considered inappropriate and beneath the dignity of a president's high office for him to speak directly to the people on matters of policy. Even the notoriously down-to-earth Andrew Jackson made relatively few speeches while he was in the White House; he appealed for popular support indirectly, via written messages and proclamations. On the eve of the Civil War Lincoln declined to discuss at public meetings the issues at stake and was applauded for doing so.[9]

Although he was not completely immune to the nineteenth-century tradition in such matters, Theodore Roosevelt was much less inhibited than most of his predecessors had been. Despite his party's large majorities in both the House and the Senate, Roosevelt's legislative recommendations inevitably brought him into conflict with conservative congressional leaders and he did not hesitate to use direct appeals to the people as a means of bringing pressure to bear on recalcitrant legislators:

> We succeeded in working together, although with increasing friction, for some years, I pushing forward and they hanging back. Gradually, however, I was forced to abandon the effort to persuade them to come my way, and then I achieved results only by appealing over the heads of the House and Senate leaders to the people, who were the masters of both of us.[10]

The passage of the Hepburn bill in 1906 is, in part, testimony to Roosevelt's legislative leadership and to his skill in using the presidency, as he put it, as a 'bully pulpit'. In its time regarded as a landmark reform measure the Hepburn Act sought to make a reality of government regulation of the railways. Those who controlled the railways were accused by their progressive critics of using their monopoly powers to exploit consumers and to discriminate in favour of large producers.

In his annual message to Congress in 1904 Roosevelt recommended legislation designed to allow the Interstate Commerce Commission to intervene in the process of deciding railroad rates. An initial bill passed swiftly in the House, but was rejected by the Senate. The Senate nevertheless agreed to conduct hearings on the matter of railway regulation and while these were underway Roosevelt embarked on speaking tours across the country. The purpose of the President's speeches was to arouse and educate the public on the issue and to appeal for support over the heads of Congress.

In deference to the earlier tradition, Roosevelt abstained from speeches on the question while the Hepburn bill was before the Senate. Eventually however, after much subterranean manoeuvring, the continued resistance of the Republican leadership in the Senate, intensive lobbying by the railroad corporations, plus the hostility of many newspapers, Roosevelt got his way – a remarkable result, explained in large part, by his success in arousing public opinion.[11]

Appealing to their constituents as a means of bringing members of Congress into line has become a commonplace strategy for modern presidents. Furthermore, the potential inherent in such approaches has been vastly enhanced by the invention of radio and television. The practice of popular leadership in this sense however dates back only as far as Theodore Roosevelt, who thereby grafted onto the presidency an essential means of alleviating that 'sickness of ungovernability' to which the American political system is so prone.[12]

In the long term probably nothing has done more to extend the boundaries of executive power and authority than the entrance of the United States onto the world stage at the turn of the nineteenth and twentieth centuries. The retreat from isolation began with the Spanish–American War of 1898 under President McKinley, but gathered great momentum when Theodore Roosevelt occupied the White House.[13] Indeed, there was little chance of the United States remaining on the sidelines in international affairs when the President was of the view that: 'It is a contemptible thing for a great nation to render itself impotent in international action, whether because of cowardice, or sloth, or sheer inability or unwillingness to look into the future.'[14]

Shortly after Roosevelt became President it became apparent that his remarkably open-ended theory of executive power applied as much to international affairs as it did to domestic policy. He believed he had a right to take whatever foreign policy action he deemed necessary in the nation's interest, provided such action was not proscribed by the Constitution.[15]

An immediate priority was the construction of a canal between the Atlantic and Pacific oceans. Panama provided the most suitable site for such a canal and after the collapse of negotiations with Colombia, of which Panama was then part, the Roosevelt administration gave tacit support to Panamanian, secessionist revolutionaries. When a revolution began in November 1903 American warships effectively prevented Colombia from putting the revolution down; Panama became independent and the canal was built, an outcome which Roosevelt regarded as his most important achievement in foreign affairs. Others saw the brutal treatment of Colombia as a particularly shameful episode in the history of American foreign policy.[16]

Further evidence of an aggressive, imperialistic foreign policy, conducted with scant reference to Congress, was revealed by the Santo Domingo affair. By 1903 Santo Domingo (otherwise known as the Dominican Republic), plagued by a succession of corrupt dictators, was unable to honour its debts to various European powers. Fearing intervention from the latter, President Roosevelt audaciously expanded the Monroe Doctrine by his so-called 'corollary'. This was included in a message to Congress where Roosevelt denied that the United States had any territorial ambitions in the western hemisphere and assured the countries of Latin America:

> If a nation shows that it knows how to act with reasonable efficiency and decency in social and political matters, if it keeps order and pays its obligations, it need fear no interference from the United States. [However,] chronic wrongdoing, or an impotence which results in a general loosening of the ties of civilized society may . . . ultimately require intervention by some civilized nation, and . . . the Monroe Doctrine may force the United States, however reluctantly, in such flagrant cases of such wrongdoing or impotence, to the exercise of an international police power.[17]

This outrageously presumptuous extension of the Monroe Doctrine was put into effect in 1905 when Roosevelt imposed upon Santo Domingo an agreement whereby the United States took control of the former's custom houses, gave the Dominican government 45 per cent of the receipts and used the rest to pay off foreign creditors. The US Senate baulked at Roosevelt's high-handed action and refused to ratify a treaty sanctioning the arrangement. Undeterred by such legislative faint-heartedness, Roosevelt implemented the agreement anyway, boasting later, 'I put the agreement into effect, and I continued its execution for two years before the Senate acted; and I would have continued it until the end of my term, if necessary, without any action by Congress.'[18]

Roosevelt's freebooting style in the making of foreign policy, his lack of concern for constitutional niceties and his uninhibited exercise of executive power can also be seen in his responses to the outbreak of war between Japan and Russia. He secretly agreed to support the Japanese if any European powers went to the aid of the Russians and he entered into a secret executive agreement that gave approval to the establishment of a Japanese military protectorate in Korea. Without consulting his Cabinet or Congress, he arranged the Russo–Japanese peace conference at Portsmouth, New Hampshire in 1905.

Two years later the President, again without consulting his Cabinet colleagues or Congress, despatched the US fleet around the world as a show of American strength. As he left office, Roosevelt exulted in his virtually one-man conduct of foreign policy:

> The biggest matters, such as the Portsmouth peace, the acquisition
> of Panama, and sending the fleet around the world, I managed
> without consultation with anyone; for when a matter is of capital
> importance, it is well to have it handled by one man only.'[19]

'Strict constructionists' in the modern Republican Party, that is
to say those who prefer to read the Constitution literally, might
well reflect on the record of one of the party's great icons, Theodore Roosevelt. In both domestic and foreign policy Roosevelt
stretched the Constitution far beyond what many would regard as
reasonable limits. Unlike the situation faced by Lincoln – the president with whom Roosevelt most wished to be identified – there
was no desperate national emergency to excuse his extravagantly
unconstitutional conduct.[20] The crisis over Panama, for instance,
was not comparable with the Civil War. No doubt a canal was
necessary for the future prosperity of the United States, but it was
farcical for Roosevelt to compare his plight at the time with that of
Lincoln forty years previously: 'I have had a most interesting time
about Panama and Colombia. My experiences in these matters
give me an idea of the fearful times Lincoln must have had in
dealing with the great crisis he had to face.'[21]

In Roosevelt's defence it should be noted that, although he
unashamedly lusted after power while in the White House, there
were limits to that craving. This became apparent when innumerable political allies pleaded with him to seek a third term, pressures which the President resolutely refused saying: 'I believe in a
strong executive; I believe in power; but I believe that responsibility should go with power, and that it is not well that the strong
executive should be a perpetual executive.'[22] From time to time,
Roosevelt's critics suspected him of megalomania, but such suspicions could ultimately be said to be without foundation when despite many urgings he readily surrendered his high office.

The success of the US Constitution and of the United States itself
has required each new generation to reinterpret the basic law
drawn up by the Founding Fathers. By the end of the nineteenth
century prevailing conceptions of the place of the president in the
American political system were no longer adequate to the problems
that the country faced both at home and abroad. By his vigorous

example Roosevelt helped to change those conceptions and thereby played a large part in the foundation of the modern presidency.

The rhetorical presidency begins with the first Roosevelt; he discussed substantive policy matters with the public and successfully appealed for their support over the heads of members of Congress, a strategem that has become essential to the exercise of presidential power. Under Roosevelt's jurisdiction the presidency became a 'bully pulpit' and the chief executive a national policy leader to an extent far greater than before. He urged a legislative programme on Congress, set precedents for government intervention in the economy and energetically pursued the national interest in international affairs.

Roosevelt, however, was an instinctive president. He came to the White House without any preconceived model of presidential power and responded to the problems of governance on an *ad hoc* basis. His ruminations on the Constitution were often half-baked and almost all of his contributions to the theory of the presidency were *ex post facto* rationalizations made in his autobiography after he left office. Above all else Roosevelt was a man of action. In other words, he acted first and offered the theoretical justification later, if at all. Providing a doctrinal foundation for the modern presidency was left to Roosevelt's greatest political rival, Woodrow Wilson.

Woodrow Wilson, 1913–21

Woodrow Wilson's name is always somewhere near the top in presidential 'greatness' polls. Nevertheless his contribution to the development of the presidency has been less than fully recognized. Most political scientists, after a passing reference to Theodore Roosevelt and Wilson, date the beginning of the modern presidency from 1933 and the arrival of Franklin Roosevelt in the White House. This is to give insufficient weight to the first Roosevelt and to underestimate gravely the importance of Wilson.

Both the Roosevelts were distinguished practitioners of the arts of presidential leadership, but Wilson was that and much else besides. Unlike the other two he entered office armed with a long thought out and carefully elaborated theory of presidential power. Furthermore, before he became politically active in 1910 Wilson had been anything but a cloistered academic quietly cultivating his ideas in private.

In 1885 he indicated that although his first ambition, a career in politics, was probably beyond his reach, he hoped that he would be able,

> to contribute something to the political knowledge and the political science of the country, to the end that our forms of government and our means of administration may be perfected . . . it is my heart's desire that I may become one of the guides of public policy by becoming one of the guides of public thought.[23]

By the early twentieth century Wilson had triumphantly achieved this secondary ambition; for more than twenty years he had been publicizing his political ideas through books, articles and public speaking. First as a professor at Princeton and then as president of that university he became an important opinion leader, assiduously propagandizing on behalf of a strong national government with the presidency at its core as the principal source of leadership. Wilson, in other words, was one of the architects of the modern presidency, providing not only precedents while in office, but before that detailed theoretical justifications for the wide-ranging exercises of presidential power that he and others pursued in office.

From his precocious youth, Wilson had been obsessively concerned with leadership and the absence of opportunities for leadership in the United States: 'No subject in the entire realm of political administration had more vitally engaged his thought.'[24] In early published essays Wilson vaunted the accomplishments and skills of great leaders of the past, while in his first important published work he advanced Cabinet government as a mechanism that would make possible responsible leadership in the national political system, replacing the rule of 'scheming, incompetent tradesmen, whose aims and ambitions are merely personal . . . [with those of] broad minded, masterful statesmen, whose sympathies and purposes are patriotic and national'.[25]

Congressional Government, Wilson's first book, was heavily critical of the Founding Fathers and of the Constitution they had devised. They had so parcelled up power and responsibility as to make leadership virtually impossible:

> The forms of government in this country have always been unfavorable to the easy elevation of talent to a station of paramount auth-

ority; and those forms in their present crystallization are more un-
favorable than ever to the toleration of the leadership of the few.[26]

In the 1880s the president had become a mere cypher completely
subservient to Congress, whereas the latter, dominated by 'petty
barons' – the chairmen of standing committees – was bereft of
genuine leaders. Neither in the House nor in the Senate was there
any individual who could be identified as *the* leader of the chamber, nor was there a small group of dominant figures, comparable
to a British Cabinet, able to impose themselves on the legislature
as a whole.

The absence of leadership possibilities in the national government continued to preoccupy Wilson throughout the remainder of
the nineteenth century. In a speech, 'The nature of democracy in
the United States', first delivered and published in 1889, Wilson
expressed concern at the strains being placed on existing political
structures by factors such as the growth of popular education, the
spread of newspapers and the influx of immigrants. These developments had created pressing problems of organization and
leadership:

> We are conscious of oneness as a nation, of vitality, of strength, of
> progress; but are we often conscious of common thought in the
> concrete things of national policy? Does not our legislation, rather
> wear the features of a vast conglomerate? Are we conscious of any
> national leadership; are we not, rather, dimly conscious of being
> pulled in a score of directions by a score of crossing influences and
> contending forces?

The checks and balances in the American system were likely to
lead to, 'paralysis in the face of emergencies'. Leadership needed
to be concentrated in contrast to the present arrangements where
no one in Congress,

> stands for the nation. Each man stands for his part of the nation –
> and so management and combination, which may be effected in the
> dark are given the place that should be held by centered and respon-
> sible leadership, which would of necessity work in the focus of the
> national gaze.[27]

In a speech, 'Leaderless government', delivered in 1897, Wilson
reiterated his indictment of the American system. At the heart of
his condemnation lay the charge that the United States was literally 'leaderless'. The president was unable to give a lead in public
affairs. His scope for originating legislation was no more than that

of Queen Victoria; the veto power was only of marginal use and his constitutional right to suggest legislation to Congress was, in practice, largely meaningless for Congress jealously guarded its legislative prerogatives and was not compelled to heed presidential suggestions.[28]

At the turn of the century Wilson's thinking underwent change. For more than twenty years he had bemoaned the absence of opportunities for 'centered and responsible leadership' in the American system, whereas in the preface to a new edition of *Congressional Government*, written in 1900, Wilson argued that the war with Spain in 1898 had set in train changes in the distribution of power that might outdate his earlier ideas. The war had brought the United States into international politics and:

> when foreign affairs play a prominent part in the politics and policies of a nation, its Executive must of necessity be its guide: must utter every initial judgement, take every first step of action, supply the information upon which it is to act, suggest and in large measure control its conduct. The President of the United States is now, as of course, at the front of affairs.[29]

By the time Wilson delivered the lectures that were to be published in 1908 as *Constitutional Government in the United States* he had become even more optimistic about the possibilities of leadership. In contrast to his earlier mechanistic view of the constitution he now saw it in organic terms, as being capable of growth and evolution to take account of new circumstances. This adaptability had made it possible for the president to become:

> The leader of his party and the guide of the nation in political purpose, and therefore in legal action.

> [The president was now seen] as the unifying force in our complex system.

> [The president's] is the only national voice in affairs. Let him once win the admiration and confidence of the country and no other single force can withstand him. . . If he rightly interprets the national thought and boldly insists upon it, he is irresistible; the country never feels the zest for action so much as when its President is of such insight and calibre. Its instinct is for unified action and it craves a single leader.

> [The president's] office is anything he has the sagacity and force to make it.

The President is at liberty, both in law and conscience to be as big a man as he can.

The Constitution bids him speak, and times of stress and change must more and more thrust upon him the attitude of originator of policies. His is the vital place of action in the system.[30]

Wilson elaborated further on his now remarkably expansive and modern view of the presidency in a letter written in 1913 as he prepared to take up office. Passivity in the White House in the manner of James Buchanan or William Howard Taft would no longer suffice, for presidents were now expected to be real leaders, willing to shoulder a wide range of responsibilities:

He is expected by the nation to be the leader of his party as well as the chief executive officer of the government, and the country will take no excuses from him. He must play the part and play it successfully, or lose the country's confidence. He must be prime minister, as much concerned with the guidance of legislation as with the just and orderly execution of the law; and he is spokesman of the nation in everything, even the most momentous and most delicate dealings of the government with foreign nations.[31]

All this was a far cry from the Whiggish notions of the Founding Fathers who had seen only a limited role for the chief executive. The new Wilsonian vision either explicitly or implicitly conferred upon the man in the White House all the roles and responsibilities we associate with the presidency today.

Wilson's unbending determination to be a president in accordance with the theoretical model he had spent many years developing quickly became apparent. He sought to make himself the prime mover in the making of public policy. He believed that to achieve this the president had to dominate the legislative process; he must become chief legislator, a prime minister in all but name. Theodore Roosevelt had to some extent blazed the trail; he had been active in pressing legislative proposals on Congress and had achieved some notable successes, but Wilson's approach was far more ambitious.

He began with the inspired revival of a custom that had elapsed more than a century before, that of presidents addressing Congress personally. Wilson believed he could use such occasions to help bridge the gap that the Constitution had created between the legislative and executive branches; they were a means of demonstrating that:

the President of the United States is a person, not a mere department of Government hailing Congress from some isolated island of jealous power, not speaking naturally with his own voice – that he is a human being trying to cooperate with other human beings in a common service.[32]

In these addresses Wilson urged upon Congress the legislative proposals, proposals which he had previously formulated with his allies in the legislature. When his bills were before Congress, he monitored their progress closely, conferring regularly with committee chairmen and, in the early years at least, meeting with individual members in a room at the Capitol. Fifty years later Lyndon Johnson spoke of the desirability of presidents developing an 'almost incestuous' relationship with Congress and their need 'to build a system that stretches from the cradle to the grave, from the moment a bill is introduced to the moment it is officially enrolled as the law of the land'.[33] Wilson was no Johnson; he was not so manically obsessed with the minutiae of policy-making. Nevertheless he involved himself in the detail of the legislative process to a degree that no president had done before.[34]

To supplement this unprecedented personal involvement Wilson followed the example of Theodore Roosevelt in using his formidable oratorical powers to drum up support among the public for his measures. As he had done as Governor of New Jersey, he took to 'the stump' as a way of bringing recalcitrant legislators into line. Wilson also drew on his New Jersey experience in making deft use of the Democratic caucus in the House of Representatives to advance his programme.

At the beginning of his first term in particular, Wilson was a remarkably successful leader of the legislature, securing the passage of a number of landmark measures, including a major tariff reform bill, the Federal Reserve Act, the act setting up the Federal Trade Commission and the Clayton Anti-Trust Act. These early successes in addition to numerous other legislative triumphs suggest that no chief executive has played a larger part than Wilson in establishing the crucial presidential role of chief legislator. In the words of otherwise not very sympathetic biographers, 'it was [Wilson] who set the stage for what is now generally regarded as one of the most important functions of the President: the formulation of a legislative program, and the exertion of his power to secure its passage.'[35]

Wilson's style as chief legislator was not, however, without its flaws and whilst his successors learned much from his early success there were also important lessons to be drawn from the disastrous conclusion to his presidency. In 1908 he had argued that the presidency required 'a man who understands his own day and the needs of the country, and who has the personality and the initiative to enforce his views both upon the people and upon Congress'.[36] The key word in this quotation is 'enforce'. The future president apparently believed that a chief executive with the right combination of talents would be able to impose his will on both the people and the legislature.

This was, at the least, a suspect view, as Edward House, the President's friend and adviser pointed out in conversation:

> We talked much of leadership and its importance in government. He has demonstrated this to an unusual degree. He thinks our form of government can be changed by personal leadership; but I thought the Constitution should be altered, for no matter how great a leader a man was, I could see situations that would block him unless the Constitution was modified.[37]

As House suggests, Wilson was unduly optimistic about what could be achieved by 'great' leadership; even the most talented of presidents have relatively few opportunites for imposing their will on the American political system. Effective leadership from the White House requires not so much force as an ability to cooperate and negotiate with other leaders who share authority and power with the president. Relations between the executive and legislative branches are complicated by the fact that 'their formal powers are so intertwined that neither will accomplish very much, for very long, without the acquiescence of the other.'[38] In seeking congressional cooperation presidents are obliged to engage in rather subtle processes of give and take: to bargain, to accommodate and to compromise. However, such tasks did not come easily to a man of Wilson's temperament.

He was anything but a gregarious man, tending to be stiff and aloof in face-to-face situations with people outside his intimate circle of friends and relations. As Arthur Link noted, Wilson 'was definitely not a hale fellow well met: in ordinary social relations he was shy retiring and diffident'.[39] To his critics, President Wilson came across as a fiercely opinionated, intellectually overbearing man, with a powerful moral streak and an inclination to see himself as an instrument of God's will.

Compromise did not come easily to Wilson. It was not that he was incapable of compromise; he had, on occasion, spoken of the merits of such tactics and he had himself made more than a few compromises in his struggle to reach the White House. But once he had achieved high office and was in a position to wield power, compromise became increasingly difficult for him. In the early stages of the formulation of a policy, he might be amenable to adjustments and concessions, but once he had decided on his position, opponents were treated as either knaves or fools and compromise with them became impossible.

When we add to these characteristics Wilson's often expressed contempt for Congress in his pre-presidential writings and speeches it is not difficult to see why many members of the legislature became resentful of his leadership. At first this was confined to mutterings on the sidelines, but eventually it was to play a major part in destroying Wilson's most cherished dream, the participation of the United States in the League of Nations. Wilson's defeat on this issue was to set back the development of the presidency for more than a decade.

When the United States entered World War I Wilson, unlike Lincoln, was careful to seek congressional approval for many of the various administrative arrangements needed to place the country on a war footing.[40] In the conduct of international affairs, on the other hand, he had no doubts as to the primacy of the president's role. Even in *Congressional Government* where he had been so gloomy regarding the great power of Congress and the weakness of the president he had found some grounds for optimism in the foreign policy area. The chief executive's right to initiate negotiations with foreign powers, so Wilson argued,

> affords him a chance to get the country into such scrapes, so pledged in the view of the world to certain courses of action, that the Senate hesitates to bring about the appearance of dishonor which would follow its refusal to ratify the rash promises or to support the indiscreet threats of the Department of State.[41]

The Spanish–American War and Roosevelt's aggressive assertion of the power of the president in foreign policy-making had given Wilson further encouragement leading him to say in 1908:

'The initiative in foreign affairs, which the President possesses without any restriction whatever, is virtually the power to control them absolutely.'[42]

In office Wilson did his utmost to live up to this sweeping affirmation of presidential rights in the making of foreign policy, treating congressional opposition with disdain, ignoring the State Department and declining to consult with his Cabinet. Congressional resentment at Wilson's acting like a 'divine right monarch' in foreign affairs reached new heights with the President's handling of negotiations over the Treaty of Versailles.[43] At the end of his second term when Wilson was inevitably weaker *vis-à-vis* Congress than he had ever been and under the added pressure of serious illness, all the limitations in his style of leadership came to the fore. If he had been stiff, uncommunicative and domineering in dealing with the legislature before, these tendencies now became even more marked.

Utterly convinced that his plan for a League of Nations was right, that God willed it and the people of America and the world demanded it, Wilson declined to give an inch to his many critics. His preparations for the Paris Peace Conference incensed not only the Republicans in the Senate, but also many of his own friends and followers. They were shocked by his insistence on attending the conference in person, his refusal to include any senators of either party in the American delegation and his unwillingness to discuss his plans before he left.

After his return from Paris with the Treaty, Wilson became engaged in a bitter struggle with the Senate over ratification. That struggle centred primarily on the case for and against certain reservations that some senators wished to add to the Treaty, the most important of which were, significantly, concerned with preserving the rights of the Senate. During this historic confrontation public and Senate meetings reverberated with impassioned complaints against President Wilson's lack of respect for legislative prerogatives and his autocratic style. For his part, the President, now a sick and broken man. steadfastly refused to compromise on the proposed reservations even though these were really only restatements of constitutional realities.

Wilson has been widely accused of self-immolation. According to Link, he 'proceeded by his own hand to remove the corner stone of his edifice of peace' while Thomas Bailey argues that the President 'slew his own brain child'.[44] Whether these verdicts are correct or not it is undeniable that the failure of the Senate to ratify the Treaty of Versailles was one of the most calamitous rebuffs that any president has ever suffered at the hand of Congress.[45] Not only was it a devastating blow to Wilson personally it was also an enormously important institutional defeat that prepared the way for more than a decade of weakness in the executive branch.

Woodrow Wilson's contribution to the institutional development of the American federal government was mixed. He succeeded brilliantly in making the presidency the 'vital place of action in the system'; in other words, the principal source of that effective national leadership that, he believed, the United States so badly needed. In office he proved to be for the most part,

> an able administrator, a shrewd leader of his party, a sensitive 'spokesman for the real purpose and sentiment of the country,' an impressive head of state, and, thanks to his academic theory of the President as a prime minister in relation to Congress, a genuinely effective leader of legislation.[46]

In adroitly exercising these functions Wilson did much to lay the foundations of the modern presidency; in the end, however, he overreached himself.

His inordinate faith in the power of leadership led him to believe that a president with sufficient determination and talent could override, once and for all, the checks and balances in the Constitution. But in this he was mistaken; outstanding presidents may temporarily bridge the separation of powers during 'honeymoon' periods or crisis situations, but inevitably such episodes are short-lived and when they end the Constitution comes back into full play. To put it another way, presidents may momentarily gain mastery over the policy-making process. They may sideline Congress for a while, but it is always only for a while. Even in the making of foreign policy where the president's constitutional position is strongest he cannot afford to underestimate the power of congressional resistance.

In the traumatic closing months of his second term, Wilson also placed too much reliance on what he perceived as his place at the head of public opinion. In his ruminations on leadership over the years he had put public oratory at the forefront of the qualities required of great leaders. And when he became more optimistic about the possibilities for leadership in the American system he laid great stress on what a president could accomplish if he gained control over public opinion: 'If he rightly interprets the national thought and boldly insists upon it, he is irresistible.'[47]

Like Theodore Roosevelt before him and many presidents since, Wilson was also inclined to make much of the chief executive's position as the only political leader with a national constituency, in contrast to members of Congress who represented only partial interests. He also emulated Roosevelt in constantly seeking to pressure legislators into cooperation by appealing over their heads to their constituents.[48]

In the early years of his presidency such tactics had paid off handsomely. His impressive oratorical skills had allowed him to marshall public opinion behind his legislative programme and to break the gridlock of the American political system. But the possibilities inherent in such tactics are not without limits and, in any case, Wilson's hold on public opinion became increasingly tenuous in later years.

As Robert Dahl has recently argued, the notion of the president possessing a national mandate is of doubtful logic.[49] Furthermore, Wilson's claim to a popular mandate in support of his policies was often insecurely founded. As Governor, President and would-be world leader he made a habit of asserting that he spoke on behalf of public opinion, but the substance behind these bold claims was not always evident.[50] He was, for instance, first elected to the presidency by a minority vote; his re-election in 1916 was secured with 51 per cent of the total vote; he failed in his appeal for a vote of confidence in the mid-term elections of 1918 and he could not have derived much comfort from the 1920 presidential election when his party's candidate was overwhelmingly defeated.

None of this is to deny Wilson's major role in the development of the presidency. As that most distinguished of Wilson scholars, Arthur Link observed:

> Few men have come to the presidency with bolder schemes of leadership or made greater contributions to the development of effective national government in the United States than Woodrow Wilson . . . historians a century hence will probably rate his expansion and perfection of the powers of the presidency as his most lasting contribution.[51]

That contribution, it should be noted, includes much more than the forceful, resourceful leadership from the White House that Wilson exemplifies; account must also be taken of the elaborate theorizing and the progamme of educating his compatriots that he engaged in for years before he became president. Even now many of Wilson's ideas are of interest to commentators and political scientists. More than a hundred years after first publication, *Congressional Government* is constantly cited in the literature of American politics. Beyond that Wilson clearly exerted a large influence on many of his successors, including Richard Nixon and, most importantly of all, Franklin Roosevelt.

Franklin Roosevelt, 1933–45

Notwithstanding the existence of some eminent predecessors no president has had a greater impact on the development of his office than Franklin Roosevelt. He revitalized and substantially enlarged the presidency and exercised the powers of the office with a skill unmatched before or since.

Testimonies to FDR's importance in the history of the presidency are numerous. In common with many other political scientists Clinton Rossiter attributes to Roosevelt the creation of the modern presidency while William Leuchtenberg describes him as 'the architect of a new political era' who has cast a giant shadow over every president since.[52] In the same vein Richard Neustadt's classic work, *Presidential Power*, has Roosevelt as its hero; he, we are led to believe, provides the model of an ideal president:

> [His] methods were the product of his insights, his incentives, and his confidence. No President in this century has had a sharper sense of personal power, a sense of what it is and where it comes from; none has had more hunger for it, few have had more use for it, and only one or two could match his faith in his own competence to use it. Perception and desire and self-confidence, combined produced their own reward. No modern President has been more nearly master in the White House.[53]

Evidence to support the high praise heaped upon Roosevelt by so many scholars is considerable. He was, without question, an exceptional president. He took up office when the country was in the depths of the Great Depression, the very foundations of the capitalist system apparently crumbling and national self-confidence at a dangerously low ebb. One in four Americans was out of work; national income had declined precipitously; two-thirds of the banks were shut while the remainder were operating under severe restrictions; the New York Stock Exchange meanwhile closed down on the morning of the new president's inauguration.

In his inaugural address Roosevelt gave clear indications of his determination to respond to this desperate situation by offering strong leadership from the White House. He aimed to make it, in Woodrow Wilson's words, 'the vital place of action in the system'. The crisis, Roosevelt was certain, could not be met as his predecessor seemed to believe by mere exhortation. 'This nation,' he said, 'asks for action, and action now!' and he gave Congress due warning of his readiness to meet that demand:

> It is to be hoped that the normal balance of executive and legislative authority may be wholly adequate to meet the unprecedented task before us. But it may be that an unprecedented demand and need for undelayed action may call for temporary departure from that normal balance of public procedure. I am prepared under my consti-tutional duty to recommend the measures that a stricken nation in the midst of a stricken world may require.

If Congress declined to accept his proposals, Roosevelt went on,

> I shall not evade the clear course of duty that will then confront me. I shall ask the Congress for the one remaining instrument to meet the crisis – broad executive power to wage a war against the emer-gency as great as the power that would be given me if we were in fact invaded by a foreign foe. . . . The people of the United States have asked for discipline and direction under leadership. They have made me the present instrument of their wishes.[54]

These riveting statements with their clear echoes of Lincoln, The-odore Roosevelt and Wilson set the stage for an unparalleled ex-hibition of strong executive leadership. Roosevelt moved swiftly and decisively to deal with the immediate banking crisis, issuing executive orders, submitting a bill to Congress and making a radio broadcast to restore public confidence.

Within hours of the opening of a special session of Congress, con-vened at the President's behest, emergency banking legislation was passed and during the next 'hundred days' fifteen major reform bills were passed including the Agricultural Adjustment Act, the act establishing the Tennessee Valley Authority, the Federal Emergency Relief Act and the National Industrial Recovery Act. Even after the 'honeymoon' period, in circumstances less favourable to the executive branch, Roosevelt's command of the legislative process remained impressive. In the period 1934–6 further major legislation was passed including the Wagner Act guaranteeing the rights of organized labour, a tax reform bill, the act setting up the Works Progress Administration with its gigantic programme of public works and, most significantly of all, the Social Security Act. The latter, providing for a federal system of old age pensions and unemployment insurance, was a near revolutionary development in the provision of welfare services by the federal government.

Most of the techniques employed by Roosevelt in his spectacularly successful efforts to gain control of the legislative process had been used before, but in his hands they acquired a new potency. He revived Wilson's practice of addressing Congress in person and he made extensive use of special messages, often backing them up with draft bills which administration supporters would then introduce. The President dispatched members of his staff to Capitol Hill to lobby on behalf of his proposals; he arranged also for the distribution of patronage as a way of lubricating the legislative process. In addition, Roosevelt himself met with congressional party leaders, committee chairmen and individual members of the legislature.

In his face-to-face encounters with legislators Roosevelt's personality was one of his greatest assets. The warmth of his smile in combination with his charm, his bonhomie, his optimism and his likeability made him, for most people at least, a difficult man to refuse. In his personal dealings with legislators inclined to be prickly and self-important and with perspectives quite different from his, Roosevelt demonstrated a rare ability to tend egos and to smooth feathers:

> He was a master at the art of providing congressional gratification – at the easy first name, the cordial handshake, the radiant smile, the intimate joke, the air of accessibility and concern, the quasi-confidential interview, the photograph at the White House desk, the headline in the hometown newspaper.[55]

As noted earlier in this chapter, legislative leadership also depends on a president's ability to marshall and manipulate public opinion. Much will turn on his capacity to appeal to the people over the heads of Congress. FDR carried the presidency to new heights in this respect. His appearances in public had electrifying effects. The personality characteristics so impressive in private were no less so on the public stage. His audiences were stirred by the timbre of his voice and reassured by his beaming countenance. On public platforms Roosevelt, despite his physical disability, exuded energy, determination and confidence, convincing many of his hearers that under his dynamic leadership the United States could fight its way out of the Depression.

The press and other forms of media provide additional means whereby presidents can reach out to and communicate with the public at large. Theodore Roosevelt, that earlier exponent of the rhetorical presidency, had skilfully manipulated the press to his advantage. The desirability of a good relationship with the press was very evident to Woodrow Wilson, but he had singularly failed to bring it about. Franklin Roosevelt, by contrast, took up where his cousin had left off and was especially impressive in his dealings with the press. Remarkably, press conferences were held roughly twice a week throughout his presidency; the tone was set at the first such gathering in the Oval Office:

> Mr Roosevelt was introduced to each correspondent. Many of them he already knew and greeted by name – first name. For each he had a handshake and the Roosevelt smile. When the questioning began, the full virtuosity of the new Chief Executive was demonstrated. Cigarette-holder in mouth at a jaunty angle, he met the reporters on their own grounds. His answers were swift, positive, illuminating. He had exact information at his fingertips. He showed an impressive understanding of public problems and administrative methods. He was lavish in his confidences and 'background information'. He was informal, communicative, gay. When he evaded a question it was done frankly. He was thoroughly at ease. He made no effort to conceal his pleasure in the give and take of the situation.[56]

Roosevelt's consummate skill in handling the press added a powerful dimension to his leadership. This was further enhanced by his legendary mastery of radio. As Governor of New York he had countered legislative opposition by appealing directly to the people through radio addresses and he now developed this revolutionary new technique further with his highly effective 'fireside chats' with the American people.

None of the techniques used by Roosevelt so far discussed was without precedent. Each one had been used by previous presidents – even radio was, in a sense, an extension of what had gone before, making possible communication with the people on a scale far beyond that available to earlier presidents. However, one of Roosevelt's genuine innovations was his extension of the range of what is known as legislative clearance, which significantly strengthened the president's control over the legislative process.

In the earlier age of Congress-centred government, executive agencies dealt directly with congressional committees. The Budget and Accounting Act of 1921 changed that in one important respect by requiring presidents to prepare a unified budget and providing for the Bureau of the Budget to coordinate, on the chief executive's behalf, appropriations requests emanating from government agencies. This change strengthened the arm of the president, but Roosevelt went further; during his administration the Bureau of the Budget became a clearing house not just for appropriations bills, but for all legislation coming out of government departments and agencies. Richard Neustadt has emphasized the significance of this development:

> The Roosevelt clearance system, thus established, incorporated its financial precursor but was no mere extension of the budget process. On the contrary, in form and fact and terms of reference this was Roosevelt's creation, intended to protect not just his budget but his prerogatives, his freedom of action, and his choice of policies, in an era of fast growing government and of determined presidential leadership.[57]

The role of the Bureau of the Budget was also widened in another way that added weight to the president's position. The Bureau already advised the chief executive on whether he should veto appropriations bills, but now this responsibility was extended to include all manner of bills. This made it possible for the veto to be wielded more systematically and more effectively. Roosevelt had always seen great potential in the president's constitutional right to veto legislation. The veto power, he believed, 'was among the presidency's greatest attributes, an independent and responsible act of participation in the legislative process, and a means of enforcing congressional and agency respect for presidential preferences or programs'.[58]

No president has made wider use of the veto than FDR. Previously chief executives had used it sparingly, with the exception of Grover Cleveland who wielded it extensively against private pension bills. In the twentieth century, prior to Roosevelt's arrival in the White House, presidents vetoed about nine bills per year whereas he, during twelve years in office, vetoed no less than 635. According to one source, Roosevelt's enthusiasm for the veto extended to asking his staff to find legislation that he might veto 'in order to remind Congress that they were being watched'.[59]

No president has been a more effective chief legislator than Franklin Roosevelt; he passed with flying colours 'the classic test of greatness in the White House'.[60] On the other hand, there was little that was completely new in his approach. As Edward Corwin noted:

> While Franklin D. Roosevelt's accomplishment as legislator first and last surpassed all previous records, yet the story of it, so far as it is of interest to us, offers little of novelty. Old techniques were sharpened and improved, sometimes with the aid of modern gadgets – for example, radio. But for the most part, except for the dimensions that the familiar sometimes attains, the pleasure afforded by the study of it is that of recognition rather than of surprise.[61]

Roosevelt's principal contribution lay in the scale of his activities as chief legislator. He recognized it as his most important role, understanding that strong executive leadership of the sort that the nation required was not possible without command of the legislative process. FDR devoted more attention to legislation than any president had done before; he fired off more messages to Congress, introduced more bills and exercised his veto more often.[62]

Arising from this phenomenal legislative activity Roosevelt presided over a massive expansion in the scope of the national government. Under his aegis the United States turned its back on the *laissez-faire* attitudes of the past and moved towards a positive state. Like his cousin Theodore, FDR believed that the federal government had a special responsibility for the public welfare. It could not sit idly by in the face of the widespread and multiform distress caused by the Depression; it was obliged to take steps to address these problems:

> Government has a final responsibility for the well-being of its citizenship. If private cooperative endeavor fails to provide work for willing hands and relief for the unfortunate, those suffering hardship

from no fault of their own have a right to call upon the Government for aid; and a government worthy of its name must make fitting response.[6]

For Roosevelt and those around him, the 'fitting response' demanded relief programmes to help get the unemployed back to work. It required also a safety net of welfare services to protect the citizenry from the vagaries of economic forces – old age pensions, aid for the disabled and for dependent children, and unemployment compensation. Furthermore, industry and commerce could no longer be allowed to operate in a context largely free of govermental control. The government was obliged to intervene in business affairs on behalf of the national interest; regulation was required to protect the collective bargaining rights of employees, to supervise the stock market and to bring order to the banking system.

These and the many other programmes that comprised the New Deal represented a fundamental shift in American attitudes towards the state with the federal government now expected to meet a whole new range of responsibilities. Many new agencies were required as well as a vast increase in the size of the federal civil service. In addition to his responsibilities as chief legislator and principal policy-maker, it fell to the President to coordinate and direct the enormous governmental apparatus that his policies had created. At an early stage it became evident that this was beyond the competence of the chief executive as presently constituted.

The Brownlow Committee set up by Roosevelt in 1936 to consider the case for reorganizing the executive branch stated, 'The President needs help. His immediate staff assistance is entirely inadequate.' Presidents had always had staff to assist them, but these had been remarkably few in number. Indeed when Roosevelt first became President the White House staff consisted of thirty-seven people, only nine of whom were of professional rank.[64] In the early years of his presidency Roosevelt informally developed a sizeable staff of advisers and assistants, but the emergence of the Executive Office of the President (EOP), as suggested by the Brownlow Committee, increased substantially the numbers and the importance of presidential staff.

The Reorganization Act of 1939 formally established the EOP. This new body was to include the White House Office, comprised of the president's personal aides and assistants. Also included was the Bureau of the Budget, transferred from its previous illogical home in the Treasury. The Bureau was also greatly strengthened and its functions were widened. It would now not only prepare the president's budget and be involved in legislative clearance. It would, in addition, be responsible for assisting the president with administrative management. The remaining three components of the EOP in its original form were to be the National Resources Planning Board, the Liaison Office for Personnel Management and the Office of Government Reports.

The establishment of the EOP was a crucial turning-point in the history of the American political system and, insofar as he was its instigator, one of Roosevelt's most significant contributions to the development of the presidency. As John Hart says, 'It is difficult to imagine how the presidency could have survived as an effective institution in American government without the addition of an enhanced presidential staff.'[65] Presidents have the gravest difficulties as it is in gaining control of a notoriously fractious political system; without the expertise and assistance of the EOP they would be helpless and the United States would be truly ungovernable.

During the late 1930s President Roosevelt began to turn his attention from domestic to foreign affairs. Earlier in the decade, in the face of the Depression, Congress had willingly conceded the initiative to the executive in domestic policy, but it was unwilling to allow such leeway in the making of foreign policy. The Italian invasion of Ethiopia in 1935 led to the passage of neutrality legislation by Congress aimed at preventing the president from intervening on either side.

In the following year, however, support for the President's authority in international affairs was forthcoming from a surprising source, the US Supreme Court. In a decision of great importance, discussed more fully in Chapter 5, *United States* v. *Curtiss-Wright Export Corporation* case, the Court gave powerful backing to the President's claim to direct foreign policy. A majority of the justices understood the need for statutory restraints on the executive in domestic affairs, but saw foreign policy in a different light; they conceded the 'plenary and exclusive power of the President as the sole organ of the federal government in the field of international relations – a power which does not require as a basis for its exercise an act of Congress'.[66]

Notwithstanding the weight of the Court's influence, as the 1930s drew to a close, it took all of Roosevelt's leadership skill to overcome popular and congressional resistance to the United States becoming involved in the rapidly developing crises in Europe and the Far East. In 1940, through an executive agreement Roosevelt exchanged American destroyers for leases on British bases. This action was widely interpreted at home and abroad as a step towards American intervention on the side of Britain and France. These suspicions gained further ground in 1941 when Roosevelt obtained from Congress Lend-Lease legislation. However, it took the Japanese attack on Pearl Harbor to sunder finally the log-jam of isolationism and resistance to Roosevelt's foreign policy on Capitol Hill and in the country at large: 'Only on the day of infamy did Franklin Roosevelt's triumphant third term war leadership really begin.'[67]

Once the United States had entered the war the growth of the presidency proceeded by leaps and bounds. Congress delegated extensively to the executive branch and Roosevelt himself assumed a dominant role in the conduct of the war, surpassing the examples even of Lincoln and Wilson. The federal bureaucracy was expanded even further to facilitate the waging of war and the President claimed that the circumstances of total war required him 'not only to direct military operations abroad but to manage economic and social affairs at home'.[68] In the face of this new emergency Congress broadly acquiesced and the enlargement of the presidency proceeded even further.

Franklin Roosevelt was an exceptional man and his influence on the development of the presidency was unquestionably vast; however, it is possible to read too much into his incumbency. Too little account is sometimes taken of the precedents set by others and insufficient attention paid to the unusually fortuitous circumstances he enjoyed and the failures that he experienced.

It is an exaggeration to say that FDR 'created' the modern presidency. He had many sterling qualities but in no sense was he an original thinker; he had no preconceived theory of the presidency to guide him as he took up office. What Roosevelt did possess was a formidable gift for leadership plus a clear understanding of what the likes of Theodore Roosevelt and Wilson had done in their pioneering efforts to be strong, reforming chief executives. To a large extent FDR followed where others had led; eminent predecessors blazed the trails upon which he built multi-lane highways. Rather than making Roosevelt the father of the modern presidency it is more appropriate to say, 'It was with Theodore Roosevelt and Woodrow Wilson that the modern concept of the strong presidency was born, and during the New Deal and its afterglow that the doctrine was crystallised.'[69]

The extravagant accolades accorded Roosevelt by American academics also give insufficient weight to the extraordinary good fortune that he enjoyed. Luck is a major element in the success or failure of any president, but FDR had far more luck than most. Popular landslides and giant congressional majorities gave him advantages that few presidents have had. Moreover, his stunning early successes as a chief legislator have to be seen against a background of desperate crisis when the American people were crying out for leadership and Congress virtually threw itself into the President's arms. And then when Roosevelt's leadership was threatened late in his second term international affairs followed by the onset of war hugely reinforced his position.

The challenges that Roosevelt faced in his second term tend to be overlooked or downplayed by his supporters. By the end of 1938 his mastery of Congress appeared to be a thing of the past. In part this was due to the usual cyclical shifts in the balance of power between Congress and president. However, Roosevelt had also brought some of these difficulties on his own head by – in a manner not dissimilar to Wilson's over the Treaty of Versailles – catastrophically overreaching himself with his plan to 'pack' the Supreme Court.

Briefly stated, the plan was intended to be a vehicle for circumventing the Court's notorious opposition to the New Deal by allowing the President to appoint a number of new justices. Unfortunately for Roosevelt his much vaunted skill in dealing with Congress and marshalling public opinion seemed to desert him at this stage. His carefully collaborative style in dealing with the legislature was abandoned as the President put together his court-packing plan in secret and sprang it suddenly on Congress much to the chagrin of his own party leaders, committee chairmen and rank-and-file Democrats. Many members of the legislature saw Roosevelt's high-handed behaviour as evidence of a president wilfully overstepping the boundaries of the Constitution.

No less surprising was the President's loss of his command of public opinion as it became increasingly apparent that the American people were not happy with his assault on the judicial branch. Congress refused to agree to the plan, but voluntary retirements from the Court allowed FDR to claim that, although he had lost the battle, he had won the campaign. It was for all that an important defeat. This episode fed the ever-present suspicions among congressmen of executive constitutional usurpation, divided the Democratic Party and badly eroded Roosevelt's public support. It also brought to an end his mastery of Congress, a situation that was alleviated only by war.

Finally, it is as well to bear in mind that the overwhelming majority of American political scientists and historians write from a position of philosophical sympathy for Roosevelt and his aims. In short, a large proportion of those who have written on the presidency have been liberal Democrats, a fact not unconnected with the excesses of esteem bestowed on Roosevelt. Making the presidency a fount of 'moral leadership' and greatly expanding the scope of the federal goverment evokes praise among those of a liberal persuasion, but is received much less sympathetically by conservatives. The enormous enthusiasm for Roosevelt and all his works in the academic community reflects, in part, the ideological preferences of that community. As students of politics concerned with maintaining achievable standards of objectivity we need to guard against using yardsticks that by definition favour presidents who are liberal Democrats and condemn their conservative counterparts.

Notes

1. Sidney Milkis and Michael Nelson, *The American Presidency: Origins and Development*, Congressional Quarterly Press, Washington DC, 1990, pp.116–67.
2. *Congressional Government*, Houghton Mifflin, Boston, 1925 (first published 1885), pp. 253–4.
3. Letter to George Otto Trevelyan, 19 June 1908 in Hermann Hagedorn (ed.), *The Theodore Roosevelt Treasury*, G.P. Putnam's Sons, New York, 1957, p. 195.
4. Wayne Andrews (ed.), *The Autobiography of Theodore Roosevelt*, Charles Scribner's Sons, New York, 1958, pp. 197–8.
5. Henry F. Pringle, *Theodore Roosevelt: A Biography*, Harcourt, Brace and Company, 1956, p. 191.

6. Edward S. Corwin *The President: Office and Powers*, New York University Press, New York, 1957, p. 154.
7. As quoted in Milkis and Nelson, *op. cit.* p. 201.
8. Andrews, *op. cit.*
9. Jeffrey Tulis, *The Rhetorical Presidency*, Princeton University Press, Princeton, 1987, p. 29. The great exception to this pattern of restraint was Andrew Johnson who went about the country vigorously defending his policy towards the South and bitterly attacking his opponents. The unacceptability of this conduct is to be seen in one of the articles of impeachment brought against Johnson. The President was castigated for, 'intemperate, inflammatory, and scandalous harangues . . . indecent and unbecoming in the Chief Magistrate of the United States' (Tulis, pp. 90–1).
10. Andrews, *op. cit.*, p. 195.
11. Milkis and Nelson, *op. cit.*, p. 196.
12. Tulis, *op. cit.*, p. 4.
13. Woodrow Wilson, *Congressional Government*, Houghton Mifflin, Boston, 1925, p. xix.
14. Andrews, *op. cit.*, p. 268.
15. Corwin, *op. cit.*, pp. 442–3.
16. To Roosevelt's chagrin the Wilson administration later apologized to Colombia and agreed to pay an indemnity.
17. Quoted in Milkis and Nelson, *op. cit.*, p. 206.
18. Arthur Schlesinger Jnr, 'Congress and the Making of American Foreign Policy' in Rexford Tugwell and Thomas Cronin (eds), *The Presidency Reappraised*, Praeger, New York, 1974, p. 88.
19. *ibid.*, p. 89.
20. See Clinton Rossiter, *The American Presidency*, Harcourt Brace and World, New York, 1964, p. 103.
21. As quoted in Samuel Eliot Morison and Henry Steele Commager, *The Growth of the American Republic*, Oxford University Press, New York, 1942, vol. 2, p. 404.
22. Hagedorn, *op. cit.*, p. 195.
23. Arthur Link (eds), *The Papers of Woodrow Wilson*, Princeton University Press, Princeton, 1966–, vol. 4, p. 255.
24. Ray Stannard Baker, *Woodrow Wilson: Life and Letters*, William Heinemann, London, 1932, vol. 4, p. 98.
25. Link, *op. cit.*, vol. 1, pp. 493–510.
26. Wilson, *op. cit.*, p. 203.
27. Link, *op. cit.*, vol. 6, pp. 221–39.
28. *ibid.*, vol. 10, p. 291.
29. *op. cit.*, pp. xx–xxi.
30. Columbia University Press, New York, 1908, pp. 60, 68–70 and 73.
31. Link, *op. cit.*, vol. 27, pp. 99–100.
32. *ibid.*, p. 270.
33. Doris Kearns, *Lyndon Johnson and the American Dream*, New American Library, New York, 1976, pp. 236–7.

34. Stephen Wayne, *The Legislative Presidency*, Harper and Row, New York, 1978, p. 15.
35. Alexander and Juliette George, *Woodrow Wilson and Colonel House*, Dover Publications, New York, 1964, p. 58.
36. *Constitutional Government in the United States*, Columbia University Press, New York, 1908, p. 65.
37. As quoted in Charles Seymour (ed.), *The Intimate Papers of Colonel House*, Ernest Benn, London, 1926.
38. Richard Neustadt, *Presidential Power*, John Wiley and Sons, New York, 1976, p. 105.
39. Arthur Link, *Wilson: The Road to the White House*, Princeton University Press, Princeton, 1947, p. 95.
40. Rossiter, *op cit.*, p. 105.
41. *op. cit.*, pp. 233–4.
42. *Constitutional Government in the United States*, *op. cit.*, p. 77.
43. Arthur Link, *Wilson the Diplomatist*, Johns Hopkins University Press, Baltimore, 1957, p. 23.
44. *Woodrow Wilson and the Great Betrayal*, The Macmillan Company, New York, 1945, p. 277.
45. See my 'Henry Cabot Lodge and the League of Nations', *Journal of American Studies*, vol. 4, no. 2, February 1971.
46. Rossiter, *op. cit.*, p. 104.
47. *Constitutional Government in the United States, op. cit.*, p. 68.
48. Wilson employed this tactic as Governor of New Jersey and even threatened to use it on an international scale by appealing to the European masses over the heads of their rulers. Georges, *op. cit.*, p. 202.
49. 'The Myth of the Presidential Mandate', *Political Science Quarterly 104*, Fall 1990, pp. 355–72.
50. On one famous occasion Wilson claimed to speak 'for the silent mass of mankind everywhere'. Georges, *op. cit.*, p. 195.
51. *Wilson: The New Freedom*, Princeton University Press, Princeton, 1956, p. 145.
52. *The American Presidency, op. cit.*, p. 142; *In the Shadow of FDR*, Cornell University Press, Ithaca, 1983, p. x.
53. *op. cit.*, p. 229.
54. As quoted in Morison and Commager, *op. cit.*, p. 589.
55. Arthur Schlesinger Jnr, *The Coming of the New Deal*, Houghton Mifflin, Boston, 1959, p. 536.
56. As quoted in William Leuchtenberg, 'Franklin Roosevelt: The First Modern President' in Fred Greenstein (ed.), *Leadership in the Modern Presidency*, Harvard University Press, Cambridge, Mass., 1988, p. 25.
57. Richard Neustadt, 'Presidency and Legislation: The Growth of Central Clearance', American Political Science Review, vol. 48, no. 3, September 1954. p. 650.
58. *ibid.*, p. 656.
59. Marcus Cunliffe, *American Presidents and the Presidency*, Fontana/Collins, London, 1972, p. 267.

60. James MacGregor Burns, *Roosevelt: The Lion and the Fox*, Harcourt, Brace, New York, 1956, p. 186.
61. *op. cit.*, p. 272.
62. Wayne, *op. cit.*, p. 16.
63. Greenstein, *op. cit.*, p. 24.
64. Stephen Hess, *Organizing the Presidency* (revised edition), Brookings, Washington DC, 1988, p. 23.
65. *The Presidential Branch*, Pergamon Press, New York, 1987, p. 35.
66. Schlesinger, *The Imperial Presidency, op. cit.*, p. 102.
67. James MacGregor Burns and Michael Beschloss, *The New Republic*, 7 April 1982, pp. 19–22.
68. Milkis and Nelson, *op. cit.*, p. 273.
69. James Sundquist, *The Decline and Resurgence of Congress*, Brookings, Washington DC, 1981, p. 9.

4

The Constraints on the Presidency

Franklin Roosevelt was an exceptionally fortunate president. He was elected and re-elected with large majorities and is party's margins of superiority over the opposition in Congress were usually vast. He also derived enormous benefit from being president during periods of national emergency. First the Depression and then World War II placed in abeyance many of the constraints on presidential power that bedevil chief executives in normal circumstances. And yet, despite his great good fortune and his many personal strengths, Roosevelt's mastery of the American political system was never complete. Even at the height of his powers he suffered set-backs, he lost control of Congress in his second term, he was often baulked by the Supreme Court and regularly frustrated by the bureaucracy.[1]

The fact that such a talented and greatly advantaged president should have so much difficulty in consistently asserting his authority is testimony to the fractious nature of the political system and its inherent tendency towards ungovernablity. In the United States, cultural and constitutional factors ensure that formal political power is not concentrated in the executive to the degree that is the case in the United Kingdom. Such power is fragmented and scattered in the American system; it is distributed centrifugally rather than a centripetally; it is shared among many leaders rather than concentrated in the hands of a few.

None of this is at all helpful to executive leadership and modern presidents are expected to be leaders. It is incumbent upon them to provide policies and programmes, to offer solutions to the nation's problems. Yet if presidents must lead, the widespread sharing of power severely limits their attempts to meet that responsibility. As Richard Neustadt has recently said:

> The President and Congress are at once so independent and so intertwined that neither can be said to govern save as both do. And even when they come together they face other claimants to a share in governing: the courts, the states, the press, the private interests, all protected by our Constitution, and the foreign governments that help to shape our policy. All these are separate institutions sharing each other's powers. To share is to limit; that is the heart of the matter.[2]

Presidents must face the realities of all this sharing of power as they seek to govern. Those who share power with them possess the capacity to thwart presidents, to prevent them from reaching their objectives. The man in the White House must gain the agreement or at least the acquiescence of these other leaders if he is to impose his preferences, his will on the political system. In short, presidents are anything but all-powerful rulers, or even prime ministers; they are closer to Gulliver figures – giants in theory, but in practice subject to a multitude of restraints. In domestic policy, in particular, the principal focus of this chapter, it is not at all appropriate to speak of an 'imperial' presidency; it makes more sense to use expressions such as the 'fettered', the 'tethered', or the 'impossible' presidency.[3]

Political culture and the Constitution

The American political culture is at the root of many of the restraints on presidential leadership. Political culture has been defined as 'a set of widely shared beliefs, values and norms concerning the relationship of citizens to their government and to one another in matters affecting public affairs.'[4]. Political culture is concerned with how people think about politics, not in a partisan sense, but in terms of what they expect of the political system. It deals with such questions as – how far should government intrude into the lives of the citizenry and how should political leaders act?

More than most, it would seem, Americans tend to be suspicious of all forms of authority and especially sceptical about government, constantly perceiving it in a negative light.[5] Thus James Madison, in Number 51 of the *Federalist Papers* saw government as a consequence of the imperfections of human nature: 'If men were angels, no government would be necessary.'[6] Similarly, two centuries later, Ronald Reagan based his 1980 appeal to the electorate in part on the slogan, 'Government is not the solution to our problems. Government is the problem.'

These negative attitudes towards government are deeply rooted in the American past. Those who established the United States were descendants of settlers who had left the Old World in search of religious and political freedom, economic opportunity and equality. These early settlers hoped to create a society different in important respects from those they had left, one

> where authority was distrusted and held in constant scrutiny; where the status of men flowed from their achievements and from their personal qualities, not from distinctions ascribed to them at birth; and where the use of power over the lives of men was jealously guarded and severely restricted. It was only where there was this defiance, this refusal to truckle, this distrust of all authority, political or social, that institutions would express human aspirations, not crush them.[7]

It was with such attitudes in mind that Americans began their experiments with constitutional forms in the late eighteenth century. Their purpose was to construct political mechanisms that would allow for the essential minimum level of government without encroaching upon the people's hard-won liberties. Even after the chastening experience of life under the Articles of Confederation they had no intention of erecting an all-powerful central state apparatus comparable to that in Britain. The Constitution drawn up in 1787 was designed to provide, in James Madison's words, for a 'compound republic' where 'the power surrendered by the people is first divided between two distinct governments, and then the portion allotted to each subdivided among two distinct and separate departments'.[8]

Madison's comment encapsulates the two main principles of the Constitution, federalism and the separation of powers. On American soil political leaders were to be given no open-ended grants of power; on the contrary, they were to be hedged in by a complex, decentralized and fragmented system where formal powers were shared among many leaders.

The Constitution has undergone much development in the last two centuries, but the concerns and fears that motivated the Founding Fathers have not lost their relevance. Americans continue to be sceptical about the virtues of government and near paranoid in their attitudes towards political leaders. As Barbara Kellerman has said:

> It would be difficult to exaggerate the importance on our political life of this resistance to leadership, this need to contain the authority of our leaders. It permeates our national traditions, customs, and ideals, and influences the character and form of our government. As much as anything else our basic antiauthority and even antigovernment attitude defines our political culture.[9]

Presidents, in particular, need to be keenly aware of these sentiments; they are expected to lead, but they must guard against the ever-present suspicions of executive dictatorship. It is not that Americans are immune to the appeals of strong leadership; those who display such qualities are often the subject of much admiration although, typically they are long dead like Washington, Lincoln or Roosevelt, or they can be safely admired from a distance like Winston Churchill, Margaret Thatcher or Mikhail Gorbachev. It is also the case that the American people have occasionally, in crisis situations, been prepared to shelve their traditional fears; in such circumstances they have been willing to set aside constitutional niceties and to ignore, momentarily, their longstanding antiauthority obsessions. Thus Lincoln during the Civil War, Wilson during World War I and Franklin Roosevelt in an era of domestic and international crisis, were all temporarily permitted to exercise strong leadership from the White House.

Such presidents were briefly allowed to override the constitutional arrangements providing for the sharing of power, but significantly, in each case, such episodes were followed by periods of anti-executive backlash: witness the attempt to use the impeachment process against Lincoln's successor, Andrew Johnson; the defeat of Wilson over the Treaty of Versailles and the routing of his party in the 1920 election. Charges of executive dictatorship flew thick and fast during Franklin Roosevelt's second term and badly undermined his authority. This has led James MacGregor

Burns and Michael Beschloss to argue that FDR's main problem

> was the system through which [he] was trying to exert leadership –
> the edifice of fragmented and dispersed powers so craftily devised
> by the framers of the Constitution. Roosevelt mistakenly felt that he
> could continue indefinitely to bridge – through personal leadership,
> improvisation, management, manipulation – the power fissures deep
> in the system. Hence his failure during his second term was not
> simply a series of personal frustrations but the encounter of a leader
> with an anti leadership system.[10]

Woodrow Wilson before Roosevelt and Lyndon Johnson after him
made similar mistakes of judgement and suffered accordingly. Furthermore that same anti-leadership system rooted in the American
political culture continues to dog presidents to this day.

The Congress

Like so many other presidents, Wilson, Johnson and Roosevelt
badly underestimated Congress as a limit on their freedom of action. Convinced of their constitutional superiority and sustained by
their claim to a popular mandate, innumerable chief executives
have come to regard congressional resistance to their wishes as
perverse and illegitimate. They have also been inclined to assume
that determined and resourceful leadership from the White House
will in itself be sufficient to force the legislature into line.

Such misplaced optimism has been reinforced by the knowledge
that the balance of power between the executive and the legislature in the national political system in the twentieth century has
shifted sharply in favour of the presidency. However, notwithstanding such development, it remains the case that Congress continues to be a major restraint on the presidency. It is a legislature
with teeth; it is far removed from a parliamentary poodle or a mere
captive of the executive branch. Unlike the situation in the United
Kingdom, the executive has no near monopoly of power, rather, it
is obliged to share power with, among others, the legislature.

The powers of Congress

Included among the prerogatives bestowed upon Congress by the
Constitution is a primary role in the legislative process, control

over the purse strings and the right to approve or disapprove senior executive appointments. With regard to legislation the Constitution goes so far as to say 'All legislative Powers herein granted shall be vested in a Congress of the United States.' Despite such phraseology, presidents in the modern age have been allowed to build substantially on their ostensibly minimal constitutional prerogatives with regard to law-making. Indeed the situation has been reached today where the president is clearly the dominant partner in the legislative process; most major legislative initiatives come from him and little legislation of real consequence is likely to pass without his support.

Nevertheless, if Congress has largely surrendered the positive power to initiate legislation to the executive, its role remains substantial and it can be an insurmountable negative force. Any bill proposed must navigate a complex network of committees and sub-committees that offer innumerable opportunities for delay, dilution or defeat. The president's chances of succeeding with his legislative programme are helped if his party has majorities in Congress, but even then he is obliged to approach the legislature more or less cap in hand. The opposition is, in any case, often in charge of one or both houses. Not since 1957 has a Republican president enjoyed the luxury of both houses controlled by his party and Presidents Nixon, Ford and Bush have been required to work with both the House and the Senate in Democratic hands throughout their years in office.

As George Bush found out in 1990, the legislature's 'power of the purse' is also not to be underestimated. Apart from the annual budgetary process important policy changes will invariably carry revenue and expenditure implications and Congress jealously guards its constitutional rights in such matters. The Budget Committees, the Senate Finance Committee, the House Ways and Means Committee, the Appropriations Committees in both houses and their sub-committees are all major power centres quite capable of inflicting severe damage on the executive branch.

The right to appoint executive officials is formally vested in the president, but he is obliged to share that power with the Senate. Many of his appointments are routinely approved, but from time to time important changes are forced. President Carter's nomination of Theodore Sorenson as Director of the CIA proved unacceptable to the Senate as did George Bush's nomination of John Tower to be Secretary of Defense. Similarly the president's power to appoint justices to the United States Supreme Court is circumscribed by the need for Senate approval and Presidents Johnson, Nixon and Reagan all suffered humiliating Court-nomination defeats.

The structure of Congress

Congress is, without doubt, the most daunting obstacle that a president faces in the making of domestic policy. Success or failure in his relations with Congress will make or break his presidency. The national legislature is endowed with important formal powers and the president's difficulties in dealing with it are greatly compounded by the structure of the institution. Congressional power is intensively fragmented and dispersed rather than being centred in a small group of leaders as in a parliamentary system. In the 1880s Wilson bemoaned the lack of central leaders in the legislature, but recognized that there were congressional 'barons'. These were chairmen who ran their specialist committees as personal fiefdoms and dominated policy-making in the area covered by that committee. Congressional 'barons' were still around until the early 1970s and for all their failings gave the legislature a degree of coherence. In recent years, however, the president's difficulties in dealing with the legislature have been worsened by the absence of genuinely consequential leaders, by a further diffusion of the power of Congress.

In trying to meet his responsibility to govern, a president must deal not with a select group of legislative leaders, but with a multiplicity of party and committee leaders. His starting-point will be the congressional leaders of his own party, but their cooperation alone will not get him very far. The influence of such leaders on their followers is limited and they may be quite helpless in the face of recalcitrant committee and sub-committee chairmen.

In parliamentary systems with strong parties, party leaders can control committees by ensuring that good party loyalists are appointed as chairmen, but in the United States party leaders in the legislature are far weaker. To be a committee chair in Congress is, of course, to be a political actor of great consequence. If not as powerful as they once were, committee chairs still 'exercise an almost decisive control over bills assigned to [their] committees. [They] normally determine when and if the committee will meet, which bills it will consider and the order of their consideration, whether public hearings will be held', as well as various other matters that may be crucial to the success or failure of a particular piece of legislation.[11] In short, chairmen, even yet, dominate the proceedings of committees, those sub-units of the legislature that carry enormous clout in the specialist areas that fall within their purview. To be the chairman of the House Agriculture Committee, for example, is to be a major player in agriculture policy-making – deferred to by presidents, Cabinet members, pressure group leaders and congressional colleagues alike.

Traditionally, seniority has been the source of a committee chairman's considerable influence. Even today a standing committee chairman is virtually certain to be the member of the party that holds a majority in the chamber who has served on the committee longest. Length of service also plays a part in determining members' speaking opportunities, their committee assignments and the quality of their office space. Seniority as an organizing principle has been cherished as a bulwark of legislative power. With some plausibility defenders of the principle argue that if committee chairmanships were decided by party leaders as in parliamentary systems, executive dominance of the legislature would inevitably follow, thereby bringing about that concentration of political power that Americans so abhor.[12]

While a case can be made for seniority as an organizing principle, it also carries disadvantages. Apart from the obvious problem of elderly decrepit members clinging on to important positions, seniority, when it was fully operative, could be savagely disruptive of parties and, in the right circumstances, a major impediment to presidents seeking acceptance of their programmes. The principle allowed committee chairmen to go their own way without reference to party majorities or the wishes of party leaders. In 1960, for instance, the Democrats won the White House with John Kennedy as their candidate; simultaneously, the Democrats retained control of both the House and Senate, but major committee chairmanships were held by Southern conservatives unrepresentative of the country as a whole and deeply hostile to the President's programme.

Another hazard of the seniority system in the past was the possibility of tyrannical behaviour by chairmen in their dealings with their colleagues. Unscrupulous chairmen, secure in their seniority, could act as they chose without fear of reprisal. It was the outlandish behaviour of some chairmen that helped to precipitate a period of congressional reform in the early 1970s.

Congressional change in the 1970s

The architects of congressional reform in the 1970s were bent on making the legislature a more democratic institution in two senses: they wished to make it more responsive to the public outside and less subject to the whims and arbitrary actions of senior members inside. The Legislative Reorganization Act of 1970, for example, made voting in the House, both in committee and on the floor, open to public scrutiny. The same act curbed some of the powers of chairmen in relation to members of their committees. Further change in 1973 opened up committees in the House to the public in almost all circumstances. In the same year the House Democratic caucus agreed the so-called Sub Committee Bill of Rights. Hitherto the chairmanships of sub-committees were in the gift of the chairmen of the main committee in question, allowing the latter to appoint cronies and ideological allies. Chairmen were now to be deprived of that power; it was instead given to the members of the majority party on the main committee. Other provisions of this reform reinforced the powers of sub-committees, making them more independent and less subject to manipulation by main committee chairmen.

The most telling change of all in the early 1970s was the weakening, although not the jettisoning it should be emphasized, of the seniority factor in the determination of committee chairmanships. Instead of allowing seniority to follow an inexorable course as in the past, procedural changes in both houses by both parties now made it possible to take other considerations into account. Challenges became feasible and if necessary ballots could be held to decide contested appointments. In 1974 the House Democratic caucus actually removed three standing committee chairmen and, in 1985, another House chairman was deposed. Other than these examples the seniority principle has since been consistently respected in the appointment of all standing committee chairmen, a fact that might seem to lead to the conclusion that the changes involved were not especially meaningful in the long run.

Such a conclusion is unwarranted. The possibility of ballots being held has, in conjunction with other assaults on the power of chairmen, transformed the relationship between them and junior colleagues. According to one source: 'Changes in the procedures and traditions surrounding the selection of committee chairs, when combined with the other reforms of the early 1970s, clearly altered their status and authority.'[13] As a smaller body the Senate is less dependent on formal rules than the House, nevertheless it too has experienced a comparable transformation in recent decades. In the 1950s the proceedings of the Senate were dominated by an inner club, or oligarchy of senior members, most of whom were from the South. The power and position of these men was sustained by a system of unwritten rules, or folkways that decreed that junior members should be seen but not heard and required them to be elaborately deferential to senior colleagues.[14]

The Senate of today is an infinitely more egalitarian institution. Even as early as the mid-1970s former Senator Mansfield could claim:

> There is no longer an inner club dictating the Senate's affairs. No senators are more equal than others. Assignments are made on the basis of geography. Seniority is still a factor but in a declining sense. There is no such thing now as a super senator or a second rate senator. They all participate.[15]

The democratization of the Senate has gone even further since Mansfield made his comment. It is now a notably individualistic institution where even the most junior members can play a full part and party leaders are at best first among equals.

The changes that have occurred in the structure of Congress in the last fifteen to twenty years have been in many ways beneficial. It is a more democratic institution. To foreign observers especially it is startlingly open to public scrutiny and the opportunities for participation by junior members are clearly greater than ever before. From the president's perspective, however, the 'new' Congress poses even more problems than its predecessors: the changes that have taken place have enhanced the diffusion of power and further complicated an already difficult relationship between the White House and Capitol Hill. President Carter gave an indication of this when he said of his problems in dealing with Congress:

I learned the hard way that there was no party loyalty or discipline when a complicated or controversial issue was at stake – none. Each legislator had to be wooed and won individually. It was every member for himself, and devil take the hindmost! Well-intended reforms in the organisation of Congress and of the Democratic party had undermined the power of party leaders. The situation was completely different from the time of Lyndon Johnson's Presidency, when he, the Speaker of the House, and the Chairman of the House Ways and Means Committee could agree on a tax or welfare proposal and be certain that the House of Representatives would ratify their decision.[16]

It is true that not all the reforms contributed to increased fragmentation; some had a centralizing rather than a decentralizing effect.[17] In some respects, for instance, congressional parties were strengthened. Legislative party caucuses had, prior to the 1970s, become largely moribund organizations in both the House and the Senate. However, changes in party rules in the House and changes of practice in the Senate have revived the caucus (or conference as it is known to Republicans). Now these bodies meet far more frequently and have a greater role in congressional proceedings. In addition, the powers of the Speaker, the principal leader of the majority party in the House have been significantly extended, although it remains the case that a Speaker's 'success rests less on formal rules than on personal prestige, sensitivity to members' needs, ability to persuade and skill at mediating disputes and constructing winning coalitions'.[18]

Nevertheless, the overall effect of the changes has been to atomize the power of Congress further than before. Individualism among members of Congress has also been substantially heightened in recent years by electoral considerations. In sharp contrast to the situation in the United Kingdom, those contesting elections to the national legislature in the United States have generally had to do so individually rather than collectively. This means that a candidate is forced, from the beginning, to put together a personal organization to win a nomination. And even after the nomination has been secured, that same candidate remains largely dependent on his or her own efforts. The aid that they will receive from their party will be at best limited, and success or failure in the general election will turn on their own ability to raise money and put together an effective, personal organization.

Members of Congress obliged to campaign individually are unlikely to be particularly responsive to the appeals of party or president once they reach Washington. This is not a new problem, as James MacGregor Burns demonstrates in recounting his experience in contesting a congressional election in the late 1950s. He regarded himself as a good party man, but had to run his election campaign virtually on his own – raising money, recruiting helpers, placing advertisments and putting out personal campaign literature. Burns goes on to say:

> As I fell back increasingly on family, friends, neighbors, and unorganized Democrats and fellow liberals throughout the district, I developed something of the loneliness and the psychology of the long distance runner, or at least of the single-minded political entrepreneur. If I had won, I would have felt loyal to my personal coalition, not to a party.'[19]

Thirty years later the inclination towards individualism among national legislators arising from electoral factors is even more marked. Campaigning for Congress these days requires enormous amounts of money, most of which candidates must raise themselves, from Political Action Committees and individual contributors. Their ability to meet this requirement depends on their success in selling themselves personally. Similarly, an effective candidate must be adept before television cameras; in commercials and news broadcasts he or she must project a suitable personal image.

The emphasis on personal qualities continues in office where legislators quickly learn that their chances of re-election have little to do with party affiliation or their stands on the issues of the day. Success will depend largely on the member's personal record in attending to the specific needs of his or her constituents; bringing benefits to the district or state and providing ombudsman services. Particularly in the House of Representatives, constituency service is regarded as the key to re-election and arguably as a result of this strategy almost all incumbents seeking re-election to the House are successful.[20]

In short, in the US Congress the president of the day faces a formidable adversary: an institution of awesome power and a structure not at all helpful to productive presidential–congressional relations. The president cannot meet his responsibilities if Congress will not cooperate, but that cooperation has been made more difficult to achieve by rule changes and electoral considerations that have together created a legislature with an intensely individualistic ethos.

Nowhere are these problems more evident than in the making of economic policy. The management of the economy is primarily the responsibility of the president and his perceived success or failure in this endeavour is crucial to his standing in the public opinion polls and his, or his party's, future electoral success. Yet if the president is held responsible for the state of the economy, he is denied control of the levers of macroeconomic policy-making: 'His authority over the economy does not equal his responsibility for its condition.'[21]

Monetary policy, for example, is largely determined by the actions of the Federal Reserve System, an independent regulatory agency. Fiscal policy, on the other hand, is ultimately decided by the legislature. The president's staff prepares a budget in his name for submission to Congress, but if it is the chief executive who proposes it is the legislature that disposes. The crucial decisions on taxes and appropriations, in other words, are taken on Capitol Hill rather than in the White House. In the making of American economic policy Congress is a major player.

The differences between the United Kingdom and the United States in the processes of budget-making are striking. In Britain, the process is under the control of leading members of the Cabinet, fortified by a disciplined bureaucracy and a legislature that invariably rubber-stamps executive initiatives. As one disgruntled Member of Parliament has recently put it:

> [In the United Kingdom] an executive prepares in secret, then announces the Budget as a fait accompli. Legislative scrutiny takes the form of a couple of days reactive parliamentary 'debate' and a farcical Finance Bill Committee in which not a single serious amendment is accepted by Government before the entire package is rubber-stamped by an uninterested parliamentary majority.[22]

In the United States the legislature is anything but a rubber stamp and the budgetary process is far from firmly under executive control. Even before the budget emerges from the White House for congressional scrutiny pressure groups and vested interests within the federal bureaucracy may have forced concessions on the president. And then, once the executive stage has been completed, the budget has to negotiate a lengthy, laborious and perilous legislative phase that may conclude with final outcomes markedly different from the president's original intentions.

Budget-making, in other words, provides an acid test of a president's ability to govern in the realm of domestic policy. Throughout both the executive and congressional stages of that process, what is at isssue is whether the chief executive can impose his economic policy priorities and goals rather than being obliged to accept those of other political actors – lobbyists, bureaucrats and members of Congress.

The federal judiciary

By comparison with the legislature, the judiciary is a far less important constraint on the power of the president. In the first place, although the Constitution provides for a three-way sharing of power in the national government, the judicial branch is weaker than its two rivals. As Alexander Hamilton said two centuries ago, the judiciary is the 'least dangerous' branch. Unlike the executive and the legislature, federal judges have

> no influence over either the sword or the purse; no direction either of the strength or of the wealth of the society, and can take no active resolution whatever. It may truly be said to have neither FORCE nor WILL but merely judgment; and must ultimately depend upon the aid of the executive arm even for the efficacy of its judgments.[23]

This has proved to be something of an overstatement, but there is no doubt that the lack of any independent means of enforcing its decisions has always been a constraint on the power of the United States Supreme Court. President Jackson made this abundantly clear in reference to a Court ruling which he deplored and declined to put into effect: 'John Marshall has made his decision, now let him enforce it.'

Despite such defiance it is the case that in some situations the Supreme Court can defeat the policy intentions of chief executives. An obvious instance is the judicial resistance to Roosevelt's New Deal programme. Undaunted by massive electoral support for FDR and his party the Supreme Court struck down key enactments such as the legislation setting up the National Relief Administration.[24]

Even when the United States was at war President Truman was thwarted on a major policy issue by the Court. When industrial strife erupted in the steel industry during the Korean War, Truman, on national security grounds, issued an executive order authorizing the seizure of steel mills and providing for their operation by the national government. The Supreme Court decided that the President's action was an unconstitutional usurpation of the power of the legislature. Truman gave way, the mills returned to private ownership and the strike went on.[25] In later years, President Nixon was first denied an injunction to prevent the publication of the top secret Pentagon Papers and then, in the throes of the Watergate crisis, was compelled by the Supreme Court to release tape recordings of conversations in the White House.[26]

It is also possible in some areas of public policy for the federal judiciary to be the predominant player, to be effectively *the* policymaker. At the end of the nineteenth century, by its decision in *Plessy* v. *Ferguson* (1896), the Supreme Court sanctioned state-ordered racial segregation throughout the nation. Then, in 1954, by their decision in *Brown* v. *The Board of Education at Topeka, Kansas*, federal justices overturned Plessy and in effect remade federal law. Similarly, in recent decades the federal courts have had a decisive role in other crucial areas of national social policy, including capital punishment, abortion, affirmative action and the rights of suspects in criminal cases. To its critics the federal judiciary may, in such cases, appear to usurp the policy-making functions of the executive and the legislature.

Conservatives were deeply troubled by the 'judicial activism' of the Warren Court (1953–69) in social policy matters and Richard Nixon, soon after his election in 1968, turned his attention to the Supreme Court. The appointment process provides a means whereby chief executives can influence the pattern of federal court decisions, but there are difficulties with this strategy; a president's nominees may be rejected by the Senate and even those who are confirmed may fail to live up to expectations. The most obvious example of this hazard was Earl Warren, appointed Chief Justice by Eisenhower, but who became a bitter disappointment to him. Warren Burger, Nixon's nominee to replace Warren was confirmed, but he proved to be less than satisfactory to the President and his fellow conservatives. And then to Nixon's chagrin his attempts to fill a further vacancy, to place on the Court another 'strict constructionist', in other words, a justice, who would not stray from literal interpretations of the Constitution, was met by two successive Senate rejections.[27]

The federal judiciary's dependence on the executive branch for the enforcement of its rulings may give the president opportunities to exercise influence. These days presidents are unlikely to go as far as Andrew Jackson in naked defiance, but much may be achieved by footdragging, by less than enthusiastic enforcement. Eisenhower, for instance, did not approve of the Brown decision and did what he legitimately could to slow down its enforcement. According to his Attorney General, 'After the Court decision [President Eisenhower] realized that it then became his job as head of the executive branch of government to enforce it. And he went about doing that in what he thought was the right way – it was a long-term way.'[28] President Nixon endeavoured to undermine later Court decisions regarding desegregation in education by curtailing the role of the Department of Justice in bringing prosecutions and by cutting back on the funding available to the Department of Health, Education and Welfare for the purposes of integration.

Presidents may also try to influence the Court by filing *amicus curiae*, or friend of the court, briefs. In addition, they may use the 'bully pulpit' to arouse public opinion against particular decisions. Theoretically, they may, working through Congress, attempt to engineer constitutional amendments overturning judicial decisions. They can also try to get Congress to narrow the appellate jurisdiction of the Court to exclude it from particular policy areas.[29]

President Reagan, although having little success, used several of the above techniques in pursuit of his social agenda. Nevertheless a large element of luck plus the professionalism of Reagan's staff enabled his administration to exploit the appointments process to good effect. Candidates for the federal judiciary at all levels were subjected to 'the most thorough and comprehensive system for recruiting and screening federal judicial candidates of any administration ever'.[30] To be appointed as a federal judge during the Reagan years it was not enough to be a Republican, it was also necessary to be a 'strict constructionist' and to be otherwise in sympathy with the President's judicial philosophy.

Liberals derived satisfaction from Reagan's failure to win congressional approval for his social agenda, in other words his preferred positions in regard to issues such as abortion, school prayer, bussing, pornography and affirmative action. But the Reaganites knew that most of these issues would be decided by the federal courts rather than the legislature. As the President himself observed:

> In many areas – abortion, crime, pornography, and others – progress will take place when the federal judiciary is made up of judges who believe in law and order and a strict interpretation of the Constitution. I am pleased to be able to tell you that I've already appointed 284 federal judges, men and women who share the fundamental values that you and I so cherish, and that by the time we leave office, our administration will have appointed some 45% of all federal judges.[31]

In fact Reagan was able to appoint a chief justice, three associate justices and altogether over 50 per cent of the federal judiciary. Despite the Bork defeat, he was able to give the Supreme Court a conservative majority and when he left office eight out of thirteen Federal Appeals Courts had Reagan-appointed majorities. Many of these appointees are likely to hand down decisions broadly in line with Ronald Reagan's social agenda. In other words, what President Reagan failed to gain in Congress in the short term he may win, in the long run, via the judiciary.[32] Eventually it should become apparent that Reagan succeeded rather better than most chief executives in coping with the limits on the presidency posed by the federal judiciary.

The federal administration

Article II of the Constitution says 'The executive Power shall be vested in a President', and in academic and popular parlance the president is often referred to as the chief executive. Furthermore, in the annual government organization manual, a schematic diagram places the president at the apex of the federal administrative structure; he, we are led to believe, directs and controls a vast army of federal bureaucrats organized in departments, agencies and bureaus. These diagrams are misleading, for if power is intensely fragmented and diffused in Congress it is hardly less so in the federal administration. This allows presidential appointees and career bureaucrats alike to become serious restraints on the president's freedom of action.

If the president is to meet his responsibility to govern he must be able to impose his choices, his policies on the political system. But his ability to do so will depend in part on his gaining the cooperation of a gigantic, amorphous administrative branch. That cooperation will not be obtained without difficulty and for some presidents their most daunting task is:

> [not] to persuade Congress to support a policy dear to his political heart, but to persuade the pertinent bureau or agency or mission, even when headed by men of his own choosing, to follow his direction faithfully and transform the shadow of the policy into the substance of a program.[33]

All democratic systems of government encounter difficulties in ensuring that what civil servants do conforms with the wishes of their elective superiors, but the problems are especially acute in the United States. In Britain, civil servants are often accused of trying to manipulate government ministers and in some situations they may have an undesirably large role in policy-making. Yet by comparison with its American counterpart, the civil service in Britain is much more centralized and hierarchical in its structure and consequently more easily subject to control by elected officials. This is made possible by different cultural attitudes, secrecy in government and the sinews of party.

Senior administrators in the United Kingdom are not above attempting to influence the shape of policy, but once the policy has been made they accept that it is their responsibility to bring about its implementation. There is little incentive in the British context for disaffected administrators to try to achieve their ends by making informal alliances with members of the legislature. Budgetary and legislative control lies with a Cabinet backed by a highly disciplined party, parliamentary committees are pale versions of those found on the other side of the Atlantic and back-bench legislators lack real weight.

The opportunities for bureaucrats in the United Kingdom to subvert or negate the wishes of elected officials are far fewer and more limited in scope than is the case in the diffused, more open and non-hierarchical structures of the federal administration in the United States. In the latter the political culture, the constitution and the weakness of party combine to create circumstances where appointed officials and bureaucrats are able to undermine or defeat what presidents are attempting to achieve.

Since the creation of the Executive Office of the President (EOP) in 1939 presidents have been provided with staff to assist them in their attempts to come to grips with the federal administration. The agencies that make up the EOP comprise a 'presidential branch' committed to aiding the president in his efforts to impose his preferences and his will on that 'maze of personalities and institutions called the government of the United States'.[34] The EOP provides the president with helpers, with eyes and ears as he struggles to keep control of the policy agenda. Those who work in this 'presidential branch' are in a real sense *his* people, he hires and fires them and his relationship with them is 'almost monarchical'.[35]

The relationship between presidents and Cabinet members is rather different, as President Johnson explained:

> When I looked out at the heads of my departments, I realized that while all of them had been appointed by me, not a single one was really mine. Here I was working night and day to build the Great Society, conquering thousands of enemies and hurdling hundreds of obstacles, and I couldn't even count on my own administrative family for complete support. I felt like a football quarterback running against a tough team and having his own center and left guard throwing rocks at him.[36]

Presidents appoint Cabinet members and others to run departments and expect them to use their positions to aid the fulfilment of the president's purposes. However, neither Cabinet secretaries nor departments are answerable only to the White House. Members of the Cabinet are nominated by the president, but their appointments have to be confirmed by the Senate. Departments are established in the first place by Act of Congress and they remain subject to congressional oversight. Their budgets are closely controlled by Congress and any departmental legislative proposals are subject to congressional scrutiny and approval.

Federal agencies are often not easily moved in new directions by the outsiders that presidents set over them. Indeed there is an ever-present danger of those outsiders – Cabinet and sub-Cabinet appointees – 'going native' and accepting departmental rather than presidential priorities. Within departments, career bureaucrats exercise great influence and these men and women may well not share the partisan or policy preferences of their supposed political masters. Furthermore, they will inevitably develop close relationships with important members of relevant congressional committees and with the leaders of constituent groups served by the department. This will lead to the formation of issue networks or sub-governments – essentially, triangular groupings of elites embracing bureaucrats, congressmen and pressure group leaders who share a community of interest and are in a position to distort the policy-making process to their collective advantage. The most notorious of these powerful informal alliances is the military industrial complex, but this is only one of many such groupings that a president must accommodate as he seeks to bring about policy change. As Bradley Patterson, a member of Eisenhower's staff has said:

> Cabinet members are beset from every side by Congressional pressures, by the pressures of special constituencies, by the pressures of their bureaucracies, by the pressures of the press, by the pressures of foreign nations, heaven knows what other sources – all of these pressures tending to grind special axes and sort of turn their heads away from the President who put them in office and to whom they're responsible.[37]

The unreliability of Cabinet members and other appointees is a mark of the diffusion that is a characteristic of the political system as a whole and the federal administration at large. But the diffusion goes further, extending down into the structure of departments, compounding the difficulties that presidents face in trying to get the bureaucracy to do what they want it to do. In reflecting on his frustrations in these matters Franklin Roosevelt said:

> The Treasury is so large and far-flung and ingrained in its practices that I find it almost impossible to get the action and results I want – even with Henry [Morgenthau] there. But the Treasury is not to be compared with the State Department. You should go through the experience of trying to get any changes in the thinking, policy, and action of the career diplomats and then you'd know what a real problem was. But the Treasury and the State Department put together are nothing compared with the Na-a-vy. The admirals are really something to cope with – and I should know. To change

anything in the Na-a-vy is like punching a feather bed. You punch it with your right and you punch it with your left until you are finally exhausted, and then you find the damn bed just as it was before you started punching.[38]

At the beginning of his presidency Roosevelt's problems were made worse by the fact that the civil service was largely made up of Republicans unlikely to be sympathetic to a reforming Democrat in the White House. According to Raymond Moley, a presidential adviser, 'A considerable proportion of them had been appointed during the preceding twelve years of Republican rule. . . . What we called the Civil Service was, in the main, merely a mass of Republican appointees frozen into office by act of Congress.'[39]

When Richard Nixon was in office he faced the same problem of a bureaucracy largely made up of civil servants affiliated to the opposition party; according to one study, published in 1971, only 5 per cent of career foreign service officers in the State Department regarded themselves as Republicans. Another source established that no more than 17 per cent of senior career administrators in a range of departments and agencies dealing with domestic affairs, were Republicans.[40] Some of Nixon's attempts to bring order to the federal administration certainly went beyond the bounds of legality, but his conviction that the federal bureaucracy was packed with administrators holding policy views antithetical to his own was founded in fact. More recent research suggests that the ideological composition of the civil service has changed yet again, this time in a rightwards direction. This, we can be sure, will present difficulties to a Democratic president in the future.

President Reagan's record in coping with these perennial problems was mixed. His detached style and his fondness for delegation created problems in his second term when he was less well served by his staff. During the first term, however, leading Reaganites demonstrated an unusual awareness of, and provided a sophisticated response to the problem of how to curb the tendency of federal administrators to go their own way.

The dangers inherent in the situation had been brought home to senior figures in the Reagan camp like Martin Anderson who had served in the Nixon administration. In Nixon's first term reasonably careful consideration was given to Cabinet appointments, and appointments at the sub-Cabinet level were also subject to vetting, but responsibility for selecting the remaining 2,000 political appointees was delegated to Cabinet members. The President furthermore grandly told his Cabinet to appoint on the basis of ability first and loyalty second. Subsequently, Nixon was horrified to find out that only 50 per cent of the 2,000 appointed were actually Republicans.[41] The adverse consequences of such loose rein appointment procedures were not lost on Anderson:

> The US Government is so large and so complex that it takes thousands of dedicated, competent, loyal people to turn campaign promises into national policy . . . [but during the Nixon years] the departments were staffed primarily with people with an agenda different from that of the White House. . . . We argued over what to do rather than about how to do it. The departments and agencies were full of people who basically disagreed with many of Nixon's policies. They were nice people, competent people, but we wasted a great deal of time arguing with them, cajoling them, persuading them. I recall going to policy meetings with a dozen or more people where I would be the *only* person in the room supporting President Nixon's policy position.[42]

The Reagan forces took a number of steps designed to deal with the sort of problems that Nixon had encountered. Edwin Meese, Counselor to the President, and ideologically a close ally of Reagan's, helped with the selection of Cabinet members and worked with Pendleton James, the White House personnel director, to ensure that not only sub-Cabinet appointments, but also the 2,000 lower level political positions went, as far as possible, to candidates who were both competent and ideologically sound.

Elaborate precautions were also taken to guard against the danger of senior members of the administration 'going native' or becoming, in Reagan's own words, 'captives of the bureaus or special interests in the departments they are supposed to direct'.[43] Transition task forces were set up to advise newly appointed Cabinet members on policy and personnel. Cabinet members and other senior administrators were also obliged to attend indoctrination sessions where major figures from the President down lectured them on the virtues of teamwork and exhorted them to remain faithful to the principles of Reaganism.

Cohesion in the Reagan administration was also enhanced by a system of Cabinet councils; these covered broad policy areas affecting several departments and brought together senior White House staff with Cabinet members. This helped to counter not only the 'going native' effect, but also the inevitable antagonism between presidential advisers and departmental secretaries that had weakened other administrations. All Cabinet council meetings took place in the west wing of the White House within a few feet of the Oval Office. The symbolic importance of Cabinet members being regularly drawn into the White House ambit was stressed by Martin Anderson:

> Just the act of having to leave their fiefdoms, get into a car, and be driven to the White House was a powerful reminder to every member of the cabinet that it was the president's business they were about, not theirs or their department's constituents.[44]

Overcoming the constraints

The catalogue of constraints on the power of the president so far discussed is necessarily brief and incomplete; the states, the media, interest groups, international organizations and foreign governments all possess a similar capacity. Indeed, given the plethora of potential obstacles that stand in their way it sometimes seems almost miraculous that presidents accomplish anything at all of significance in domestic policy. Most presidents fail to deal effectively with these difficulties; however, a select few, at least briefly, overcome the inherent tendency towards ungovernability in the system sufficiently to meet their responsibilities.

As the example of Franklin Roosevelt makes clear, crisis circumstances may be a great help to the chief executive; in the face of an emergency the restraints decline in significance. Anti-authority attitudes may, for the moment, be suppressed while Congress, the judiciary and the administration are likely to be less obstructive than in quieter times. What, however, about non-crisis situations? How do presidents cope then? Much will depend on the stock of 'presidential capital' available to the executive. Capital in this sense is an amalgam of support for the president's party in the legislature, his standing in the public opinion polls and the margin of his victory at the previous election. In most situations, the president's party support in Congress will be the most important ingredient of capital.[45]

Any president's success or failure in mastering the political system will also be heavily dependent on that greatest of all imponderables – luck. Particularly in the present age of international interdependence, his authority may be undermined or strengthened by developments over which he has no control.[46] Massive rises in the price of oil crippled presidents in the 1970s, whereas in the decade that followed changes within the Soviet Union presented their successors with extraordinary opportunities.

Another factor of great importance to a chief executive's ability to grapple with the limits on his power is the quality of his staff. If he is to govern effectively the expertise of those who work in the Executive Office of the President will be crucial. And given the essential need to develop a productive relationship with Congress a strong legislative liaison operation will be indispensable.

Success in the White House moreover requires a clear understanding by both the president and his staff that in the American system of shared powers there is little scope for issuing orders or commands; as Richard Neustadt tells us, 'presidential power is the power to persuade'.[47] Harry Truman summed up the central dilemma of presidential power when, in reference to his successor, he said, 'He'll sit here, and he'll say, "Do this! Do that!" *And nothing will happen.* Poor Ike it wont be a bit like the Army. He'll find it very frustrating.'[48] There is little doubt that the government of the United States bears little resemblance to the army. Military organizations have hierarchical structures; senior officers at the apex issue commands which are relayed down to those who are obliged to carry them out. Even in military organizations subordinates are not above evading or diluting orders from on high, but given the extent of relatively rigid discipline the scope for such activity is minimal.

Presidents, on the other hand, must persuade rather than order other political actors to do what they want them to do. Chief executives need the cooperation or acquiescence of other members of the political elite, but such people are unlikely to be responsive to presidential directives. Members of Congress, judges, senior bureaucrats and other leaders share power with the president rather than holding their jobs at his discretion. As Neustadt says, 'When one man shares authority with another, but does not gain or lose his job on the other's whim, his willingness to act upon the urging of the other turns on whether he conceives the action right for him.'[49]

In order to persuade other political leaders to cooperate with him the president must bargain, he must make deals, he must negotiate with those with whom he shares power. 'Bargaining is a generic term referring to several related types of behavior. In each case, an exchange takes place: goals or resources pass from a bargainer's hands in return for other goals or resources that he or she values.'[50]

Bargaining takes place in all political systems but nowhere is it more pervasive than in the United States:

> the politician is, above all, the man whose career depends upon successful negotiation of bargains. To win office he must negotiate electoral alliances. To satisfy his electoral alliance he must negotiate alliances with other legislators and administrators, for his control depends on negotiation. Most of his time is consumed with bargaining. That is the skill he cultivates; it is the skill that distinguishes the master politician from the political failure.[51]

Bargaining skill is indispensable in a chief executive obliged to operate in a pluralist system of decision-making, where power is diffused and decentralized, where there is a multiplicity of significant power-holders rather than just a few. The president is the chief bargainer in the American political system. Without bargaining skills, a president will be a nonentity in the White House, unable to control other political leaders and incapable of meeting his responsibility to govern.

In negotiating with members of Congress the president and his staff have a variety of bargaining counters available. He might agree to appear in the constituency of a committee chairman at election time to provide him with highly visible support. Patronage in the form of federal jobs for the friends and followers of members of Congress can be used for bargaining purposes. The chief executive can use his influence to channel campaign contributions in the direction of favoured legislators; by working through party leaders, he may help a congressman to achieve a desirable committee post. A president's support for a legislator's pet bill may be vital to its passage. Similarly, appropriations for projects in a member's constituency may stand or fall depending on signals from the White House. Some of the benefits used for bargaining purposes may appear trivial to the outside observer, but they are important for all that:

> It might be something as unobtrusive as receiving an invitation to join the President in a walk around the White House grounds, knowing that pictures of the event would be sent to hometown

newspapers along with hints from 'White House sources' that the President valued and frequently sought this man's advice.'[52]

Such 'small potatoes' of presidential beneficence can be vital in the endless pursuit of congressional cooperation. Some bargains, of course, are implicit rather than explicit. A congressman's support for the president on a particular issue may not represent a straightforward *quid pro quo*; it could well be a mark of his gratitude for favours bestowed upon him in the past.

Bargaining is an unavoidable necessity in American politics and negotiating skill is a central component of presidential power. It is not to be assumed, however, that it provides a complete explanation. There are many reasons apart from the trading of favours why a legislator or bureaucrat may accede to the wishes of the man in the White House. They may be responsive to his charm, his charisma, his intellectual quality, his symbolic position as chief of state or his standing in the Washington community. Members of the political elite may give a president their support out of friendship, or because they find him to be a likeable person. They may be moved by a sense of party loyalty. They may be intimidated by the president's apparent command over public opinion, a position that he may seek to reinforce by using television, radio and public speechifying in general.

The latter strategy has become especially significant in the years since Richard Neustadt's book, with its emphasis on bargaining, was first published in 1960. Ever since the time of Theodore Roosevelt presidents have resorted to the 'bully pulpit' in their efforts to overcome the limits on their capacity to govern. In their public utterances they have flaunted their claim to a national mandate, cast aspersions on the parochialism of legislators and denounced the 'special interests'. The possibilities inherent in such approaches have, of course, been greatly magnified by the onset of television.

Since the 1950s presidents with the necessary gifts have been able to appeal over the heads of Congress to the whole nation simultaneously via television, yet television, while sometimes a boon to the man in the White House, may also become a burden. Television executives and commentators are in a position to influence the national agenda in ways that presidents may find objectionable. Thus the change in United States policy towards South

East Asia in the late 1960s was partly forced on President Johnson by those who worked in television.[53] It was television that, to Richard Nixon's chagrin, kept the issue of Watergate before the public long after it would have disappeared in the pre-televison age. Similarly televison, by relentlessly harping on the Iran hostage question contributed much to the downfall of President Carter.

The constant scrutiny of the White House by the media in general and television in particular limits the president's freedom of action and may ultimately destroy him. Nevertheless, in the right hands television can be a devastatingly effective presidential resource and Reagan's spectacular success in changing the terms of debate in 1981, and in obtaining a tax reform bill in his second term, owed much to his extraordinary skill as a television communicator. His successor, by contrast, suffered the ignominy of making a televised appeal for support over the heads of Congress during the 1990 budget crisis which backfired badly. It was reported that after Bush's address an overwhelming majority of those voters who contacted their congressman or senator urged them to vote against rather than for the President on this issue.[54] According to Thomas Edsall this was a particularly

> grave blow to the core of presidential power. In the American system of checks and balances, presidential authority in domestic matter depends heavily on the power of the bully pulpit, now especially through television, to control the direction of domestic policy.[55]

If an American president is to govern, if, in other words, he is to gain acceptance of his policies, he must master an extraodinarily fragmented and fractious political system. Most of those who have held this great office in the twentieth century have failed to achieve such mastery; they have remained baffled and frustrated by the immense problems of presidential power. A handful of outstandingly able presidents have enjoyed a degree of success, but even they have been dependent on large elements of good fortune.

Notes

1. This chapter draws on material that first appeared in Ch. 2 of my book, *Ronald Reagan and the American Presidency*, Longman, London and New York, 1990.

2. *Presidential Power and the Modern Presidents*, Free Press, New York, 1990, p. x.
3. The adjectives in inverted commas appear in the titles of books on the presidency. Neustadt, in the updated version of his classic study *Presidential Power* says that 'presidential weakness was the underlying theme' of the original and is still his theme thirty years later (p. ix).
4. Herbert McClosky and John Zaller, *The American Ethos*, Harvard University Press, Cambridge, Mass., 1984, p. 17.
5. See Samuel Huntington, *American Politics: The Promise of Disharmony*, Harvard University Press, Cambridge, 1981 and H. G. Nicholas, *The Nature of American Politics*, Oxford University Press, Oxford, 1986.
6. Rossiter edition, The New American Library, New York, 1961, p. 322.
7. Bernard Bailyn, *The Ideological Origins of the American Revolution*, Harvard University Press, Cambridge, Mass., 1967, p. 319.
8. Rossiter edition, *op. cit.*, p. 323.
9. *The Political Presidency: Practice of Leadership*, Oxford University Press, New York, 1984, pp. 3–4.
10. *The New Republic*, 7 April 1982, pp. 19–20.
11. Jack Plano and Milton Greenberg, *The American Political Dictionary* (6th edition), Holt, Reinhart and Winston, New York, 1982, p. 164.
12. Barbara Hinckley, *The Seniority System in Congress*, Indiana University Press, Bloomington, 1971, p. 3.
13. Lawrence Dodd and Bruce Oppenheimer, *Congress Reconsidered* (3rd edition), Congressional Quarterly Press, Washington DC, 1985, p. 47.
14. See Donald Matthews, *US Senators and Their World*, Vintage Books, New York, 1960.
15. 'Senate More Democratic Now, Mansfield Claims', *Wisconsin State Journal*, 17 September 1976, section 1, p. 15.
16. *Keeping Faith*, Collins, London, 1982, p. 80.
17. See Kenneth Shepsle, 'The Changing Textbook Congress' in John Chubb and Paul Peterson (eds), *Can the Government Govern?*, Brookings, Washington DC, 1989.
18. Roger Davidson and Walter Oleszek, *Congress and Its Members*, Congressional Quarterly Press, Washington DC, 1985, p. 176.
19. *The Power to Lead: The Crisis of the American Presidency*, Simon and Schuster, New York, 1984, p. 148.
20. In 1988, for example, 402 out of 409 incumbents seeking re-election were returned to office.
21. Louis Koenig, *The Chief Executive*, Harcourt Brace Jovanovich, New York, 1986, p. 254.
22. Graham Allen MP, letter to *The Guardian*, 31 October 1990, p. 20.
23. Rossiter edition, *op. cit.*, p. 465.
24. *Schecter Poultry Corp.* v. *United States*, 295 US 495 (1935).
25. *Youngstown Sheet and Tube Co.* v. *Sawyer*, 343 US 579 (1952).
26. *New York Times* v. *United States*, 403 US 713 (1971) and *United States* v. *Nixon*, 418 US 683 (1974).

27. See Henry Abraham, *Justices and Presidents* (2nd edition), Oxford University Press, New York, 1985, Ch. 2.
28. As quoted in David O'Brien, *Storm Center: The Supreme Court in American Politics*, W. W. Norton, New York, 1986. p. 318.
29. See Richard Hodder-Williams, 'Ronald Reagan and the Supreme Court' in Joseph Hogan (ed.), *The Reagan Years*, Manchester University Press, Manchester, 1990.
30. Stephen Markman quoted in David O'Brien, 'The Reagan Judges: His Most Enduring Legacy' in Charles O. Jones (ed.), *The Reagan Legacy*, Chatham House, New Jersey, 1988.
31. Presidential message to the National Convention of the Knights of Columbus, 5 August 1986.
32. See especially O'Brien, *op. cit.*, 'The Reagan Judges . . .'.
33. Clinton Rossiter, *The American Presidency*, Harcourt Brace, New York, 1956, p. 59.
34. Richard Neustadt, *Presidential Power*, John Wiley and Sons, New York, 1960 and 1976, preface to the original edition np.
35. Theodore Lowi, *The Personal President*, Cornell University Press, Ithaca, 1985, p. 142.
36. Doris Kearns, *Lyndon Johnson and the American Dream*, New American Library, New York, 1976, p. 253.
37. Quoted in P. G. Henderson, 'Organizing the Presidency for Effective Leadership: Lessons from the Eisenhower Years', *Presidential Studies Quarterly*, Winter 1987.
38. Neustadt, *op. cit.*, p. 110.
39. Stephen Hess, *Organizing the Presidency*, Brookings, Washington DC, 1988, p. 23.
40. Joel Aberbach and Bert Rockman, 'Clashing Beliefs in the Executive Branch: The Nixon Administration Bureaucracy', *American Political Science Review*, vol. LXX, no. 2, June 1976.
41. Bruce Oudes (ed.), *From the President: Richard Nixon's Secret Files*, André Deutsch, London, 1989, p. 87.
42. Martin Anderson, *Revolution*, Harcourt Brace Jovanovich, New York, 1988, p. 195.
43. Television address, 3 November 1980.
44. Anderson, *op. cit.*, p. 226.
45. Paul Light, *The President's Agenda*, Johns Hopkins University Press, Baltimore, 1982, pp. 14–15.
46. See Richard Rose, *The Postmodern President*, Chatham House, New Jersey, 1988.
47. *Presidential Power, op. cit.*, p. 100.
48. *ibid.*, p. 77.
49. *ibid.*, p. 102.
50. Davidson and Oleszek, *op. cit.*, p. 398.
51. Robert Dahl and Charles Lindblom, *Politics, Economics and Welfare*, Harper and Row, New York, 1953, p. 336.
52. Kearns, *op. cit.*, p. 248.

53. See Austin Ranney, *Channels of Power: The Impact of Television on American Politic*, Basic Books, New York, 1982.
54. *Time* (international edition), 22 October 1990, p. 56.
55. 'The Gridlock of Government', *The Washington Post*, National Weekly Edition, 15–21 October 1990, p. 6.

5

The President and Foreign Policy

The previous chapter discussed some of the limits on the power of US presidents in domestic affairs. Many of those apply in the making of foreign policy. The anti-authority political culture is no less relevant; the powers of Congress in the foreign policy realm are substantial; the structure of the legislature is equally troublesome and by no means can the Department of State always be relied on to implement the president's programme.

Despite the leeway accorded him during wartime and at moments of crisis the president of the United States is constrained in international affairs to a degree that chief executives elsewhere would find intolerable. His position, for example, is not at all comparable to that of a British prime minister. As one scholar puts it:

> The prime minister appoints people to office without worrying about parliamentary confirmation, concludes treaties without worrying about parliamentary ratification, declares war without obtaining parliamentary assent, is safe from parliamentary investigation and in many respects has inherited the authority that once belonged to absolute monarchs. Congress pusillanimous as it often is, is far more independent of the head of government, far more open to a diversity of ideas, far more capable of affecting executive policies, far better staffed and paid and far more disposed to check, balance, challenge and investigate the executive branch than Parliament.[1]

It is nevertheless the case that in the endless struggle between the executive and the legislature over the conduct of foreign policy the superiority of the presidency has long since been established. There remains in place a significant sharing of powers, but the largest share rests with the president. Congress may restrain him, they may prevent him from doing what he wants to do, but initiatives, crisis responses and leadership must come from him.

Foreign policy and the Constitution

The constitutional division of reponsibility between president and Congress in the making of foreign policy will be discussed here under five subheadings: treaty-making; the war power; the power of the purse; foreign aid and foreign trade.

Treaty-making

The president is clearly expected to be the principal player in the negotiation of treaties with foreign powers even though the Constitution prescribes an important role for the Senate: '[The president] shall have Power, by and with the Advice and Consent of the Senate, to make Treaties, provided two-thirds of the Senators present concur.' These few words do not define at all precisely the sharing of power between the chief executive and the Senate in this key area of foreign policy. Disputes over the nature of this division were inevitable and none was more bitter than the one that broke out after World War I between President Wilson and the Senate over the Treaty of Versailles.

Long before that Wilson had convinced himself of the primacy of the president in foreign affairs and his dominant role in the treaty process:

> The initiative in foreign affairs, which the President possesses without any restriction whatever, is virtually the power to control them absolutely. The President cannot conclude a treaty with a foreign power without the consent of the Senate, but he may guide every step of diplomacy, and to guide diplomacy is to determine what treaties must be made, if the faith and prestige of the government are to be maintained. He need disclose no step of negotiation until it is complete, and when in any critical matter it is completed the government is virtually committed. Whatever its disinclination the Senate may feel itself committed also.[2]

As a scholar Wilson took the view that the president's control over diplomacy was virtually total; initiatives were the prerogative of the chief executive, the Senate had no right to be consulted during the process of negotiating a treaty and was confined to saying yes or no to the finished product. This theoretical notion of presidential supremacy was to prove decidedly over-optimistic in practice. As we saw in Chapter 3, at the end of World War I many senators were disinclined to accept such a heavily restrictive interpretation of their place in the treaty process. They were deeply affronted by Wilson's refusal to discuss his plans with them before he left for Paris and by his unwillingess to keep them informed during the course of the negotiations.

The President's principal opponent in what was to be an ugly battle with the Senate was Henry Cabot Lodge, the leader of the Republican majority. Lodge too had written earlier about these matters, but he argued that the Senate's power in the making of treaties was:

> equal to and coordinate with that of the President, except in the initiation of a negotiation which can of necessity only be undertaken by the President alone. The Senate has the right to recommend entering upon a negotiation or the reverse. . . . [It also has] the right to amend. . . . It is also clear that any action taken by the Senate is a part of the negotiation . . . the action of the Senate upon a treaty is not merely to give sanction to the Treaty, but is an integral part of the treaty making and may be taken at any stage of a negotiation.[3]

Each man overstated his case, but it was, to say the least, politically imprudent of Wilson as president to be so dismissive of the role of the Senate. Notwithstanding the president's right to initiate negotiations, in treaty-making, as in so many other areas, there is a sharing of power that presidents and their staff cannot afford to ignore. Senate resentment generated by Wilson's determination to monopolize the treaty process contributed to his humiliating defeat over the Treaty of Versailles.[4] Subsequent presidents, conscious of the disaster that befell Wilson, took steps to avoid making the same mistakes. Senators were consulted and involved in the deliberations leading to agreements such as the UN Charter, the NATO treaty, and, more recently, the Panama Canal treaties.

It has been possible for presidents to escape from the difficulties that the Senate may present in treaty-making by using executive agreements instead. These are understandings between the heads of national governments, that may be either written or oral and do not, as such, require Senate consent, although congressional approval may become necessary if funding is required. One of the best examples is Roosevelt's destroyers-for-bases exchange with Churchill in 1940; others include the Yalta and Potsdam agreements at the end of World War II, the Vietnam peace agreement in 1973 and various military base agreements with countries such as Spain, Diego Garcia and Bahrain.[5]

It is apparent that executive agreements are sometimes concerned with the great issues of foreign policy and there are obvious negative implications for the prerogatives of the legislature, particularly if the agreements are secret. Moreover, since World War II there has been a considerable proliferation of executive agreements; according to one estimate the United States is now party to more than 4,000 compared to something like 1,000 treaties.[6] In 1972, Congress, alarmed at the ever-increasing number of executive agreements, adopted the Case Amendment; this requires the president to report the text of agreements with foreign powers to Congress. It appears, however, that the Case Amendment has been less than fully observed in practice.[7]

The war power

The sharing of power that is so much a feature of the Constitution is very evident with regard to the so-called 'war power'. The clause that vests the right 'To declare War' in Congress is sometimes taken to mean that the war power belongs exclusively to the legislature, but the matter is infinitely more complicated than that. Even though the Articles of Confederation conferred upon Congress 'the sole and exclusive right and power of determining on peace and war', those who drew up the second constitution in 1787 thought differently. They saw the necessity for a strong, but not too strong, separate, executive branch; one that possessed power, but had no monopoly of power.

At one stage the Founding Fathers gave consideration to a draft clause that would have given Congress the power 'To make war'. However, a significant amendment was introduced: 'Mr Madison and Mr Gerry moved to insert "declare" striking out "make" war; leaving to the Executive the power to repel sudden attacks.'[8] Precisely what this change meant is not entirely clear. Nevertheless it seems that the Founding Fathers were saying two things: first, that presidents must be allowed to do what was necessary when crises arose, but second they were not to be given *carte blanche* to embark on military action as they saw fit.

As we saw in Chapter 2, Lincoln, at the time of the Civil War, drew extensively on his share of the war power to justify taking actions that would otherwise be deemed unconstitutional. These included calling up the state miltias, supending *habeas corpus* and blockading the South – all without congressional approval. In defence of these steps Lincoln cited Article II of the Constitution. Included in that article is the oath of office that all presidents take swearing to 'preserve. protect and defend' the Constitution. This, Lincoln believed, made him responsible for the public safety or, in modern terminology, national security; as he saw it he had the 'duty of preserving by every indispensable means, that government – that nation of which the Constitution was the organic law'.[9] The logic of this position was undeniable – it was hardly possible to preserve the Constitution if the integrity of the nation was destroyed.

Nevertheless Lincoln's claim to the war power was alarmingly open-ended. To support his position further he argued that the commander in chief clause gave him the right to take whatever action he believed necessary to 'best subdue the enemy'.[10] Not for Lincoln the minimalist interpretation of the commander in chief clause found in the *Federalist Number 69* where Hamilton seems to suggest that the president will be little more than a formal head of the armed forces with the policy decisions remaining in the hands of the legislature.[11] In practice, however, countless presidents, Lincoln included, have pre-empted congressional control over policy.

Chief executives have repeatedly taken action and left Congress with little option except to support the president. As Wilson said a century ago in regard to treaty-making, the president's right to initiate negotiations gives him the 'chance to get the country into such scrapes, so pledged in the view of the world to certain courses of action, that the Senate hesitates to bring about the appearance of dishonor which would follow its refusal to ratify' executive initiatives.[12] In the same way presidents, sustained by their formal position as commander in chief and their right to take initiatives, have, on many occasions, unilaterally committed forces or entered into agreements; in other words they have got 'the country into such scrapes' that Congress and the nation have had little choice but to go along.

One particularly famous occasion, already referred to, occurred when Franklin Roosevelt through an executive agreement exchanged American destroyers for the lease of a number of British bases. Executive agreements are not subject to congressional approval yet this was a step fraught with momentous consequences for American foreign policy. In fact Roosevelt consulted with colleagues and congressional leaders before agreeing to the exchange, but in a formal sense he unilaterally made a dramatic and far-reaching gesture of support for the allied side in the war then underway in Europe. Robert Jackson, Roosevelt's Attorney General, drew partly on the commander in chief clause in defence of the president's action.[13]

A decade later Dean Acheson, President Truman's Secretary of State advised the President that the commander in chief clause entitled him to send American forces to South Korea without having to ask for congressional approval.[14] The President accepted this advice, thereby setting in train US involvement in a three-year war in which nearly six million Americans served and more than thirty-three thousand lost their lives even though Congress at no stage formally declared war. In much the same way Presidents Kennedy, Johnson and Nixon, acting in their role as commander in chief, committed what eventually became vast military forces to Vietnam. Once again there was a massive outpouring of men and *matériel* in a war, lasting for nearly a decade, that was never formally authorized by Congress.

Kennedy, in 1962, without consulting Congress, placed the US air force on alert and directed the navy to blockade Cuba so as to prevent the Soviet Union delivering further missiles – actions which came frighteningly close to precipitating World War III.[15] As McGeorge Bundy later explained 'the executive branch made a secret decision of the very gravest character and then carried it through, informing congressional leaders just before the President informed the country and the world, but not in any deep sense consulting with the Congress.'[16]

In 1970, President Nixon, justifying his invasion of Cambodia, informed the leader of the Republicans in the Senate that he was fulfilling the 'Constitutional duty of the Commander in Chief to take actions necessary to protect the lives of United States forces'.[17] Even later in that decade, after Congress had revolted against some of the earlier excesses of presidential power and passed the War Powers Resolution in 1973, chief executives were still taking military action with little or no reference to the legislature. Gerald Ford sent marines into Cambodia to free an American merchant ship, the *Mayaguez*, later telling Congress: 'This operation was ordered and conducted pursuant to the President's constitutional executive power and his authority as commander in chief of the United States armed forces.'[18] President Carter similarly justified his abortive attempt to rescue hostages from Iran in 1980 and President Reagan regularly drew on the same authority in defence of various military ventures – in Lebanon, Libya, Grenada and Nicaragua.

There is nothing new about all this. Theoretically, the Constitution involves a balance between 'war-declaring' by Congress and 'war-making' by the president; in practice declarations of war have been exceedingly rare. Over two centuries, the United States has been engaged in something like 130 significant military conflicts, whereas Congress has declared war on only five occasions. Furthermore, only one of those declarations, that concerned with the War of 1812, was preceded by a debate in Congress on the issue; other declarations simply acknowledged that war had begun.[19]

In early 1991 President Bush did not seek a declaration of war against Iraq. He asked Congress for authorization to use force to implement UN resolutions calling for unconditional Iraqi withdrawal from Kuwait. Resolutions giving the President authority to use force were agreed on 12 January in the House by a vote of 250–183 and by the narrow margin of 52–47 in the Senate.[20]

The power of the purse

The decision to go to war is made by the president and in many cases such decisions are not buttressed by formal declarations of war by Congress; however, the commitment of military forces incurs expenditures and the Constitution specifies that 'No money shall be drawn from the Treasury, but in consequence of Appropriation made by Law.' Congress is also empowered 'To raise and support Armies . . . [and] To provide and maintain a Navy.' The legislature, in other words, must approve all expenditures military or otherwise and control of the purse strings is arguably the most potent power that Congress possesses.

The executive branch's command of diplomacy and its scope for initiating military action is, in theory, offset by Congress's power of the purse. The executive is thereby checked by the legislature; as the Founding Fathers intended, there is a sharing of power. Unfortunately this theoretical picture is constantly marred by the fact that most military engagements are over and done with before Congress can pull the financial plug. The Cuban missile crisis, Johnson's intervention in the Dominican Republic, Reagan's invasion of Grenada and Bush's attack on Panama were all at an end before Congress had an opportunity to use its financial weapon.

Even where hostilities extend over long periods there are difficulties in using control of the purse strings to terminate a war. Once American troops are in action even dissenting legislators will be reluctant to cut off funding; it will be argued that, irrespective of the merits of the case, it is dishonourable to deprive men risking their lives for their country of financial support. It was sentiments such as these, coupled with a fear of the political backlash that might follow, that for a number of years inhibited congressional attempts to halt the war in Vietnam.

When criticisms of the war began to surface in Congress, President Johnson and his staff cited congressional votes providing funding as evidence of support for US policy in South East Asia. This was answered by George Mahon, the chairman of the House Appropriations Committee, who argued that voting money for the troops 'does not involve a test as to one's basic views with respect to the war in Vietnam. The question here is that they are entitled to our support as long as they are there, regardless of our views otherwise.'[21] Congressional willingness to provide appropriations for the war finally began to weaken substantially in the late 1960s and in 1970 the Cooper–Church Amendment was passed cutting off funds for US troops, advisers and air support in and over Cambodia. After this breakthrough, further amendments were introduced as popular and congressional disenchantment with the war mounted.

Foreign aid

Foreign aid offers another avenue available to legislators wishing to use their financial clout to influence foreign policy. Since World War II foreign aid for military or other purposes has become a major instrument of foreign policy. According to one estimate, between 1945 and 1980 the United States disbursed over $200 billion in foreign aid; the Marshall Plan alone saw the distribution of $15 billion to Western Europe in grants and loans in the period 1948–52.[22]

President Truman's aid programmes did not pass Congress without a struggle and, in the years since, the legislature has regularly declined to rubber stamp such proposals emanating from the executive branch. Some legislators have disapproved of foreign aid altogether, whereas others have been concerned to ensure that American assistance has gone to the right recipients. The former category once included Otto Passman, a legendary chairman in the 1950s and 60s of the sub-committee of the House Appropriations Committee concerned with foreign aid. Every year, irrespective of which party held the White House, Passman used his key position to impose swingeing cuts on executive branch aid proposals.

The shape of American foreign policy as reflected in its aid programmes owes a great deal to congressional influence. The fact that Israel has consistently been a recipient of massive American aid is partly, although by no means entirely, to be explained by the effectiveness of the pro-Israeli lobby in Congress.[23] In the 1980s President Reagan sought to pursue a policy of even-handedness in the distribution of foreign aid to US allies in southern Europe – Greece and Turkey. The administration's failure to accomplish this shift is, in part, explained by the large influence of the Greek–American lobby among members of Congress.[24]

Even more seriously from an executive branch perspective, President Reagan's policy in Central America was severely hampered by congressional control of the purse strings. He was determined to curtail, if not undermine, the Sandinista regime in Nicaragua by providing financial and military assistance to the Contra opposition. Many in Congress were either ambivalent about this policy or openly hostile to it and the Boland amendments were passed in an effort to modify Reagan's policy. The most important of these, that became law in 1984, stated:

> During fiscal year 1985, no funds available to the Central Intelligence Agency, the Department of Defense or any other agency or entity of the United States involved in intelligence activities may be obligated or expended for the purpose or which would have the effect of supporting directly or indirectly, military or paramilitary

operations in Nicaragua by any nation group, organization, movement or individual.[25]

Taken as read this was a very specific constraint on the executive's freedom of action in a crucial area of foreign policy. The violation of this and other Boland amendments helped create one of the most important crises of congressional/presidential relations there has been for some time – one which might have led to an attempt to impeach the President.

Foreign trade

The Constitution confers upon Congress various economic powers that can have important foreign policy consequences. Thus Article I Section 8 includes, 'The Congress shall have power To lay and collect Taxes, Duties, Imposts and Excises, . . . [and] To regulate Commerce with foreign nations.' These clauses effectively gave the legislature exclusive control over the regulation of foreign trade and, for close on 150 years, Congress generally adhered to protectionist policies; using tariffs to defend American industries and to generate revenue for the federal government.[26]

In that earlier era the writing of tariff laws provided classic exercises in pluralist politics that tended to show Congress in the worst possible light. Tariff rates were determined by irrational, unseemly, if not corrupt, procedures involving fierce lobbying and relentless bargaining at the expense of any consideration of the national interest. As a senator remarked in the 1930s:

> Logrolling is inevitable, and in its most pernicious form. We do not write national tariff law. We jam together, through various unholy alliances and combinations, a potpourri or hodgepodge of sections and local tariff rates, which often add to our trouble and increase world misery.[27]

An increasing awareness of the disadvantages of both protectionism and Congress's methods for deciding on tariff rates led to the Reciprocal Trade Agreements Act of 1934. This legislation delegated to the president the authority to negotiate reciprocal trade agreements with foreign countries that increased or reduced tariffs by up to 50 per cent. Subsequent updating legislation has maintained the principle of delegating the power of trade negotiation to the president, but with Congress continuing to supervise and often striving to restrict the freedom of manoeuvre of the executive branch.

The struggle over American trade policy in recent years has been between Republican presidents committed to free trade and a largely Democratic Congress more susceptible to protectionist influences. Ronald Reagan was an unabashed free trader:

> I am a free-trader. I firmly opposed import quotas. I believed that the new competition Detroit faced [from Japan], like all competition, was good for it and good for consumers – a spur that would motivate our auto industry to produce better cars. That's how the free enterprise system works.[28]

In Congress rather different views were advanced by the likes of Richard Gephardt, a leading House Democrat from Missouri. In 1987, the Reagan administration had to fend off Gephardt-sponsored legislation, aimed primarily at Japan, requiring tariff reprisals against countries with excessive trade surpluses with the United States.[29] Although the legislation in question passed the House, but failed in the Senate, it is the case that in recent years the influence of Congress in trade policy matters has increased:

> Senators and representatives recognize that the president is more likely than Congress to implement trade policy in the overall interest of the nation. Yet there is no evidence in congressional action during the 1980s that Congress is willing to give the president the power to do so.[30]

The Bush administration's current attempts to negotiate a free trade agreement embracing Mexico and Canada may yet fail to gain approval on Capitol Hill. The agreement with Canada is in place, and after a struggle Congress agreed in 1991 that negotiations with Mexico could proceed under a 'fast track' procedure allowing the finished treaty to be voted up or down without revisions. Given the strength of protectionist sentiment in Congress, final agreement to a treaty is by no means guaranteed.[31]

Presidential primacy in foreign policy

So far this chapter has shown that, despite the substantial constitutional prerogatives of Congress, the executive branch, in most situations, is the overwhelmingly dominant partner in the foreign policy-making process. Powerful support for such presidential primacy was provided by the US Supreme Court in 1936.

Curtiss-Wright

Congress, in 1934, in attempting to limit hostilities that had broken out between Paraguay and Bolivia, passed a joint resolution delegating to the President the authority to stop the sale of arms to either country. President Roosevelt duly imposed an embargo on the sale of arms which was then violated by the Curtiss-Wright Corporation in selling fifteen machine guns to Bolivia. When the matter became the subject of litigation it was argued that the embargo was invalid because Congress had improperly delegated power to the executive.

In their decision in *United States* v. *Curtiss-Wright Export Corporation* (1936) the Supreme Court indicated not only that the delegation was legitimate, but also came down heavily on the side of presidential supremacy in the realm of foreign policy. According to Justice Sutherland, who delivered the opinion of the Court, an important distinction had to be made between internal and external affairs; in the former case, 'the federal government can exercise no powers except those specifically enumerated in the Constitution, and such implied powers as are necessary and proper to carry into effect the enumerated powers.'

External affairs were, Sutherland insisted, a different matter. When the break with Britain occurred in the eighteenth century the United States had acquired that power to control its relations with other countries that accrue to all free and independent nations. This included, in the words of the Declaration of Independence, 'full Power to levy War, conclude Peace, contract Alliances, establish Commerce, and to do all other Acts and Things which Independent States may of right do'. These powers, according to the Court, were not derived from the Constitution, rather, they were inherent powers belonging to the United States as a sovereign nation and vested in the federal government. The executive branch of the federal government had moreover something close to a monopoly of these powers:

> In this vast external realm with its important, complicated, delicate and manifold problems, the President alone has the power to speak or listen as the representative of the nation. He *makes* treaties with

the advice and consent of the Senate; but he alone negotiates. Into the field of negotiation the Senate cannot intrude; and Congress itself is powerless to invade it. . . . It is important to bear in mind that we are here dealing not alone with an authority vested in the President by an exertion of legislative power, but with such an authority plus the very delicate, plenary and exclusive power of the President as the sole organ of the federal government in the field of international relations – a power which does not require as basis for its exercise an act of congress, but which, of course, like every other governmental power, must be exercised in subordination to the applicable provisions of the Constitution.[32]

This was surely one of the most momentous of all Supreme Court decisions and, even allowing for the qualifying clauses, it seems to undermine seriously congressional claims to a significant share in the making of foreign policy. The president 'alone' speaks and listens on the nation's behalf; he 'alone' negotiates treaties and in international relations generally he has 'plenary and exclusive' power as the 'sole' organ of the federal government. Not surprisingly, presidents from Roosevelt to Bush have derived great comfort from the Curtiss-Wright decision even though its validity has been strongly challenged by constitutional scholars.[33]

An age of crisis

When Curtiss-Wright was handed down, isolationism still prevailed in the United States; within a few years, however, President Roosevelt, fortified by the verdict of the Supreme Court, took various steps that brought America, once and for all, into the international arena. Henceforth the United States would be a principal player on the world stage with responsibilities and interests to match. That development in itself inevitably tilted the balance of power in the political system in favour of the president, a movement which for many years was accentuated by a more or less perpetual state of international crisis. As Senator Fulbright of Arkansas remarked in 1966:

In the past 25 years, American foreign policy has encountered a shattering series of crises and inevitably – or almost inevitably – the effort to cope with these has been executive effort, while the Congress, inspired by patriotism, importuned by Presidents and deterred by lack of information has tended to fall in line. The result has been an unhinging of traditional constitutional relationships.[34]

Starting with the events that led to World War II, the United States has experienced a constant series of crises in international relations. Each of these has tended to strengthen the power of the president. Modern means of warfare require rapid decisions in defence of the nation's vital interests, thereby precluding, so it is argued, the possibility of close adherence to the Constitution. As Richard Neustadt noted in 1963, 'when it comes to action risking war, technology has modified the Constitution.'[35] Many of the crises that presidents have had to confront in the last fifty years have been real enough, but some have been manufactured or overstated, undoubtedly with an eye to the advantages that follow.[36]

A related factor contributing to the growth in executive dominance in foreign policy is the example set by that most influential of modern presidents, Franklin Roosevelt:

> The towering figure of Franklin Roosevelt, the generally accepted wisdom of his initiatives of 1940 and 1941, his undisputed authority as Commander in Chief after Pearl Harbor, the thundering international pronouncements emanating from wartime summits of the Big Two or the Big Three – all these gave Americans in the postwar years an exalted conception of presidential power.[37]

Whilst some presidents since have had no desire to emulate Roosevelt in domestic policy, they have all sought to follow him in international relations. From Harry Truman in Korea to George Bush in the Persian Gulf, presidents have drawn strength from the Roosevelt example; the precedents he set have helped them to respond to crisis situations as they have seen fit and encouraged them to run American foreign policy without being too particular about congressional sensitivities in such matters.

Some presidents have also evaded congressional restraints by using the Central Intelligence Agency as an instrument of foreign policy. The CIA was originally intended to be only an intelligence-gathering body, but it has been repeatedly involved in covert operations; it has destabilized governments, provoked coups and revolutions and even plotted political assassinations. Responsibility for this fundamental change of function has been attributed to Eisenhower who, it is alleged, 'silently turned the CIA into the secret army of the executive branch'.[38] As such, the agency lists among its achievements the restoration of the Shah of Iran in 1953, the unseating of the government of Guatemala in 1954, and the overthrow of Allende in 1973.[39] Among its abortive adventures the two most notable are the Bay of Pigs fiasco of 1960 and the Iran-Contra affair in the 1980s.

Congressional inadequacies

Presidential dominance is also partly explained by congressional cooperation that, on occasion, has come close to abdication. Legislative prerogatives, in other words, have not always been usurped; they have sometimes been delivered to the executive on a plate. There are also entirely legitimate reasons why legislators should defer to presidents in such matters. Even notably outspoken, independent-minded members of Congress have convinced themselves that the legislature is ill suited to the task of conducting American foreign policy and that such matters are best left to the president.

Former Senator Barry Goldwater, for example, has argued:

> Our founding fathers made foreign policy an executive branch responsibility. . . . The direction of [the armed] forces and the daily control of foreign affairs rest with the President. The founding fathers well understood that Congress lacked the capacity for swift and decisive decision making that is essential to protect the nation in times of crisis.[40]

The late Senator John Tower also stressed the advantages of leaving the direction of foreign policy in the hands of the chief executive. Only the president has a national mandate, the information, the personnel, the expertise and the capacity for the confidentiality required to formulate an overall strategy for the nation. Domestic policy could be reasonably dealt with on a piecemeal basis with mistakes being rectified as required, but such procedures were not conducive to the development of a satisfactory foreign policy:

> Five hundred and thirty-five Congressmen with different philosophies, regional interests and objectives in mind cannot forge a unified foreign policy that reflects the interests of the United States as a whole, nor can they negotiate with foreign powers, or meet the requirement for diplomatic confidentiality. They are also ill-equipped to respond quickly and decisively to changes in the international scene. The shifting coalitions of Congress which serve us so well in the formulation and implementation of domestic policy, are not well suited to the day-to-day conduct of external relations.[41]

There is surely something to be said for such arguments. The very structure of Congress is antithetical to the development of a coherent policy towards the outside world; the legislature is handicapped by the fragmentation that arises from weak parties, a membership infinitely responsive to partial interests and a multiplicity of committees and sub committees with overlapping jurisdictions.

International relations specialists maintain that coherence is a necessary requirement of a satisfactory foreign policy yet the legislature's parcelling out of responsibility for such matters to a plethora of sub-units is not helpful. It has been estimated that in 1977, jurisdiction over foreign affairs in the Senate was shared between half of twenty-two standing and special committees. And that takes no account of the further breakdown into sub-committees. The Foreign Relations Committee, for instance, had nine sub-committees whereas the Appropriations Committee had three sub-committees dealing with national defence and foreign policy. Meanwhile the House of Representatives had no less than fifty-six sub-committees, 'active in some dimension of foreign affairs'.[42]

The vulnerability of Congress to partial interests was an especial concern of another former senator, Charles Mathias: he drew attention to the adverse consequences for American foreign policy that follow from the pressures that some ethnic groups are able to bring to bear on the policy process. Jewish-Americans, Greek-Americans, Irish-Americans and other ethnic groups have, according to Mathias, been able to impose distortions on American foreign policy which have sometimes been damaging to the national interest.[43]

The Jewish-American example illustrates Mathias's case well. The leading lobby for this ethnic group is the American Israel Public Affairs Committee (known as AIPAC, it is *not*, however, a political action committee). This organization has a staff of more than one hundred, boasts a membership of 55,000 households and in 1991 had a budget of $12 million. AIPAC in the thirty-seven years of its existence has assiduously cultivated the support of leading members of Congress. Senators are normally expected to be more immune to lobbyists than representatives, but the comment that follows illustrates the fear that AIPAC invokes even in the Senate:

'My colleagues think AIPAC is a very, very powerful organization that is ruthless, and very, very alert,' says [one] senator who like so many on the subject of AIPAC, asks that his name not be named. 'Eighty per cent of the senators here roll their eyes on some of the votes. They know that what they're doing isn't what they really believe is right, but why fight in a situation where they're liable to get beat up on. There's no countervailing sentiment,' this senator adds, noting that the small but ardent circle of pro-Israel activists, unlike its Arab–American counterpart, gives millions of dollars every election cycle to candidates for office.[44]

In short, congressional attitudes towards the Middle East and its many problems have for years been influenced by one of the most potent of pressure groups of all, the pro-Israel lobby. That lobby by definition relentlessly pursues the interests of one nation to the exclusion of all others and the legislature has accordingly tended to be especially sympathetic to Israel. Presidents, too, have generally favoured Israel since World War II, but their national responsibilities place a greater onus on them to develop a foreign policy that is in the best interests of the United States.

A recent example of an executive/congressional clash of this nature occurred in September 1991 when President Bush battled with the pro-Israel lobby over his proposal to delay loan guarantees of $10 billion to Israel. These guarantees were required to assist the settlement of Soviet Jewish emigrants, but the administration took the view that a congressional debate followed by a favourable vote on this issue at this time would critically undermine current American efforts to convene a Middle East peace conference. Initially, it appeared likely that the notorious weight of the pro-Israel lobby in Congress would defeat the President's request for delay. However, after a veto threat and an appeal to the people over the head of Congress, Bush got his way. The President's success on this occasion owed much to his success in the Gulf War, his high standing in the public opinion polls and the disintegration of the Soviet Union. Another president at another time would, no doubt, have failed.[45]

A further weakness of Congress in the making of foreign policy is that its members tend to specialize in destructive criticism and have no great incentive to be constructive. Such behaviour is encouraged by the very nature of the American political system with its separation of powers and the absence of a career link between the legislative and executive branches. Members of Congress can make a career out of harrying, criticizing and obstructing the executive; even when they help in the formulation of policy it is not a policy that they will have to implement. By contrast, members of the House of Commons are restrained by the experience of government they may have had in the past, or the hope that they may at some time in the future become part of the executive themselves.[46]

By the late 1960s presidential primacy in foreign affairs seemed to have been fully established. The Curtiss-Wright decision, the precedents set by FDR, an almost permanent state of international crisis and the inadequacies of the legislature appeared to have irreversibly altered the constitutional balance. However, disillusionment arising from the catastrophic Vietnam war and the Watergate scandal helped create a determination to restore some balance to the political system.

Restoring the balance

The Imperial Presidency

In his book, *The Imperial Presidency*, Arthur Schlesinger Jnr argued that the forms of the Constitution had been overtaken in recent years by 'a conception of presidential power so spacious and peremptory as to imply a radical transformation of the traditional polity. . . . The constitutional Presidency . . . has become the imperial Presidency and threatens to be the revolutionary Presidency.'[47] Foreign policy, most notably executive decisions to go to war, was primarily responsible for the emergence of the imperial presidency and the principal villains of the piece were Presidents Johnson and Nixon.

As a member of the Senate Johnson had enthusiatically endorsed President Truman's sending troops to Korea without congressional approval and then as president himself he proved to be even less inhibited than his predecessor. Ever since the 1950s, the United States had had some sort of military presence in Vietnam, but under Johnson this limited involvement was transformed into an enormous commitment. US bombing of Vietnam began in Febuary 1965 and by the end of that year there were 184,300

American troops in the country, a number which rose to more than 500,000 before Johnson left office in 1969. This was military conflict on a vast scale yet launched by the executive branch with no more than a fig leaf of congressional authorization – the Gulf of Tonkin Resolution. This measure, which Johnson treated virtually as a blank cheque allowing him to do whatever he decided was necessary in Vietnam, had been 'rushed through Congress in August 1964 in a stampede of misinformation and misconception, if not of deliberate deception'.[48]

Johnson's failure to seek a declaration of war or to otherwise engage in meaningful consultation with Congress, plus his intolerance of dissent within his administration, led Schlesinger to suggest that the President conducted himself more like an eighteenth-century British monarch than a republican chief executive. Yet if Johnson's behaviour was outrageous, Nixon's was deemed to be even worse. Notwithstanding his massive widening of the war Johnson had declined advice that he carry the war further into neighbouring Laos and Cambodia.

Richard Nixon, on the other hand, constantly citing the commander in chief clause as his authority, and treating Congress with contempt, invaded Cambodia, a neutral country. He claimed that he was entitled to do so because of the threat to the lives of American troops posed by enemy Vietnamese using Cambodia as a sanctuary. Subsequently, and again without any approval from Congress, Nixon launched intensive bombing raids against Cambodia and another neutral country, Laos.

As we have seen, many presidents before Johnson and Nixon had pushed their war power to extreme limits, including Lincoln, Franklin Roosevelt and Truman, but these, so it is often argued, were significantly different cases. Lincoln and Roosevelt faced desperate situations where the very survival of the nation was at risk and even Truman could claim that he acted with the authority of the United Nations. Johnson and Nixon, by contrast:

> surpassed all their predecessors in claiming that inherent and exclusive presidential authority, unaccompanied by emergencies threatening the life of the nation, unaccompanied by the authorization of Congress or the blessing of an international organization, permitted a President to order troops into battle at his unilateral pleasure.[49]

The disastrous course of events in South East Asia in conjunction with the Watergate revelations undermined confidence in American political institutions in the early 1970s and gave credibility to allegations of presidential excess. In this new climate of opinion the arguments in favour of a significant foreign policy role for Congress were treated with more respect than had been the case for some time.

The case for a significant Congressional role

Those who doubt whether Congress has much to contribute to foreign policy are prone to argue that the president has access to superior sources of expertise and information, is able to operate with secrecy and dispatch and has a perspective which is national rather than narrowly parochial.

That the executive has an information advantage is undeniable, but too much can be made of this. Information in itself is certainly no guarantee of wise decision-making. During the Vietnam War the executive was supported by droves of experts and specialists drawing on mountains of information. Many of those advising President Johnson assured him that the war could be won. In the long term, however, it seems hardly disputable that the handful of critics in Congress who opposed the war from the start were, despite their supposed information deficiency, correct. As Schlesinger scathingly commented:

> no episode in American history had been more accompanied by misjudgment, misconception and miscalculation than the war in Vietnam. Information? The newspapers and magazines provided far more accurate information about the progress of the war in Indo-China than Top Secret cables from Saigon.[50]

Members of the national legislature in the United States have access to not inconsiderable sources of information. They may have personally garnered expertise and understanding after many years on a specialist committee or sub-committee and, unlike their counterparts elsewhere, they are flanked by large personal and committee staffs with the capacity and resources for serious research. Members of the Senate Foreign Relations Committee, for instance, are unlikely to be helpless, exposed amateurs constantly upstaged by professionals from the executive branch.

Crisis situations demand secrecy and dispatch and the executive is clearly better able than the legislature to meet these conditions. However, two points should be borne in mind: first, crises can be manufactured and second, by no means is foreign policy about crisis response alone. Senator Fulbright, a former chairman of the Foreign Relations Committee, provides a good example of a contrived crisis that occurred in 1965.

One afternoon in April, congressional leaders were summoned to an emergency meeting at the White House. They were told that the revolution that had broken out in the Dominican Republic was endangering American lives and a force of marines would be landed in Santo Domingo that night to provide the necessary protection. No one in the congressional delegation expressed disapproval of this unilateral executive action. A few months later investigations by the Foreign Relations Committee revealed that the real purpose of sending 22,000 marines to the Dominican Republic was to prevent the setting up of a left-wing government. In other words, a crisis had been fabricated to make possible a military intervention into a neighbouring country – an action that Fulbright, and conceivably other congressional leaders, would have disapproved of if they had been given time to ascertain the full facts.[51]

It is obvious that there is much more to foreign policy than responding to crisis situations. According to one definition, foreign policy means 'those external goals for which the nation is prepared to commit its resources'. Many such goals – deterring the Soviet Union, settling the Palestinian–Israeli dispute, establishing a New World Order – are long rather than short-term objectives. Similarly, national security policy, which may be included as part of foreign policy, is concerned with the military dimension of defending and advancing the national interest: 'it involves preventing threats to national security; collecting and digesting information about the behavior of potential enemies; creating and maintaining necessary miltary alliance systems; supplying friendly countries with arms aid, [etc.].'[52] These too are largely long-term matters; only in some circumstances do they require the immediate, decisive responses that only executives can provide.

Even allowing for the unwieldy, if not chaotic, structure of Congress many of the great issues of American foreign policy can be properly dealt with in the legislature. In some respects indeed,

Congress provides a more appropriate forum than the executive branch. A successful foreign policy needs to rest on a consensus of opinion in the nation at large and the legislature can play an important part in creating and sustaining such a consensus. As Averell Harriman said on one occasion, 'No foreign policy will stick unless the American people are behind it and unless Congress understands it the American people aren't going to understand it.'[53] Members of Congress, furthermore, are notoriously close to their constituents; they are in touch with public opinion in a way that bureaucrats, presidential advisers and even presidents are not.

The development of consensual support requires a basic understanding of the issues, and of their pros and cons, by the public in general. Congress, particularly in the age of television, can help raise the level of public understanding. Televised congressional committtee hearings have, from time to time, shown Congress at its best; they have been impressive vehicles of public education. The Watergate hearings, for example, provided a national seminar on the conduct of American politics; the interested public was able to learn in copious detail what had been taking place at the heart of the political system. The Iran–Contra hearings, held in 1987, similarly brought before the people details of dubious activities within the executive branch, while also providing a forum for the consideration of American policy towards Nicaragua.

The extended hearings on the war in Vietnam conducted by the Senate Foreign Relations Committee in the 1960s contributed to the eventual change in public policy. In contemplating what results might follow from embarking on these hearings, Senator Fulbright remarked:

> It is our expectation that these proceedings may generate controversy. If they do, it will not be because we value controversy for its own sake, but rather because we accept it as a condition of intelligent decision–making, as, indeed, the crucible in which a national consensus as to objectives may be translated into a consensus of policy as well.[54]

Conceivably, in the early years, American public opinion was behind the massive commitment of military forces to Vietnam; however, the hearings later held by the Senate Foreign Relations

Committee demonstrated that if such a consensus had existed before, it was now collapsing.

In the battles between presidents and Congress over the conduct of foreign policy, chief executives constantly point to their possession of a national mandate. The concept of a presidential mandate is decidedly dubious in itself and, to revert to the Vietnam example, Richard Nixon, in his first term, 1969–73, could not reasonably claim a mandate for his policy in South East Asia. In the 1968 campaign Nixon constantly presented himself as the candidate who would bring the war to a conclusion and, 'by late September he was talking almost exclusively about ending the war'.[55] In the 1968 election Nixon won no more than 44 per cent of the total vote (approximately 16 per cent of the total population) and in office showed few signs of bringing the war to a speedy conclusion; full-scale hostilities went on throughout Nixon's first term and, despite a programme of 'Vietnamization', by the end of 1972 there were still 140,000 US troops in Vietnam.

It is also worth bearing in mind that while it is reasonable for the president to stress that he, unlike legislators, is answerable to a national constituency, presidential elections are only one way whereby public opinion is represented. Members of Congress are representative of public opinion organized and quantified in a different, but no less legitimate manner. And in the case of House members, they can argue that they are especially close to the grass roots with popular 'mandates' which are subject to renewal every two years.

Congressional reassertion and the War Powers Resolution

The case for a significant congressional role in the formulation and implementation of foreign policy gained a new plausibility in the 1970s. After thirty years of obeisance to the White House, legislators began to consider how presidential excess might be curbed and congressional, constitutional prerogatives reasserted. During this period, a wide range of legislation was introduced, designed to rein in the executive branch: 'The thrust of the legislation was to restrict the President's ability to dispatch troops abroad in a crisis, and to proscribe his authority in arms sales, trade, human rights, foreign assistance and intelligence operations.'[56]

The most important of an estimated 150 such restrictions was the War Powers Resolution of 1973. The immediate inspiration for this law was President Nixon's incursion into Cambodia in 1970 (see page 120). In more general terms, however, this was an attempt by Congress to prevent presidents from going to war without congressional approval. It sought to specify, in other words, the circumstances under which a chief executive could commit American forces to military action.

The War Powers Resolution stated that a president could involve armed forces in hostilities *only* under certain conditions: (1) a formal declaration of war by Congress; (2) some other form of 'specific statutory authorization'; (3) when a 'national emergency' was deemed to exist. The first two of these were mere restatements of the constitutional position and it was the third that was of especial significance. In an attempt to avoid a repetition of those many occasions when the executive alone had decided when a 'national emergency', or crisis, existed, the new legislation defined it as a situation 'created by attack upon the United States, its territories or possessions, or its armed forces'. This definition, it should be noted, would have excluded ventures such as Lyndon Johnson's dispatch of marines to the Dominican Republic, ostensibly to protect American citizens living there. Even more interestingly, the Resolution would have also denied legitimacy to the Kennedy administration's response to the crisis over missiles in Cuba. Kennedy was reacting to a 'perceived threat of attack' rather than an actual attack.[57]

The War Powers Resolution required further that when the president was responding to a 'national emergency' as defined above, he was obliged, insofar as it was possible, to consult with Congress beforehand. Failing that, he had to report his action to Congress within forty-eight hours. Once armed forces had been committed, Congress could demand their withdrawal at any time by passing a concurrent resolution of both houses which, by definition, is not subject to a presidential veto. The troops would in any case have to be withdrawn after sixty days, with a possible thirty-day extension, unless, in the interim, a declaration of war, or some other form of congressional authorization had been agreed. Not suprisingly, President Nixon declared the War Powers Resolution passed in October 1973 to be unconstitutional and duly exercised his veto. The veto was overridden, but the view that the legislation represents an illegitimate infringement of the president's freedom to act as commander in chief and head of the executive branch persists to this day: 'Presidents Nixon, Ford, Carter and Reagan have all believed that the War Powers Act is unconstitutional and incompatible with the ability of a strong president to carry on his duties as required.'[58]

It has also been argued that in some situations the War Powers Resolution extends rather than limits the freedom of the president:

> He could so firmly commit the nation's forces and prestige during the ninety-day period that Congress would find it politically and militarily impossible to reverse the operation. What begins as marginal or contrived has the potential of deteriorating into a genuine emergency, compelling congressional support. As the sixty- to ninety-day period deadline grew near, legislators might 'rally round the flag' rather than independently debate the wisdom and the merits of President's decision.[59]

There is much force to this argument, given the closeness of members of congress to their constituents and the propensity of the American people to confer overwhelming support on military interventions by the president irrespective of the circumstances. Recent examples of such occurrences include the invasion of Grenada and Bush's incursion into Panama. It is noteworthy that both of these military actions were quickly completed. If either had dragged on for a considerable length of time, popular support might have been eroded and the legislature would probably have become less passive.

There are other flaws in this legislation. For instance, it is not at all clear with whom in Congress the president is obliged to consult, nor is it evident what form that consultation should take. Consultation with all members of Congress is out of the question, but are party leaders to be consulted, committee chairmen, or what? Will a briefing as to what is about to take place be sufficient, or does consulation require much more than that? The Resolution seemed to go so far as to require that those who were consulted had to agree to the proposed course of action, but if that is so how were legislators to obtain the information they would require to make an informed decision in a crisis situation?[60]

In short, there are many difficulties with the War Powers Resolution. Right-wing academics, Cabinet members and White

House spokesmen regularly denounce it as unconstitutional, and an intolerable, dangerous restraint on the president's freedom to respond to crises. Presidents also constantly ignore or skirt around its provisions. Nevertheless the Resolution is symbolic of the efforts to restore the constitutional balance in the 1970s.

By no means were those efforts inconsequential; a new mood of congressional assertiveness in foreign policy did prevail throughout the 1970s and 1980s. During that period legislators showed a new determination to prevent presidents from inflicting upon them the sort of indignities they had suffered at the hands of Lyndon Johnson and Richard Nixon.

It may be that this era is about to come to an end. The War Powers Resolution grew out of the national trauma of the Vietnam War. Even though it was a gross oversimplification, that war was perceived as a presidential war and the Resolution was a way of preventing such a catastrophe from happening again. The Gulf War, on the other hand, is popularly seen as a wondrous success brilliantly engineered from the White House. In this new atmosphere, highly favourable to the presidency, the War Powers Resolution may become increasingly irrelevant.

Conclusions

Those who fought to restore the balance of the Constitution in the making of foreign policy were, from the beginning, bound to fail. Whatever the Constitution says and notwithstanding the case for a significant, congressional role the supremacy of the executive in the formulation and implementation of foreign policy is inevitable. As E.S. Corwin said, 'The verdict of history, . . . is that the power to determine the substantive content of American foreign policy is a *divided* power, with the lion's share falling usually, though by no means always, to the President.'[61] Corwin wrote those words many years ago, but nothing has happened since to detract from their wisdom. Congress was then and remains today very much a secondary partner in these matters. The legislature has the scope to make difficulties at the margin, to create embarrassments, to cause delays and occasionally to thwart the president altogether, but the overall direction of foreign policy is clearly the executive's responsibility.

There is much to deplore in how some presidents have exercised that responsibility, but it is much more difficult to deny their *right* to do so. Those inclined to insist that Congress be treated as an equal partner must contend with a formidable body of argument and precedent. They must first answer weighty historical figures such as John Marshall (later Chief Justice of the Supreme Court), who in 1799 said, 'The President is the sole organ of the nation in its external relations, and its sole representative with foreign nations.'[62] Alexander Hamilton in the *Federalist Number 74* also needs to be answered:

> Of all the cares or concerns of government, the direction of war most peculiarly requires those qualities which distinguish the exercise of power by a single hand. The direction of war implies the direction of the common strength; and the power of directing and employing the common strength forms a usual and essential part in the definition of the executive authority.[63]

Beyond that, those who insist on an equal role for Congress must deal with the implications of the Curtiss-Wright decision. This ruling, which the Supreme Court, despite many complaints, has shown little sign of repudiating, has given impressive and enormously influential support to the executive branch in its constant struggles with the legislature over the conduct of foreign policy. And then there are the precedents set by those giants of American history, Abraham Lincoln and Franklin Roosevelt. Both vigorously expanded the president's war power in successfully asserting their right to exercise control at a moment of high crisis in the history of the United States. It is often argued, usually by commentators of a liberal persuasion, that other less admirable presidents have illegitimately called upon the Lincoln and Roosevelt examples to defend their own less worthy actions. Theodore Draper, for instance, scorns Reagan who, 'apparently mistook himself for Lincoln and the covert operation against Nicaragua for the Civil War'.[64]

Lincoln's excesses of presidential power can be excused, so the argument goes, on the grounds that he faced the ultimate crisis, the destruction of the nation itself. Similarly, Roosevelt's many actions of dubious constitutionality are made acceptable by the fact that he was grappling with the Third Reich. On the other hand, Lyndon

Johnson and Richard Nixon in South East Asia and Ronald Reagan in Central America, so we are told, did not face comparable situations. These tend, however, to be *ad hominem* arguments. We may not accept that the cases are parallels, but that is a matter of subjective judgement.

Long before Lincoln became president he warned against conceding too much freedom in war-making to the executive. He hypothesized a situation where the president wished to invade Canada to counteract a threatened British invasion of the United States and went on 'how could you stop him? You may say to him, "I see no probability of the British invading us," but he will say to you, "Be silent; I see it, if you don't." '[65] Lincoln later lost his qualms about presidential war-making, but his earlier point remained valid and relevant to the 1980s. In that later period Reagan was effectively saying to his opponents that although they disagreed he happened to regard Nicaragua as a serious threat to the security of the United States, 'Be silent; I see it, if you don't.' Like Lincoln in 1861 and Roosevelt in 1940–1 Reagan in the 1980s believed that a crisis existed in Central America entitling him to take steps to deal with the situation.

Even the most fervent advocate of the rights of the legislature would not deny the president's authority to respond to genuine crises, to meet immediate threats to the national security; it was, after all, agreed in the Constitutional Convention that the executive had 'the power to repel sudden attacks'. In the eighteenth century, and even much later, that could reasonably be confined to a concern with the nation's immmediate borders whereas 'to repel sudden attacks' in the late twentieth century has quite different ramifications. As a State Department spokesman said in 1966:

> In 1787 the world was a far larger place, and the framers probably had in mind attacks upon the United States. In the 20th century the world has grown much smaller. An attack on a country far from our shores can impinge directly on the nation's security.[66]

Such reasoning no doubt lay behind John Kennedy's announcement in 1962 that the launching of a nuclear missile from Cuba against any part of the Western Hemisphere would be construed as an attack by the USSR on the USA and would be answered in kind.[67]

It also needs to be remembered that a case can be made for a president in some circumstances operating outside the law and even the Constitution. At first sight this seems to be a shocking and unacceptable proposition. The rule of law is assumed to be an essential requirement of any democratic system. How, therefore, can it possibly be legitimate to permit the person in whom is vested the responsibility to execute the laws to violate those laws himself? Intensely negative reactions to such a line of argument are especially likely in the United States, a nation which takes great pride in its written Constitution, where the majority of legislators are lawyers and individual citizens are inclined to be excessively litigious.

It is nevertheless necessary to take into account presidential prerogative. Executive prerogative was discussed by John Locke, one of the most important intellectual influences on the Founding Fathers. Locke insisted that the rule of law should, in normal circumstances, prevail, but he also recognized that emergencies could occur where the executive would have 'the power to act according to discretion for the public good, without the prescription of law and sometimes even against it'.[68] Crises, in other words, might arise where in order to preserve the nation itself the executive would be entitled to take illegal and even extra-constitutional action. A case in point was Lincoln's reaction to his perception of a dire threat to the integrity of the state.

Ronald Reagan in his attempt to evade the provisions of the Boland Amendments, the War Powers Resolution and the Constitution can also be defended in terms of Lockean prerogative.[69] Shortly after he was inaugurated Reagan received from intelligence agencies what he regarded as:

> firm and incontrovertible evidence that the Marxist government of Nicaragua was transferring hundreds of tons of Soviet arms from Cuba to rebel groups in El Salvador. Although El Salvador was the immediate target, the evidence showed that the Soviets and Fidel Castro were targeting all of Central America for a Communist takeover. El Salvador and Nicaragua were only a down payment. Honduras, Guatemala, and Costa Rica were next, and then would come Mexico.[70]

In other words, President Reagan was led to conclude that what was happening in Central America was placing the security of the United States under real and immediate threat. He was, however, frustrated by his inability to convince either the American people or Congress of the validity of his fears.[71] There are surely parallels here not only with Lincoln's situation, but also with Roosevelt's in 1940–1. FDR was similarly frustrated by a recalcitrant, largely neutralist Congress and an apathetic public. He believed that if Britain succumbed to Hitler the United States would be next; Roosevelt took actions in accordance with that belief, sometimes with scant reference to legality. In the 1980s Reagan, a great admirer of Roosevelt, followed in his eminent predecessor's footsteps. In both cases there were many critics who denied that a threat to American national security really existed and deplored the failure of the executive to abide by the law. In the 1940s the critics tended to be Republicans, whereas in the 1980s they were more likely to be Democrats.

It is not by any means being suggested here that presidents must always be given a free hand, or that Congress has no significant role to play in the formulation and implementation of foreign policy. The complex sharing of power wrought by the Constitution remains in place and we can be sure that disputes will continue to rage as to the appropriate division between the executive and the legislature in these matters. The arguments will go on and it is highly desirable that they should do so.

The balance between the two branches has been sharply tilted by the persistence of international crisis, but it would be disastrous if the balance disappeared altogether. It is essential that the legislature goes on carping and criticizing, calling the executive to account, demanding to know what is being done in the name of the United States and helping to create consensus. If democracy is to be really meaningful it is vital that the legislature has a voice in the life-and-death decisions of foreign policy. Corwin spoke of the Constitution offering an 'invitation to struggle for the privilege of directing American foreign policy' and it is a struggle that needs to continue even though the president, in most situations, is bound to be the victor.[72]

Notes

1. Arthur Schlesinger Jnr, *The Imperial Presidency*, Popular Library, New York, 1974, p. 463. NB. Other references to *The Imperial Presidency* in this book are to the Deutsch edition, London 1974.

2. *Constitutional Government in the United States*, Columbia University Press, New York, 1908, pp. 77–8.
3. 'The Treaty Making Powers of the Senate', *Scribners Magazine*, vol. 31, no. 1, January 1902.
4. See David Mervin, 'Henry Cabot Lodge and the League of Nations', *Journal of American Studies*, vol. 4, no. 2, February 1971.
5. Louis Fisher, *Constitutional Conflicts Between Congress and the President*, Princeton University Press, Princeton, 1985, p. 272.
6. Jack Plano and Milton Greenberg, *The American Political Dictionary* (6th edition), Holt, Reinhart and Winston, New York, 1982, p. 410.
7. Fisher, *op. cit.*, p. 278.
8. Max Farrand (ed.), *The Records of The Federal Convention of 1787*, Yale University Press, New Haven, 1937, vol. 2, p. 318.
9. Schlesinger, *The Imperial Presidency, op. cit.*, p. 61.
10. See Ch. 2 above.
11. Rossiter edition, The New American Library, New York, 1961, p. 418.
12. *Congressional Government*, Houghton Mifflin, Boston, 1925, pp. 233–4.
13. Marcus Cunliffe, *American Presidents and The Presidency*, Fontana/Collins, London, 1972, p. 237.
14. Schlesinger, *The Imperial Presidency, op. cit.*, pp. 132–3.
15. Cecil Crabb and Pat Holt, *Invitation to Struggle: Congress, the President and Foreign Policy*, Congressional Quarterly Press, Washington DC, 1984, p. 10.
16. *US Congress* Hearings of the House of Representatives Sub Committee on National Security and Scientific Developments, 1970, pp. 12–13.
17. Arthur Schlesinger Jnr, 'Congress and the Making of Foreign Policy' in Rexford Tugwell and Thomas Cronin (eds), *The Presidency Reappraised*, Praeger, New York, 1974, p. 104.
18. Raymond Tatalovich and Byron Daynes, *Presidential Power in the United States*, Brooks/Cole, Monterey, 1984, pp. 331–2.
19. Crabb and Holt, *op. cit.*, p. 9; Fisher, *op. cit.*, p. 287.
20. *Insight*, 28 January 1991, p. 18.
21. Schlesinger, *The Imperial Presidency, op. cit.*, p. 291.
22. Plano and Greenberg, *op. cit.*, pp. 410 and 419.
23. Charles Mathias, 'Ethnic Groups and Foreign Policy', *Foreign Affairs*, no. 5, Summer 1981, pp. 975–98.
24. See Alex Brummer, 'How to Buy Friends and Influence History', *The Guardian*, 16 April 1985, p. 21.
25. *Congressional Quarterly Almanac 1984*, CQ Press, Washington DC, 1985.
26. David Yoffie, 'American Trade Policy: An Obsolete Bargain?' in John Chubb and Paul Peterson (eds), *Can the Government Govern?*, Brookings, Washington DC, 1985, p. 105.
27. *ibid.*, p. 106.
28. *An American Life*, Hutchinson, London, 1990, p. 241.
29. Hedrick Smith, *The Power Game*, Random House, New York, 1988, p. 145.

30. Yoffie, *op. cit.*, p. 138.
31. *The Observer* 'Mexico' Supplement, 8 September 1991.
32. *United States* v. *Curtiss–Wright Export Corp.*, 299 US 304 (1936).
33. See, for example, Richard Hodder–Williams, 'The President and the Constitution' in Malcolm Shaw (ed.), *Roosevelt to Reagan*, C. Hurst, London 1987, p. 24. In 1990 advisers to President Bush drew on the decision in defending recent Republican administrations against charges of executive usurpation of legislative powers, *New York Review of Books*, 17 May 1990.
34. 'The Fatal Arrogance of Power', *New York Times Sunday Magazine*, 15 May 1966.
35. As quoted in Donald Robinson, *To The Best of My Ability: The Presidency and the Constitution*, W. W. Norton, New York, 1987, p. 226.
36. See Theodore Lowi, *The Personal President*, Cornell University Press, Ithaca, 1985, pp. 170–3.
37. Schlesinger, *The Imperial Presidency, op. cit.*, pp. 122–3.
38. Arthur Schlesinger Jnr, *The Cycles of American History*, André Deutsch, London, 1986, p. 395.
39. See John Ranelagh, *The Agency: The Rise and Decline of the CIA*, Hodder and Stoughton, London, 1987.
40. *Goldwater*, St. Martin's Press, New York, 1988, p. 30.
41. 'Congress versus the President: The Formulation and Implementation of American Foreign Policy', *Foreign Affairs*, Winter 1981/192, pp. 239–46.
42. Crabb and Holt, *op. cit.*, p. 35.
43. Mathias, *op. cit.*.
44. Lloyd Grove, 'Israel's Force in Washington', *The Washington Post National Weekly Edition*, 24–30 June 1991.
45. *The Guardian*, 12 September 1991, p. 10; 13 September 1991, p. 9; 14 September 1991, p. 11.
46. Robert Dahl, *Congress and Foreign Policy*, W. W. Norton, New York, 1950, pp. 135–6.
47. *op. cit.*, p. viii.
48. *ibid.*, p. 179.
49. *ibid.*, p. 193.
50. *ibid.*, p. 283.
51. 'The Fatal Arrogance of Power' *op cit.*
52. Crabb and Holt, *op. cit.*, p. 6
53. Quoted in Schlesinger, *The Imperial Presidency, op. cit.*, p. 325.
54. Fulbright, *op. cit.*
55. Stephen Ambrose, *Nixon: The Triumph of a Politician 1962–72*, Simon and Schuster, New York, 1989, p. 191.
56. John Tower, 'Congress Versus The President: The Formulation and Implementation of American Foreign Policy', *Foreign Affairs*, Winter 1981/1982, pp. 239–46.
57. Crabb and Holt, *op. cit.*, p. 127.

58. Caspar Weinberger, 'Dangerous Constraints on the President's War Powers', *The Fettered Presidency*, L.Crovitz and J. Rabkin (eds), American Enterprise Institute, Washington DC, 1989, p. 97.
59. Fisher, *op. cit.*, p. 312.
60. *ibid.*, p. 311.
61. *The President: Office and Powers*, New York University Press, New York, 1957, p. 171.
62. *ibid.*, p. 177.
63. Rossiter edition, New American Library, New York, 1961, p. 447.
64. 'The Constitution in Danger', *New York Review of Books*, 1 March 1990.
65. See Ch. 2 above.
66. Quoted in Fisher, *op. cit.*, p. 293.
67. *ibid.*
68. John Locke, *The Second Treatise of Government*, Thomas Peardon (ed.), The Liberal Arts Press, New York, 1952, p. 92.
69. See Walter Berns, 'Constitutional Power and the Defense of Free Government' in B. Netanyahu (ed.), *Terrorism: How the West Can Win*, Farrar, Strauss, Giroux, New York, 1986.
70. *An American Life, op. cit.*, pp. 238–9.
71. *ibid.*, p. 479.
72. *op. cit.*, p. 171.

6

Evaluating Presidents:
The Case of Eisenhower

The presidency of Dwight David Eisenhower (1953–61) is of especial interest for two reasons. First, his historical importance is undeniable; he dominated the politics of the 1950s, won two landslide victories at the polls and was one of only four presidents in the twentieth century to serve two full terms. Second, early assessments of Eisenhower's presidency have been overtaken by a large revisionist literature that has helped to correct the historical record while adding significantly to our understanding of the nature of presidential power. In addition, these revisionist studies have given us reason to reconsider what criteria should be used in the evaluation of presidents.

The road to the White House

Eisenhower, the thirty-fourth president of the United States, served in the White House from 1953–61. Born in Texas in 1890, he grew up in Abilene, Kansas. In 1915 he graduated from West Point, the American equivalent of Sandhurst, and was a colonel when World War II began. During the war, with the help of powerful sponsors – George Marshall and President Roosevelt himself – Eisenhower moved rapidly up through the senior ranks and, by December 1944, was a five-star general. He was appointed Supreme Commander of the Allied Expeditionary Forces responsible for operation OVERLORD, the invasion of continental

Europe that began in 1944. Received as a national hero on his return to the United States at the end of the war, he became Army Chief of Staff. After a period as President of Columbia University, he was appointed commander of NATO before accepting the Republican nomination for the presidency in 1952.

The selection of Eisenhower as the Republican standard bearer casts light on the non-ideological nature of American politics and the process whereby candidates for the presidency are chosen. It seems most likely that Eisenhower had no formal connection with the Republican Party before he entered the contest for the nomination. He had held no political office, had not voted in previous presidential elections and almost certainly was not even a registered Republican. Moreover, in 1948 he had been pressed by liberal Democrats to allow his name to go forward as the nominee of their party for the presidency. There have been other 'outsider' candidates for the presidency but none can have been more completely so than Dwight Eisenhower.

When Eisenhower's name was put forward, little was known about what he actually believed in beyond an enthusiasm for free enterprise and collective security.[1] Aware of his closeness to FDR, conservative members of the Republican National Committee suspected, erroneously, that he might be a closet New Dealer. However these doubts were swept aside by other party leaders excited by the prospect of Eisenhower's drawing support from both Republicans and Democrats as well as the all-important bloc of independent voters. Obviously, his status as a war hero was one of Eisenhower's great strengths, but, on the stump, he revealed other assets. His broad grin, his warm, folksy personality and even his fuzziness on the issues allowed him to project a reassuring, avuncular image of great electoral potential.

Despite his military background, Eisenhower was unlikely to trigger those paranoid suspicions of leaders and leadership that characterize the American political culture.[2] In no sense was he a threatening figure; he had managed to convey an impression of a soldier reluctantly compelled by a sense of duty to take up politics. And his benign, unassuming persona contrasted favourably with that of another general favoured by some Republicans – Douglas MacArthur. The latter's flamboyant style, obvious political ambition and openly conservative views made him far less acceptable.[3]

The optimism of those who had pressed Eisenhower's nomination was spectacularly vindicated by the result of the 1952 election. In the face of a 2–1 disadvantage in party registration figures, Eisenhower overwhelmed Adlai Stevenson by a majority of 55.4 per cent to 44.6 per cent of the popular vote. Four years later, he was relected by a landslide of even greater proportions gaining 57.75 per cent of the popular vote as against 42.25 per cent for Stevenson.

In 1952, Eisenhower's victory was paralleled by Republican success in the congressional elections with the party winning control of both houses for the first time since 1933. This advantage was lost in 1954, but given the slender Democratic majorities in the 84th and 85th Congresses, plus the preponderance of conservative Democrats holding key positions, it was not until the last two years of his presidency that Eisenhower was confronted by a seriously hostile legislature. Furthermore, throughout his two terms he enjoyed remarkably high levels of support in public opinion polls – averaging 64 per cent approval rates in Gallup polls.[4]

The three components of 'presidential capital', that resource which does so much to determine a president's effectiveness, are the margin of electoral victory, party strength in Congress and popular approval.[5] By comparison with many presidents, especially Republicans, Eisenhower was particularly well endowed with presidential capital and it was his alleged failure to make good use of that resource that contributed much to the early criticisms of his stewardship.

Early evaluations

Shortly after Eisenhower left the White House, Arthur Schlesinger Senior conducted a presidential 'performance in office' poll among seventy-five experts, mainly professional historians. This survey placed Eisenhower, jointly with Chester Arthur, as twenty-first out of thirty-one presidents that had served so far.[6] The Schlesinger poll reflects the low view of Eisenhower's attainments widely held in the 1960s. The previous decade, so it was argued, had been a period of drift and stagnation when the country for most of the time was led by a genial, decent and popular president who was, however, bumblingly inept and ineffectual.

Supposedly, Eisenhower spent an inordinate amount of time on the golf course; insisted that his staff reduce the complexities of decision-making to one page memoranda; attempted to organize the White House on military lines and extravagantly delegated authority to subordinates. In short, Eisenhower was accused of abdicating his responsibility to provide efffective leadership. During his tenure, his critics argued, a dangerous missile gap between the United States and the Soviet Union had opened up, the rampaging of Joseph McCarthy had gone unchecked for too long and little had been done to deal with the intensifying problems of race relations.

Among students of politics the most influential critique of Eisenhower as president was that provided by Richard Neustadt in *Presidential Power* who argued that success in the White House turns on the chief executive's ability to influence effectively 'the behavior of men actually involved in making public policy and carrying it out'. Presidential power construed in this way went beyond the formalities of the Constitution. It was derived from three sources: first, the bargaining counters, or advantages, that go with the office of president; second, the perceptions of other political leaders regarding a president's skill and determination in making use of those advantages and third, his standing with the public at large: 'In short, [a president's] power is the product of his vantage points in government together with his reputation in the Washington community and his prestige outside.'[7]

As Chapter 3 demonstrated, Franklin Roosevelt is the hero of Neustadt's work and his presidency is presented in the most laudatory terms. We are led to believe that no president in the twentieth century had had a better understanding of the problems of presidential power; Roosevelt knew how to obtain power, how to hold on to it and how to make use of it. He brought to his office an ideal combination of background experience, personal qualities and ambitions that had enabled him to come to grips with the infinitely perplexing problems of presidential leadership. 'He wanted mastery, projected that desire on the office, and fulfilled it there with every sign of feeling he had come into his own.'[8]

Eisenhower is to be found at the opposite end of Neustadt's scale; a man from whom much had been expected, but who had 'exchanged his hero's welcome for much less than its full value in the currency of power'.[9] One of Eisenhower's gravest handicaps was his 'amateur' status; by comparison with Roosevelt, he badly lacked relevant experience: 'he had behind him the irrelevancy of an army record compiled for the most part outside Washington'. This backgound deprived him of an understanding of the mysteries of decision-making in the political system. In particular, he had not learned in the hard school of experience that, unlike the situation in the army, formal powers were no guarantee of power, that presidents do 'not obtain results by giving orders – or not, at any rate, merely by giving orders'.[10]

Rather than simply giving orders presidents had to persuade other political leaders, and the best known sentence in Neustadt's book is probably: 'The power to persuade is the power to bargain.'[11] We saw in Chapter 4 that bargaining is central to the exercise of presidential power; chief executives who are unwilling to bargain or who fail to deploy their bargaining resources skilfully will be ineffective in office. Their ability to gain the cooperation of congressmen, Cabinet members, bureaucrats and others will be seriously infringed. Bargaining did not come easily to Eisenhower; he found the distribution of patronage offensive and generally made evident his distaste for politics and politicians.

While Roosevelt was a master bargainer who revelled in the machinations of politics, Eisenhower regarded it as a dirty business that he wished to distance himself from as far as possible. This was not to suggest that Eisenhower lacked political ambition; despite appearances, he had lusted after the presidency for years before being elected and actively sought re-election. But, in office, he displayed no feel for political power and no delight in using it; he did not crave to master the system or to advance specific objectives: 'Roosevelt was a politician seeking personal power; Eisenhower was a hero seeking national unity. He came to crown a reputation not to make one. He wanted to be arbiter, not master. His love was not for power but for duty – and for status.'[12]

In Neustadt's view Eisenhower believed that as president he should stand aloof from the sordidities of the political struggle. He aspired to emulate George Washington – a president whose qualities of goodness and integrity inspired reverence and whose very presence at the head of affairs was a source of national reassurance. Associates of Eisenhower, urging him to seek a second term, had little difficulty in convincing him that he was needed because of his international reputation and his ability to heal divisions and reconcile differences at home and abroad. They encouraged him to believe that he, in the manner of George Washington, 'fulfilled the Presidency just by being there'.[13]

Richard Neustadt's book contributed much to the development of the so-called 'textbook presidency', the model that dominated the literature of political science and popular commentary for a long time after World War II and persists in modified form to this day. A generation of textbook writers, journalists and other commentators lavishly glorified the office of president. According to the conventional wisdom of the 1960s in particular, the United States needed leadership to enable it to cope with crises at home and abroad and only the chief executive could provide that leadership. The man in the White House needed to be dynamic, imposing, and purposeful with clear objectives and a will to govern; a man who relished the challenges of the office and who had the energy, the wit and the ambition required to override the fragmentation in the American system: 'What was needed, most texts implied, was a person with the foresight to anticipate the future and the personal strength to unite us, to steel our moral will, to move the country forward and make it governable.'[14] The textbook president was a high profile leader, a doer, an activist who eagerly seized control of the levers of poltical power – a president, in other words, in the mould of Franklin Delano Roosevelt.

The Eisenhower approach to presidential leadership

From the outset there was little chance of Eisenhower meeting the requirements of the textbook presidency. Aggressive leadership from the front was not his style. He was not driven by reformist zeal; he came to the office with no specific agenda and no great faith in what could be achieved by governmental action. Conservatives in Congress hoped Eisenhower might roll back the New Deal, but he had no such extravagant ambitions: 'His aspirations as president were limited to two overriding objectives: peace abroad and a balanced budget at home. In keeping with those aspirations, his view of the presidential role was circumscribed.'[15]

In contrast to free-booting activists like Roosevelt, and later Johnson, Eisenhower was a fastidious constitutionalist who believed that principles like the separation of power were to be taken seriously. He had been shocked by Roosevelt's usurpations of the rights of the legislature and 'brought to the White House a genuine respect for Congress and a traditionalist's conception of the separation of powers. In talks with associates he has referred to himself more than once as a "Constitutional President".'[16] Rather than manipulating, bullying and sometimes riding rough-shod over Congress, as textbook presidents were prone to do, Eisenhower deferred to the legislature, carefully consulting with its leaders and declining to crack the whip of party discipline. Most presidents resort to patronage as a means of holding their party together and bringing Congress into line, but Eisenhower disdained such tactics and regularly showed his 'contempt for the power of patronage'.[17]

Reference was made in Chapter 4 to the tendency of strong presidents to use their office as a 'bully pulpit', overcoming congressional opposition by making appeals over the heads of senators and congressmen to their constituents. Eisenhower, despite his great personal popularity was reluctant to so use his office; he was not totally averse to making such appeals, but did so only sparingly:

> As for using the power of his own personality in direct appeal to the people – to summon support, to bestir the Congress, or to rally the party – Eisenhower felt and practiced . . . constraint and diffidence. Any President, of course, enjoys unique and unsurpassed ways and occasions to command national attention, and Eisnhower used most of them at one time or another. But he never employed such resources in any coherent and sustained campaign.[18]

Contrary to the inferences of Neustadt and others, Eisenhower was not so foolish as to think that the White House could be structured along military lines, but he was a firm believer in the virtues of organization. In this, of course, he yet again differentiated himself from Franklin Roosevelt. The latter had little time for formal organization and, in the interests of maintaining his personal predominance, had delegated

> responsibility and authority in small, vague and sometimes conflicting fragments, to a point where only he could contribute consistency and direction. . . . [This] resulted in fuzzy lines of responsibility, no clear chains of command, overlapping jurisdiction, a great deal of person squabbling, and a lack of precision and regularity.[19]

Eisenhower was more appreciative of the value of team work

and believed that the size and complexity of American government made it foolhardy for one man to even try to direct all its activities. The only sensible way forward was through organization including the active and regular use of structures such as the Cabinet and the National Security Council. By working through such formal structures, not only was decision-making improved, it was also possible to offset the centrifugal tendencies that afflict all administrations.[20]

Carefully defined delegation to well-qualified subordinates was another essential feature of Eisenhower's approach to the problems of presidential governance. Given the great burdens of the office chief executives were bound to rely on trusted assistants, but this did not entail the abdication of the president's responsibility to make the decisions. Eisenhower's reliance on John Foster Dulles in the making of foreign policy was widely commented upon at the time. Some years later the former president freely admitted his dependence on the advice of his Secretary of State, but vigorously denied that Dulles made the decisions:

> Foster made no important move without consulting the President. I reviewed in advance all his major pronouncements and speeches, and when he was abroad he was constantly in touch by cable and telephone. If we did not see eye to eye – and these instances were rare – it was, of course, my opinion that prevailed; this is the way it has to be. The persistent statement that I turned foreign policy over to Dulles is – to use a more civilized word than it deserves – incorrect.[21]

Judged on its own terms rather than those held by the legion of Roosevelt *aficionados* there is much to be said for Eisenhower's approach to presidential leadership. Those terms included limited policy change ambitions; a willingness to work with Congress rather than trying to override it, plus a conviction that good government is best served by formal organization and careful delegation.

Eisenhower revisionism

Revisionist scholars such as Fred Greenstein have gone further in defence of the Eisenhower approach arguing that to picture him as an amiable, naive and rather idle chief executive, bemused and baffled by the problems of presidential power, is to deal in caricature. In truth, we are told, Eisenhower was a workaholic and a highly skilled and subtle leader. He may not have adhered to the Neustadt-sanctified Roosevelt model of presidential power, but for all that, his methods were highly effective and his achievements sufficient to place him in the front rank of modern presidents. No other president between Roosevelt and Reagan had succeeded in winning and completing two terms. Throughout those two terms Eisenhower had enjoyed extraordinary support in public opinion polls in contrast to the catastrophic collapses in such support experienced by most other post-war presidents.

Eisenhower, furthermore, compiled a record of achievement in foreign and domestic policy which, although unimpressive to observers at the time, looks much better in retrospect. In contrast to the agony of Vietnam which engulfed the United States in the 1960s, Eisenhower quickly brought the Korean War to a conclusion and no American lives were lost in combat for the next seven-and-a-half years. On the domestic front, Eisenhower's unwillingness to expand welfare programmes and his fears of inflation appeared to be better founded later than liberal pundits had allowed in the 1960s.[22]

Richard Neustadt had made much of Eisenhower's allegedly inept performances at press conferences. The President's mangled syntax, his rambling, confused and apparently ill-informed comments supposedly inflicted serious damage on his 'professional reputation' and destroyed his credibility with the all-important Washington community. Greenstein, however, sees the President's behaviour in such settings in a different light, suggesting that Eisenhower's evasive, ambivalent and sometimes seemingly uninformed remarks were actually carefully contrived answers designed to confuse his questioners and preserve his freedom of manoeuvre. Thus when, in early 1955, there was a danger that the President would be asked a question on the desperately sensitive matter of whether the United States would use tactical nuclear weapons to defend Quemoy and Matsu, Eisenhower reassured his press secretary, 'Don't worry, Jim, if that question comes up, I'll just confuse them.'[23]

Behind the genial avuncular image, it is claimed, there was a tough-minded sophisticated leader. It is denied that he delegated excessively to Sherman Adams in domestic affairs and to John

Foster Dulles in foreign policy matters. He certainly made much use of such people as advisers and as lightning rods to protect him from the odium when things went wrong, but the important decisions he made himself. It is similarly claimed that it is not true that Eisenhower had no taste or talent for politics. He refused to demean his high office by engaging in slanging matches with politicians and publicly he distanced himself from the minutiae of day-to-day politics. Behind the scenes, however, he was a hard-working deeply committed chief executive – a master, no less, of 'hidden hand' leadership.

In contrast to the confused, uncertain and somewhat incompetent figure that Eisenhower sometimes cut in public, we are told that in fact he had a clear and sharply analytical mind. In organizing the White House, in sharp contrast to Franklin Roosevelt, Kennedy and others he made careful use of his Cabinet and the National Security Council. This not only provided him with the expert advice that every modern president must have, but also helped to counteract the centrifugal tendencies that afflict all administrations.[24]

It is quite evident that Eisenhower had little taste for the style of leadership associated with Franklin Roosevelt and for long glorified by scholars such as Richard Neustadt, Arthur Schlesinger and countless others. However, according to the revisionist scholars, he was a masterly practitioner of a different, but nevertheless effective, brand of leadership. Rather than aggressively leading from the front, engaging in rhetorical bombast, vilifying opponents, trampling on congressional sensitivities and allowing himself to be seen as being deeply immersed in the detail of policy-making, Eisenhower specialized in quiet and subtle leadership, in large part exercised from behind the scenes.

To illustrate this argument Greenstein draws on the example of Eisenhower's response to the activities of Joseph McCarthy, the senator from Wisconsin who led the witch hunt against alleged communist sympathizers in government. According to Eisenhower's critics this episode showed him at his worst, revealing a president who lacked the courage, the will and the political nous to deal with the greatest domestic challenge of his administration. Greenstein's detailed investigation, based on new evidence, suggests that Eisenhower played a large part in bringing about the senator's downfall. Following his usual custom the President declined to engage in personalities by openly and directly assailing McCarthy, yet he did his utmost to undermine him by oblique comment and worked assiduously, although privately, in cooperation with Republican congressional leaders for his defeat.

In contrast to the Neustadtian picture of a president with no real feel for, or understanding of, politics the revisionists would have us believe that Eisenhower was a sophisticated and extraordinarily cunning political leader. Furthermore, according to Greenstein, no president has bettered Eisenhower in dealing with that central dilemma that faces all incumbents – how to ensure that their position as chief of state is not undermined by their role as prime minister:

> The American president is asked to perform two roles that in most democracies are assigned to separate individuals. He must serve both as chief of state and as the nation's highest political executive. The roles seem almost designed to collide. As chief of state – the equivalent of a constitutional monarch – the president is symbol of unity. He is expected by Americans to represent the entire nation. However, as poltical head of the executive branch, he has the intrinsically divisive responsibilities of a prime minister. He is expected to prevent or prosecute wars, foster a prosperous economy, and bring about desirable social conditions. If he passively sits back and assumes the stance of a genuine constitutional monarch the country is likely to founder from lack of central guidance. If, on the other hand, he conspicuously leads the polarizing process of welding policy-making coalitions, he loses his broad acceptance as leader of the entire nation.[25]

Unlike many other modern presidents Eisenhower's 'broad acceptance' was never seriously in doubt, as his consistently high public opinion poll rankings show. This latter phenomenon can be explained by the various political strategies he adopted. One of these was his use of covert leadership behind the scenes. Aggressive leadership from the front on controversial issues was bound to alienate some groups, a consequence that could be avoided, or at least ameliorated, by 'hidden hand' leadership.

Similarly, delegation to subordinates was not only desirable in itself; it made possible the use of those underlings as 'lightning rods'. The President was no less fiercely anti-communist than his Secretary of State, but, to the public and the outside world, Dulles was the harsh, intractable cold warrior while Eisenhower was the reasonable man of peace. Farmers enraged by cuts in agricultural subsidies were likely to blame Ezra Benson, the outspoken Secretary of Agriculture, rather than the President while: 'Many of the inevitable irritations produced by White House nay-saying found their target in the staff chief, Sherman Adams.'[26]

The President's apparent ineptitude at press conferences also helped to preserve his personal popularity. His rambling style, his refusal to answer some questions and the appearance he conveyed of not knowing what was going on in his administration undoubtedly damaged, as Neustadt suggests, Eisenhower's professional reputation. In other words, these performances did not impress political elites based mainly inside the Washington beltway. However out in the grass roots reactions were different. The President's folksy style was more acceptable and there was a pay-off from his avoidance of controversial questions:

> Both the calculated and unintentional aspects of Eisenhower's press conference style had the same effect as his approach to delegation of authority: they damaged his reputation among the political cogniscenti, but protected his options as a decision maker and insulated him from blame by the wider public for controversial or potentially controversial utterances and actions.[27]

The persistent refusal of Eisenhower to engage in the politics of personality, in other words, to attack his opponents personally and publicly, had the effect of distancing him from the political fray. By repeatedly saying of Joseph McCarthy 'I just will not – I refuse – to get into the gutter with that guy', Eisenhower managed to place himself above the struggle; he conveyed the image of a statesman rather than a mere politician and did not risk damaging that broad acceptance in the country as a whole that a chief of state must have.

The public popularity Eisenhower enjoyed is, of course, also partly explained by his personal attributes. His past experience as a war leader gave him a weight that few others could match and his ability to make himself acceptable to the American people in public situations was considerable. Like Roosevelt, and later Reagan, Eisenhower came across as a warm, likeable man. He projected concern and understanding and his broad grin and genial manner helped him to exude a sense of buoyant optimism.

Evaluating presidents

Apart from correcting the historical record the revisonists have added substantially to our understanding of presidential leadership. They have demonstrated conclusively that Franklin Roosevelt and his many admirers in academe had a less than complete understanding of the mysteries of presidential power. It is now evident that there is more than one way of exercising leadership from the White House. It is also apparent that some later presidents might have learned some valuable lessons from Eisenhower's example.

For instance, as the next chapter will show, Lyndon Johnson provided a classic instance of a president who allowed his chief of state role to be undermined by the divisiveness of his responsibilities as leader of the national government. By leading from the front and immersing himself in the detail of policy-making Johnson was held personally responsible when things went wrong. When, despite civil rights legislation and Great Society programmes, black unrest continued unabated, white backlash was directed at Johnson. Similarly, when the Vietnam War came to be perceived as a disastrous mistake, Johnson became the focus of blame and recrimination. These developments contributed heavily to the collapse of Johnson's standing in the public opinion polls and helped drive him from office.

Richard Nixon should perhaps have paid closer attention to Eisenhower's conduct of the presidency. In contrast to his mentor's carefully deferential attitude towards Congress, Nixon and his senior staff treated the legislature with contempt. Instead of studiously cultivating congressional leaders and trying to work with them, Nixon and his colleagues tried to govern without Congress, a strategy that even without the Watergate scandal was bound ultimately to fail.[28]

The Democratic Presidents, Kennedy, Johnson and Carter, instead of trying to emulate Roosevelt's egocentric style in organizing the presidency could have derived benefit from some of Eisenhower's thinking on these matters. He was surely right in his assertion that government had become too big and complex for one-man direction and in his belief that considered delegation in conjunction with formalized administrative arrangements was now essential.[29]

The re-evaluations of Eisenhower provided by Greenstein *et al* have drawn attention to some of the weaknesses in the over-whelmingly predominant Roosevelt/Neustadt/textbook model of the presidency, but there is one flaw that requires additional comment – the inclusion of a liberal bias. When measured against the standards set by Neustadt and others of like mind, conservative presidents, Republican presidents, are inevitably found wanting. This suggests that rather more care needs to be taken when selecting the criteria to be used in the appraisal of presidents.

The academic study of politics requires us, as far as possible, to be objective in our analyses; teachers and students alike are denied the latitude in these matters enjoyed by journalists and saloon bar pundits. Objectivity is, of course, an ideal rather than a realizable goal, but we need to avoid the danger of distortions arising from partisan or ideological preference. To state the obvious, in evaluating presidents it is not acceptable to formulate paradigms with normative requirements that chief executives of one political persuasion are bound not to be able to meet. Rigorous comparative assessment of presidents needs the establishment of criteria that are more value-free than those often used.

The 1962 Schlesinger poll, mentioned above, gave Eisenhower a very low ranking, reducing him to parity with one of the most obscure presidents of all those who have served. However, given the partisan affiliations of those polled this result is not too surprising. A few years later Thomas Bailey, in an appendix to his book, *Presidential Greatness*, drew attention to 'The bias of historians'. After conducting a straw poll of thirty leading unversities Bailey concluded that the overwhelming proportion of American historians were Democrats. They were also very likely to be advocates of social and economic reform, New Deal enthusiasts and admirers of Franklin Roosevelt.[30] As Bailey noted, further similar patterns of bias were to be found among political scientists and evidence that these tendencies persist even yet was provided by a 1984 poll among members of the American Political Science Association.[31] This revealed that political scientists in general were almost always Democrats, and specifically, 76 per cent of those who specialized in American politics identified with that party. In evaluating Ronald Reagan's 'overall performance in office' moreover there was a close correlation between assessment and party affiliation: 71 per cent of respondents who identified as Republicans rated Reagan as 'excellent' or 'good' while 29 per cent found him to be 'fair' or 'poor'. Of the Democratic identifiers, on the other hand, 96 per cent found Reagan to be 'fair' or 'poor', whereas only 4 per cent rated him as 'excellent' or 'good'.

In explaining the roots of the 'textbook' presidency tradition, Thomas Cronin stressed the importance of liberal values among those who wrote on the presidency in the post-World War II period. These were academics who favoured 'strong, activist, vigorous leadership' from the White House; they had a liberal enthusiasm for structural reforms and cherished an 'idealized view of the Roosevelt years'.[32] One of the many commentators who falls into this category is Richard Neustadt. His book, as we have seen, contains much that is heavily critical of Eisenhower; he is presented at almost every turn in a most unflattering light and the picture is only slightly modified in later editions. Neustadt's obvious lack of respect for Eisenhower's presidential style is all of a piece with his background and the normative thrust of his book. As the son of a New Deal official and a member of Truman's White House staff his book reveals unqualified enthusiasm for Franklin Roosevelt and all that he stood for whereas Eisenhower is damned as, 'a sort of Roosevelt in reverse'.

As a member of Eisenhower's staff has testified, it is undoubtedly true that Eisenhower was the obverse of Roosevelt in almost every respect:

> Where Roosevelt had sought and coveted power, Eisenhower distrusted and discounted it: one man's appetite was the other man's distaste. Where Roosevelt had avidly grasped and adroitly manipulated the abundant authorities of the office, Eisenhower fingered them almost hesitantly and always respectfully – or generously dispersed them. Where Roosevelt had challenged Congress, Eisenhower courted it. Where Roosevelt had been an extravagant partisan, Eisenhower was a tepid partisan. Where Rooosevelt had trusted no one and nothing so confidently as his own judgment and his own instinct, Eisenhower trusted and required a consensus of cabinet or staff to shape the supreme judgments and determinations. Where Roosevelt had sought to goad and taunt and prod the processes of government toward the new and the untried, Eisenhower sought to be both guardian of old values and healer of old wounds.[33]

As a liberal Democrat Neustadt is prone to emphasize the desirability of active, reforming government led by a vigorous agenda-setting chief executive:

> Energetic government and viable public policy are at a premium as we begin the seventh decade of the twentieth century. . . . The more determinedly a President seeks power, the more he will be able to bring vigor to his clerkship. . . . Most Washingtonians look to the White House for [an agenda][34]

This liberal perspective is not shared by many Americans; conservatives favour less government rather than more, are sceptical of what can be achieved by passing laws and are less likely to expect the president to become an agenda-setter. Such people were likely to applaud Eisenhower's determination to reserve 'his greatest force for keeping unwanted things from being done', and to approve his putting in place an 'Adminstration committed to conserving rather than creating, guarding rather than building'.[35]

Writing in 1976 Neustadt's view of Eisenhower's presidency is hardly less condemnatory than before. In reflecting on what he had written in 1960 he says:

> To write in Eisenhower's time after serving under Truman was to writhe with impatience at the President's concern for his extraordinary public standing, his hero's prestige, hoarding not risking it, being not doing. . . . Eisenhower's quietude seemed more conservative in terms of policy than I, for one, deemed prudent. So I still think it was. We paid a price for damming up reform until the flood of the mid-sixties.[36]

This is to condemn Eisenhower for not being a doer, an activist, a reformer, for being, in other words, a conservative Republican rather than a liberal Democrat.

What criteria, then, should we use in the evaluation of presidents? As I have argued elsewhere I share the view of Frederick Watkins and others that the proper subject of political science analysis is the decision-making process rather than the '*content* of the decisions made'.[37] Students of American politics should be primarily observers of the political decision-making machinery, trying to comprehend, among other things, the context within which that machinery operates; the relationships between its component parts and the reasons why it occasionally produces policy outcomes, but more frequently does not. The nature of those outcomes, their consequences and the merits of possible alternatives are matters of secondary concern. In other words, the principal focus of our attention should be the process of policy-making rather than the content of the policies made.

It follows that in evaluating presidents the central consideration should be how far they succeed in achieving their objectives. Whether those objectives are desirable or not is a separate, if not irrelevant matter. What is interesting about a particular president is how far he is effective in overcoming the many obstacles to presidential power discussed earlier in this book. The most important yardstick of success or failure in the White House should be effectiveness appropriately defined by Barbara Kellerman in the following terms:

> When I speak of an effective presidency, or effective presidential leadership, I am speaking here in terms of functional criteria only. I am not asking if the leadership was, for example, courageous, wise or moral, or if it led the country down the proper path. I am asking only if it was effective in the sense that the president was able to accomplish what he wanted to accomplish.[38]

Aaron Wildavsky argues along similar lines in an essay concerned with President Reagan's merits as a political strategist:

> When I speak of politicians as strategists, I mean that they have a vision, a broad sense of direction toward which they wish the nation to move, and that they use effective and creative (nonobvious) means in pursuing these ends. *Nothing is implied about the desirability of the directions chosen, for then the politicians could be strategists only by being in accord with the preferences of the analyst.* [my italics][39]

Evaluating Eisenhower

The revisionists have convincingly argued that contrary to what sometimes appeared to be the case, Eisenhower did establish a respectable degree of mastery over the political system. His style of leadership was far removed from that of Roosevelt, but he was for all that an astute, skilled and effective leader. It was not, Greenstein argues, a style suitable for effecting major changes of direction in public policy. It would not have served FDR in the 1930s, Johnson in the 1960s, or even Reagan in 1981; in each of these cases presidents were seeking fundamental change in economic and social policy and aggressive leadership from the front was required to bring that about.

Eisenhower's purposes were different and his ambitions more limited. Fundamental change was not on his agenda and he did not feel it necessary or desirable for him to be proliferating legislative initiatives. His positive domestic policy achievements were accordingly relatively few. The most important were probably the 1957 civil rights bill and the legislation leading to the construction of the interstate highway system. The first was an innocuous bill of little significance in the long term, but this could certainly not be said of the second, 'the largest public works program in the history of mankind'.[40] Other than that so much of what Eisenhower accomplished was of a negative nature, with his strategies best suited to preventing undesirable developments from occurring:

> The bipartisan bloc of conservatives who dominated his first three Congresses did not succeed in 'rolling back' the basic New Deal reforms. The liberals who were strong in his final Congress did not succeed in instituting substantial welfare-state innovations. In each case, his aim was to hold the line and he got what he wanted, as he did over the eight years in resisting pressures to increase defense spending.[41]

Such a statement of accomplishments was, however, never likely to impress liberal commentators. Liberal Democrats have a faith in what can be achieved by passing bills or other forms of governmental action that conservatives like Eisenhower do not share. Those broadly on the left of the political spectrum are inclined to assume that societal problems require activist responses, whereas their opponents may either deny that the problems exist or believe that they are not susceptible to governmental action. No doubt Eisenhower would have agreed with that noted conservative thinker of the nineteenth century John C. Calhoun when he said, 'There is often in the affairs of government more efficiency and wisdom in non action than in action.'[42]

It is of course the case that the United States had plenty of problems in the 1950s and Eisenhower was criticized for his failure to provide initiatives aimed at solving them. The revisonists have assured us that he was an effective leader, is it not therefore reasonable to criticize him for his apparent unwillingness to use his leadership skills and his massive popularity on behalf of worthy causes?

Two issues that cried out for attention during this period were civil rights and McCarthyism. Liberals had no doubts that vigorous action from the centre was required to eradicate racial discrimination. However, a conservative like Eisenhower took a different view. He was more sympathetic to the white South and seriously doubted whether race relations could be improved by governmental action. In considering the possibility of a Supreme Court judgment aimed at abolishing segregation in education he indicated his belief that:

> Improvement in race relations is one of those things that will be healthy and sound only if it starts locally. I do not believe that prejudices, even palpably unjustified prejudices, will succumb to compulsion. Consequently, I believe that federal law imposed upon our states in such a way as to bring about a conflict of the police powers of the states and of the nation, would set back the cause of progress in race relations for a long, long time.[43]

Some would argue that Eisenhower was quite wrong in his analysis. They would maintain that after he left the White House, it was demonstrated beyond dispute that court decisions and the passage of federal legislation could faciliate progress in race relations. But given Eisenhower's convictions it is inappropriate to criticize him here, at least, for his failure to initiate a programme of civil rights legislation.

The McCarthy issue has to be seen in a different light. Eisenhower agreed with McCarthy that communist influences in American institutions was a problem of the greatest importance. It had reached a point, Eisenhower said in campaigning for the presidency, where there was 'contamination in some degree of virtually every department, every agency, every bureau, every section of our government. It meant a government by men whose very brains were confused by the opiate of this deceit.'[44] But if Eisenhower agreed that there was a security problem he was unhappy with McCarthy's tactics, regarding him as an unseemly trouble-maker who caused difficulties for Congress and the Republican Party and upset members of the executive branch.[45]

Greenstein argues that Eisenhower, while refusing to attack McCarthy publicly, worked assiduously behind the scenes to bring about the Wisconsin senator's eventual defeat – this, we are led to believe, was a classic instance of the President's 'hidden hand' leadership. It did, however, take some time to come into play. In the 1952 campaign Eisenhower had given in to advisers urging him to delete a crucial paragraph from a speech to be delivered in McCarthy's home state. The paragraph in question defended George Marshall, Eisenhower's great patron, against McCarthy's scurrilous attempts to impugn his loyalty.

Once Eisenhower was in the White House, it took a long time before he was ready to move seriously against the senator; in early 1954, for instance, his henchman Richard Nixon was still making efforts to mollify McCarthy.[46] Not until late in the day when McCarthy had declined in the public opinion polls, foolishly overreached himself by attacking the army and showed signs of being in pursuit of the presidency itself, did Eisenhower finally act: 'The effort to humiliate the Army exhausted his patience. The President would still refuse to attack the senator openly. . . . He would, however, pay careful attention to Joe's every move and take several quiet steps to thwart his political power.'[47]

If effective leadership, defined as the achievement of objectives, is to be the principal yardstick of presidential success or failure it is arguable that on the McCarthy issue Eisenhower does not measure up particularly impressively. Admittedly there was some ambivalence in his position, and undoubtedly he did ultimately contribute to McCarthy's defeat. However, the fact is that McCarthy was not defeated until after he had inflicted a great deal of damage, caused much suffering to innocent people and seriously harmed the image of the United States abroad. Conceivably, if Eisenhower had moved earlier and more openly, if he had been willing to risk some of his precious public prestige, the demise of Joe McCarthy might have been brought about much earlier. On this issue at least there is some weight to the charge that Eisenhower was more concerned with preserving his standing in the public opinion polls than with putting it to use: 'In the White House, instead of using his popularity to advance the interests of his administration, he came more and more to hoard it, placing a higher premium on his adulation by the American people than on any specific achievement.'[48]

Possibly the most telling stricture against Eisenhower's eight years in office is to be derived from his own memoirs. He suggests that the verdict on his presidency would ultimately depend on whether the United States turned away from the assumptions underpinning the New Deal. If this happened, Eisenhower said,

> The years of my two terms would be counted as some of the most meaningful during our national existence . . . [if this did not occur] the growth of paternalism to the point of virtual regimentation would so condition the attitude of future historians that our time in office would be represented as only a slight impediment to the trend begun in 1933.[49]

Given the large extensions of the New Deal that took place in the 1960s it is surely the case that the Eisenhower years posed no more than a 'slight impediment' to the tradition established by Franklin Roosevelt. Not until the 1980s did any real reversal become apparent. Judging Eisenhower on his own terms, in this sense at least, his presidency was a failure.

Notes

1. Fred Greenstein, *The Hidden–Hand Presidency: Eisenhower as Leader*, Basic Books, New York, 1982, pp. 14 and 47.
2. See Ch. 4 above.
3. Robert Divine, *Eisenhower and the Cold War*, Oxford University Press, Oxford, 1981, p. 11.
4. Thomas Cronin, *The State of the Presidency*, Little, Brown, Boston, 1980, pp. 328–9.
5. Paul Light, *The President's Agenda*, Johns Hopkins University Press, Baltimore, 1982, pp. 26–34.
6. 'Our Presidents: A Rating by 74 Historians', *New York Times Magazine*, 29 July 1962, p. 12.
7. John Wiley and Sons, New York, 1976, p. 247.
8. *ibid.*, p. 230.
9. *ibid.*, p. 248.
10. *ibid.*, p. 232.
11. *ibid.*, p. 104.
12. *ibid.*, p. 233.
13. *ibid.*, p. 234.
14. Cronin, *op. cit.*, p. 78.
15. Stephen Hess, *Organizing the Presidency*, Brookings, Washington DC, 1988, p. 55.
16. Robert Donovan, *Eisenhower: The Inside Story*, Harper, New York, 1956, p. 83.
17. Emmet Hughes, *The Ordeal of Power*, Macmillan, London, 1963, p. 131.
18. *ibid.*

19. Richard Fenno, *The President's Cabinet*, Harvard University Press, Cambridge, Mass., 1963, p. 44.
20. Phillip Henderson, 'Organizing the Presidency for Effective Leadership: Lessons from the Esienhower Years', *Presidential Studies Quarterly*, Winter 1987, pp. 43–69.
21. *ibid.*
22. *ibid.*
23. Greenstein, *op. cit.*, p. 69.
24. Henderson, *op. cit.*
25. Greenstein, *op. cit.*, p. 5.
26. *ibid.*, p. 91.
27. Fred Greenstein, 'Eisenhower as an Activist President: A Look at New Evidence', *Political Science Quarterly* 94, Winter 1979–80, pp. 575–99.
28. Charles O. Jones, 'Congress and the Presidency' in Thomas Mann and Norman Ornstein (eds), *The New Congress*, American Enterprise Institute, Washington DC, 1981
29. Henderson, *op. cit.*
30. Thomas A. Bailey, *Presidential Greatness*, Appleton Century Crofts, New York, 1966.
31. Walter Roettger and Hugh Winebrenner 'Politics and Political Scientists', *Public Opinion*, September/October 1986, pp. 41–4.
32. Cronin, *op. cit.*, pp. 88–90
33. Hughes, *op. cit.*, p. 347.
34. *op. cit.*, pp. 251–3.
35. Hughes, *op. cit.*, pp. 360 and 58.
36. *Presidential Power and the Modern Presidents*, The Free Press, New York, 1990, p. 191.
37. David Mervin, *Ronald Reagan and the American Presidency*, Longman, London, 1990, p. 6.
38. *The Political Presidency: The Practice of Leadership*, Oxford University Press, Oxford, 1984, p. x.
39. *Society*, May/June 1987, pp. 56–62.
40. Stephen Ambrose, 'The Ike Age', *New Republic*, 9 May 1981.
41. Greenstein, *Hidden-Hand Leadership, op. cit.*, p. 230.
42. Margaret Coit (ed.), *John C. Calhoun*, Prentice Hall, New Jersey, 1970, p. 21.
43. Robert Ferrell (ed.), *The Eisenhower Diaries*, W. W. Norton, New York, 1981, pp. 246–7.
44. Thomas C. Reeves, *The Life and Times of Joe McCarthy*, Blond and Briggs, London, 1982, p. 439.
45. Ferrell, *op. cit.*, pp. 233–4.
46. Reeves, *op. cit.*, p. 532.
47. *ibid.*, p. 553.
48. Divine, p. 9.
49. Dwight Eisenhower, *Waging Peace: White House Years*, Doubleday, New York, 1965, p. 654.

7

The Tragedy of Lyndon Johnson

It is hardly possible to conceive of two presidents with more different styles than Dwight Eisenhower and Lyndon Johnson (1963–9). The former, despite a reputation as a moderate, was profoundly conservative while the latter was, at root, a populist. The revisionists notwithstanding, Eisenhower could not possibly be described as an activist in the White House; Johnson, by contrast, was a frenetic activist. Eisenhower was deeply sceptical of Franklin Roosevelt while Johnson idolized him. 'Hidden-hand' leadership was Eisenhower's forte whereas Johnson led vigorously from the front. While Eisenhower hoarded his public prestige Johnson recklessly squandered his. Eisenhower came to the presidency after a lifetime of military service by comparison with Johnson's three decades of experience as a professional politician.

Johnson's populist inclinations reflected his origins. He was born and raised in the then remote, inhospitable Hill Country of central Texas: 'The political heritage of Johnson's hill country was that of populism. There [he] absorbed the established concept that government existed to help the ordinary people, and that the ordinary people's basic wants were essentially the same.'[1] Johnson's father was an unsuccessful farmer and real-estate entrepreneur and for some time a member of the Texas state legislature. Educated at the Southwest Texas State Teachers College, Lyndon Johnson spent one formative year teaching poor Mexican children in southern Texas. He also taught briefly in a Houston high school before beginning his political career in 1931 as the personal secretary of

Richard Kleberg, a Texas member of the US House of Representatives.

As a congressional administrative assistant, Johnson acquired a powerful patron in Sam Rayburn, then a prominent Texan congressman and a future Speaker of the House. Rayburn's influence facilitated Johnson's appointment as the Texas state director of a New Deal programme, the National Youth Administration. This awesomely responsible job for a 26-year-old man with no previous administrative experience beyond that of running a small congressional office, involved the creation of 12,000 public works jobs for young Texans. Throwing himself into this work with the phenomenal energy and resourcefulness that characterized his whole career, Johnson was also given the opportunity to begin laying the groundwork for a personal political organization.[2]

Elected to the US House of Representatives in 1937 the hard-driving, hugely ambitious Johnson within a short while became bored and frustrated by the House's hidebound procedures and the tyranny of the seniority system: 'The House was no institution for a young man in a hurry. Within three years Johnson had become, in his words, "terribly restless and unhappy".'[3] After a first unsuccessful campaign for the US Senate in 1941 Johnson gained election to that body in 1948.

Senator Johnson

The Senate that Johnson joined in 1949 was noted for its club-like ethos and for its informal structure. Unlike the House, its membership was small, formal leadership positions counted for relatively little, and power was concentrated in the hands of an inner club, a largely Southern-based elite of senior conservatives. The position of this oligarchy was sustained by a code of folkways or informal rules that members were obliged to respect if they aspired to effectiveness in the Senate. New members were expected to serve lengthy periods of apprenticeship before they were allowed to become full participants in the proceedings of the chamber. Elaborate deference to senior members was essential and a willingness to work hard and to specialize narrowly was obligatory. In debate on the floor or in committee, senators were expected to conduct themselves in a gentlemanly fashion, disdaining ideology, treating their colleagues with studied courtesy and refraining from personal attacks. Finally, senators were required at all times to display an undying commitment to the Senate as an institution.[4]

In this rather curious, archaic environment, Lyndon Johnson found his natural political home. He had little difficulty in conforming to the folkways. He could hardly be described as a Southern gentleman but he had Southern credentials of a sort; he was only too willing to become an apprentice and he was a workaholic with a specialist interest in defence matters. Johnson also had little time for ideology and was more than ready to devote himself unstintingly to the Senate. By playing down his earlier populist views and assiduously cultivating leaders of the inner club such as Robert Kerr of Oklahoma and, most importantly of all, Richard Russell of Georgia, Johnson quickly made his mark in the Senate. Indeed within a short while he had managed to get himself elected to formal party leadership positions that members of the oligarchy like Kerr and Russell regarded as beneath them.

At a remarkably early stage Johnson became the Democratic Whip; he was subsequently elected minority leader of the Democrats and became majority leader in 1955 when his party regained control of the Senate. In other hands, these formal positions were of little account, but Johnson cunningly used them to undercut the old guard and make himself the centre of power in the Senate: 'By the middle of the [1950s] the powerful 'Senate men' who had raised Johnson to the position of titular leader found themselves reduced to lieutenants in a system directed in fact as well as in name, by the party leader – Lyndon Johnson'.[5] Johnson's extraordinarily swift rise to pre-eminence in the Senate is, in large part, explained by the force of his personality and some understanding of that remarkable and complex phenomenon is essential to the study of his presidency.

Johnson was a man of imposing physical presence; six feet four, manically energetic and irrepressibly talkative, he overpowered those with whom he came into close contact. His personality was not only outsize, it was also extremely complex, as Robert McNamara later indicated to Joseph Califano: 'I can assure you of one thing: You will never work for or with a more complicated man than Lyndon Johnson so long as you live. I guarantee it.'[6] For those with refined tastes Johnson was not a particularly attractive human being; some found the coarseness of his language distasteful, disapproved of his often uncouth behaviour and were shocked by his deceitfulness and his naked opportunism. However, behind the image that Johnson sometimes projected of a vulgar, unlettered, unscrupulous Texas 'corn pone' there was a man of great intelligence with a pronounced social conscience.

There can be no doubt regarding Johnson's intelligence. He left book reading to others, but only a man with an exceptional mind could have acquired his masterly grasp of the intricacies of American politics. This was essential to his command of the Senate and made possible his phenomenal success later as chief legislator. One distinguished historian, who served on Johnson's White House staff for three years after teaching at Princeton for more than two decades, believed the President to be the most intelligent person he had ever encountered: 'intelligent in terms of sheer IQ, a clear, swift, penetrating mind, with an abundance of its own type of imagination and subtleties'.[7]

The suggestion that Johnson was also something of an idealist with a highly developed social conscience is rather more difficult to sustain. Even if he was ultimately a political idealist there was, without doubt a dark side to his personality.[8] His climb to the top of the greasy pole was marked by ruthless and unscrupulous determination. His early political advancement was heavily dependent on his ability to ingratiate himself with powerful patrons like Rayburn and Roosevelt. In campaigning for elective office Johnson spent vast sums of money, much of it obtained from Texas oil–men and other wealthy business interests, who expected, and often received, a return on their investments.

In 1937 Johnson won election to the House of Representatives by tying himself completely to Franklin Roosevelt. As a congressman he identified himself unreservedly with the President and became known as FDR's man in Texas. Johnson's first run for the Senate in 1941 was conducted on a platform of all out support for Roosevelt. By 1948 FDR was dead and Johnson appeared to veer sharply to the right in his second attempt to win a seat in the Senate. His success in this election, moreover, involved scandalous ballot rigging in the Democratic primary.[9] Once Johnson was in the Senate his rapid elevation to the position of party leader turned on his willingness to suppress his populist leanings and to fawn upon conservative members of the inner club.

It is also the case that some of Johnson's public utterances in the

1940s and 1950s and the votes that accompanied them made him an unlikely leader in the battles for civil rights in the 1960s. For much of his long congressional career, he consistently voted against civil rights measures, including even a bill designed to outlaw lynching. In 1948 he described President Truman's modest civil rights programme as an 'effort to set up a police state' and as late as 1957 he was accused by liberals of using his position as majority leader to dilute the civil rights bill of that year.

Certainly, Lyndon Johnson's boundless political ambition led him to engage in some ethically dubious activities. And it is not at all surprising that more fastidious politicians like Dwight Eisenhower should dismiss Johnson as a 'small man . . . superficial and opportunistic'.[10] Nevertheless there is plenty of evidence to confirm the view that Johnson remained at heart an idealist; a man moved by the pain, deprivation and limitations on liberty that afflicted others and bent on doing what he could to remedy those deficiencies. This was to become apparent when Johnson finally reached the White House. In 1965, for instance, in an address to Congress urging voting rights legislation he movingly took up the battle cry of those who had marched and demonstrated on behalf of civil rights, 'we shall overcome':

> Their [the Negroes'] cause must be our cause too. Because it is not just Negroes but really it is all of us who must overcome the crippling legacy of bigotry and injustice. And we shall overcome. . . . This great, rich, restless country can offer opportunity and education and hope to all – all black and white, all North and South, sharecropper, and city–dweller. These are the enemies – poverty, ignorance, disease. They are enemies, not our fellow man, not our neighbor, and these enemies, too, poverty, disease and ignorance, we shall overcome.

Johnson went on to say that he had never expected to have the chance to contribute to the solution of these problems: 'But now I do have the chance, and I will let you in on a secret. I mean to use it. . . .'[11] This surely touches upon Johnson's great saving grace. Whatever reservations we may have regarding the tactics he used to achieve office, he clearly did not seek power for its own sake, but in order to put it to use on behalf of fellow human beings.

Throughout his life Johnson was above all else a doer, an activist. Whether teaching underprivileged Mexican children, or coaching the debate team in a Houston high school the young Johnson astounded observers by his ferocious energy and the totality of his commitment to the job at hand. As a congressman's secretary and a New Deal administrator, Johnson's drive found new outlets, whereas after an initial burst of energy and enthusiasm the confining structure of the House caused him to become frustrated and restless. The Senate, on the other hand, provided an arena admirably suited to Johnson's extraordinary talent for acquiring and making use of political power: 'Johnson was born with the instinct of power, and long before he reached the White House he knew exactly where it rested, how to obtain it, and, most important, how to exercise it.'[12]

When he arrived in the Senate, by instinct, upbringing and experience Johnson already knew that in the American context ideology was largely irrelevant and that political power had little to do with giving orders and everything to do with persuasion. To a degree that few others grasped, he understood that control came from bargaining; that the successful politician lived by the 'negotiation of bargains. . . . Most of his time is consumed in bargaining. This is the skill he cultivates; it is the skill that distinguishes the master–politician from the political failure'.[13]

If Johnson was to be master of the Senate he needed tokens of exchange for bargaining purposes. Accordingly, when he became majority leader, he manoeuvred to gain control of the processes whereby committee posts were assigned, office space was allocated and campaign funds were disbursed. To supplement these invaluable sources of patronage, Johnson brought into being a highly efficient intelligence system with his aide Bobby Baker at its centre. This gave Johnson vital insights into the needs, desires and motivations of his colleagues while allowing him to monitor the infinitely complex workings of the decision-making process. Together, Johnson's command over patronage, his intelligence system and his remarkable personality made it possible for him to dominate the proceedings of the Senate in a way that no one else had done for many years before, or would probably ever do again.

Lacking any talent as a debater Johnson was at his most formidable in dealing with individuals or small groups. In such situations he could apply what came to be known as 'The Treatment':

> The Treatment could last ten minutes or four hours. It came enveloping its target, at the LBJ Ranch swimming pool, in one of LBJ's offices, in the Senate cloakroom, on the floor of the Senate

itself – wherever Johnson might find a fellow Senator within his reach. Its tone could be supplication, accusation, cajolery, exuberance, scorn, tears, complaint, the hint of threat. It was all of these together. It ran the gamut of human emotions. Its velocity was breathtaking, and it was all in one direction. Interjections from the target were rare. Johnson anticipated them before they could be spoken. He moved in close, his face a scant millimeter from his target, his eyes widening and narrowing, his eyebrows rising and falling. From his pockets poured clippings, memos, statistics. Mimicry, humor, and the genius of analogy made The Treatment an almost hypnotic experience and rendered the target stunned and helpless.[14]

Nowhere were Johnson's amazing political skills more fully utilized than as majority leader in the Senate. His keen intelligence, his voracious appetite for detail, his disdain for ideology, his tactical cunning and his outstanding talent as a bargainer combined to make him a remarkable political force. However, those attributes that served him so well in the Senate were not, as Johnson was painfully to discover, all that was required in the White House.

In 1960 Johnson was John Kennedy's principal rival in the contest for the Democratic presidential nomination. Kennedy was nominated on the first ballot, but needed Johnson on the ticket to secure the electoral support of the South. After nearly three frustrating years as Vice President Johnson himself became President on the assassination of Kennedy in November 1963.

Johnson in the White House

1963 was a desperate year in the history of the United States; race relations were in a state of crisis with blacks pressing hard for amelioration of the many injustices they had suffered for so long; the threat of nuclear war had been only narrowly averted in the previous year and a communist takeover of South Vietnam, followed by the whole of South East Asia, seemed imminent. Then, in late November, despair enveloped much of the nation when John Kennedy, the young, vigorous and articulate chief executive, was struck down by an assassin.

For many Americans, an already dreadful situation was made worse by the thought of the White House falling into the hands of an uncouth, unprincipled, Texan wheeler-dealer. Johnson, himself, was well aware of the weakness of his position:

> I took the oath, I became President. But for millions of Americans I
> was still illegitimate, a naked man with no presidential covering, a
> pretender to the throne, an illegal usurper. And then there was
> Texas, my home, the home of both the murder and the murder of
> the murderer. And then there were the bigots and the dividers and
> the Eastern intellectuals, who were waiting to knock me down be-
> fore I could even begin to stand up. The whole thing was almost
> unbearable.[15]

Johnson, at the beginning, proved himself equal to the challenges confronting him, handling the problems of transition from
one presidency to the next with a 'brilliant display of leadership
and political skill'. He moved carefully to reassure the public and
to neutralize any suggestion of usurpation. He pleaded with Kennedy appointees to remain in office and accepted that it was his
responsibility to follow his predecessor's agenda. That agenda included a tax reduction proposal, a civil rights bill and a yet to be
formulated anti-poverty programme. John Kennedy had had many
difficulties in dealing with Congress and, according to one measure, had, in 1963, managed to get only 27 per cent of his proposals
approved by the legislative branch.[16] In the new circumstances and
under the masterly direction of Lyndon Johnson as chief legislator,
the former president's aspirations were triumphantly turned into
policy realities.

As Eric Goldman suggests, Johnson, at this early stage of his
presidency, operated in the manner of a prime minister. Unlike
most presidents, but like a prime minister he had risen through the
ranks of the legislature; he regarded Congress as his 'home' and
claimed that his feeling for its ways was 'deep in the marrow of my
bones'. For Johnson the president's main function was to be chief
legislator 'The thing that counts', he told Goldman, 'is getting
those bills through. They really do things, because they have the
stamp of the country on them.'[17]

Other outstanding chief legislators overcame opposition in Congress by appealing to the people over the heads of members of the
legislative branch. As a a former 'Senate man' himself Johnson
was disinclined to use this approach. Unlike Wilson and both the
Roosevelts, he was an indifferent public speaker; in contrast to
Kennedy he was never comfortable in front of television cameras.
Johnson, therefore, sought to work primarily from within the legis-

lature, drawing on the skills and the understanding that he had developed, the contacts that he had made and the political debts he was owed.

No other president has equalled LBJ's intimate understanding of Congress, his knowledge of how its tortuous procedures work, or his sensitivity to the needs and desires of legislators:

> He knew where every wire of power ran, whose influence was waxing or waning, the rules and habits of the committees, what each had done three years before and wanted to do next year, the skeletons and the hopes in scores of closets. . . . Johnson knew how much congressmen are like the rest of us and he knew with an instinct developed over the long years of politicking, the essential difference: congressmen want to run for office, once again, and to win. LBJ responded to this urge and to its accompanying considerations. The decades of congressional life, the national campaigns, the photographic memory, the voracious interest in political situations all counted. He had studied not only Congress but the circumstances surrounding congressmen . . . he had a surgical knowledge of states and districts, the political strengths and weaknesses of individual congressmen, their supporters and opponents back home, their allegiances, apprehensions and ambitions.[18]

This extraordinary level of understanding in combination with Johnson's bargaining resources and his talent for making use of those resources helped make him, for a while, the most formidable of chief legislators. A Kennedy tax reduction bill had been in Congress for ten months when Johnson took over; it had passed the House, but now had to negotiate the Senate where amendments significantly weakening the bill were to be expected. With Johnson in charge, debilitating amendments were beaten back and the tax cut became law.

A civil rights bill submitted by President Kennedy and strengthened, over administration objections, in the House Judiciary Committee was on the verge of passing the House when Johnson became President. Like the tax reduction bill, the real resistance to this measure could be expected from the Senate. In particular, Southern Democrats, led by Johnson's former patron Richard Russell, would inevitably mount a filibuster to prevent the passage of a significant civil rights bill. When the bill reached the Senate, Johnson adamantly rejected all suggestions of compromise with his former colleagues and negotiated deftly to win the support of his kindred spirit Everett Dirksen, the leader of the Republicans in the Senate. Eventually, after an epic filibuster lasting nearly two months, the cloture process was successfully invoked – the first occasion when a filibuster against a civil rights bill had been defeated.

The 1964 Civil Rights Act was a step of great consequence, contributing much to the breaking down of the apartheid system that still prevailed in the South. Among other things, it prohibited segregation in public accommodations; authorized the Department of Justice to bring suits in the courts to eliminate such segregation where it occurred; banned discriminatory practices in federal programmes and outlawed discrimination in employment.

In its origins, of course, the 1964 Act was a Kennedy bill and there is little doubt that it would have passed, in some form, if Kennedy had still been alive. It is also the case that the former president's tragic death in itself gave impetus to the bill. Nevertheless it was Johnson who ensured that a bill with real teeth was passed; had Kennedy still been in the White House, it seems certain that the legislation would have been seriously weakened by compromise.[19]

Johnson's other great achievement of 1964 was the Economic Opportunity Act, the main element in his war on poverty. This legislation included provision for an Office of Economic Opportunity in the EOP responsible for coordinating poverty-related programmes in government agencies. Unlike the tax reduction and the civil rights bill, the idea of an anti–poverty programme had not got beyond the drawing board during Kennedy's time. On his first day in the Oval Office, Johnson moved the proposal to the top of his agenda, enthusiastically assuring Walter Heller, the Chairman of the Council of Economic Advisors, 'That's my kind of programme. I'll find money for it one way or another. If I have to, I'll take money away from things to get money for people.'[20]

Barbara Kellerman presents the passing of the Economic Opportunity Act as a particularly notable example of effective leadership from the White House – an occasion where a president brilliantly succeeded in reaching his objective. Before Johnson entered office there was little awareness of the problem of poverty among either the public or elites. Through speeches and publicized meetings with relevant groups, Johnson made poverty a national issue; he supervised the formulation of a policy to deal with the problem and then used his mighty powers of persuasion to get other political leaders to accept that policy.[21] This policy-making *tour de force* burnished Johnson's image as a latter-day Roosevelt, as a dynamic and effective leader, in good time for the 1964 election.

With the martyrdom of John Kennedy still a potent factor and the ill-advised selection by the Republicans of Barry Goldwater as their presidential candidate, Johnson cruised to an enormous land-slide victory in 1964, winning 61 per cent of the total popular vote. This massive victory was flanked by overwhelming Democratic success in the congressional elections. In the Senate, the Democrats now had 68 seats against 32 for the Republicans, while in the House, there were 295 Democrats and 140 Republicans.

The Great Society

In early 1965 Johnson was at the height of his powers and in a position, so he hoped, to satisfy his zeal for reform, to realize his vision of a Great Society:

> I do not want to be the President who built empires, or sought grandeur, or extended dominion. I want to be the President who educated young children to the wonders of their world. I want to be the President who helped to feed the hungry and to prepare them to be taxpayers instead of tax-eaters. I want to be the President who helped the poor to find their own way and who protected the right of every citizen to vote in every election. I want to be the President who helped to end hatred among his fellow men and who prompted love among people of all races and all regions and all parties. I want to be the President who helped to end war among the brothers of this earth.[22]

In the 1990s such lofty idealism may seem ludicrously naive, but Johnson was president in a less sceptical age. One part of his vision, the protection of 'the right of every citizen to vote in every election', was significantly advanced by the passage of the Voting Rights Act of 1965. Even as late as the 1960s, blacks in Southern states were systematically deprived of the right to vote by psycho-logical and physical intimidation and discriminatory voter registra-tion practices. Congress had passed several bills designed to deal with the problem, but there had been no significant improvement. In 1960 it was calculated that 6.1 per cent of voting age blacks were registered to vote in Mississippi and 13.7 per cent in Alabama. In Dallas county, Alabama, of which Selma was the county seat, there was, in 1965, a voting age population of 14,400 whites and 15,115 blacks. The total number registered to vote was 9,877, 9,542 of whom were white and 335 black.[23]

It was outrage at figures such as these that led Martin Luther King and other black leaders, in early 1965, to make Selma the focus for voter registration drives, marches and other forms of peaceful protest. The violent responses of local law enforcement officials to their activities, widely covered on national television, helped to convince Johnson and his colleagues of the need for new legislation. Once the President had recognized the necessity for a voting rights bill, he 'threw himself with great zest and enthusiasm into the battle'. The final bill included provision for the suspension of literacy tests and for the appointment of federal registrars to supervise the registration process. That this bill made a difference is evident from the statistics. In 1965 in Mississippi there were 28,500 blacks registered to vote whereas by 1968 there was a ten-fold increase with 250,770 on the rolls. In the South overall, black registration leapt up from 28.8 per cent of the voting age population in 1962 to 66.9 per cent in 1970.[24]

Even though it was black street protest that impelled Johnson into action, it was his drive and legislative skill that made the 1965 act possible. Later he rightly saw it as the most important legislation passed during his presidency.[25] In this case Johnson was not content simply to pass a bill; he also interested himself in its implementation, checking on the appointment of registrars, encouraging civil rights groups to put forward black candidates and monitoring the improvement in black registration figures.

Such careful attention to implementation was less apparent with regard to much of the other Great Society legislation initiated by Johnson. His early success in getting what he wanted from Congress was unprecedented; in the number of bills passed at least he achieved his ambition of outdoing even Roosevelt. In 1965, the first session of the 89th Congress saw the passage of 84 out of 87 major measures introduced by the President. And by the time Johnson left office there were in place approximately 500 federal government social programmes. This torrent of legislation that rushed through Congress in a few short years included provision:

for everything from flood control to birth control to rat control. For poor children there were school breakfast, Head Start, day care, and foster grandparent programs. For the elderly, there were nursing homes, medicare and special housing. For the minorities, there were civil rights, voting rights and fair housing laws. For the consumers, there were truth-in-packaging and truth-in-lending and all sorts of safety legislation ranging from automobiles and highways to children's toys and housewives' draperies. For the environmentalists, there were scenic rivers and trails, clean air and water legislation, and any number of conservation and wilderness area preservation bills. The people in the country got rural development grants; the urban dweller a safe streets act; and the American Indians, their own Indian Bill of Rights. The federal government began training more workers than did the Fortune 500 largest corporations. Its position as the single most important factor in financing and building the homes in which most Americans live was cemented and enhanced. Legislation was passed to help drug addicts, retarded children, students, teachers and scientists.[26]

Given the pace at which this legislation was introduced, it is hardly surprising that much of it failed to achieve its objectives. Some programmes failed because the legislation had been too hastily drafted or was not adequately followed up during the implementation stage; other programmes were not backed by a consensus and many failed simply because they lacked sufficient finance. This became a particular problem as the United States became more and more deeply mired in South East Asia. By 1967 Congress was not prepared to accept a tax increase to help pay for the war in Vietnam without severe cuts in domestic expenditure. President Johnson was obliged to accept that he could not have the Great Society programmes he so cherished and a major war.

Vietnam

If the ability to master Congress is, as is often suggested, the acid test of presidential competence Lyndon Johnson was one of the most successful of modern presidents.[27] In 1964 and 1965 he commanded Congress as if he was a prime minister and, even allowing for the inadequacies of some of the legislation passed, his proposals did include bills of great consequence, such as the 1964 Civil Rights Act and the Voting Rights Act of 1965. On the other hand, when it came to that central responsibility of all modern presidents, the management of foreign policy, Johnson proved to be hopelessly out of his depth: 'In dealing with foreign policy . . . he was insecure, fearful, his touch unsure.'[28] Neither his background nor his pre-presidential experience had prepared him for the rigours of international affairs. Despite his remarkable intelligence he remained an ill-educated, unlettered, provincial politician; an undisputed master of the complexities of the American political system, but lacking in any serious understanding of the outside world.

It seemed not to occur to Johnson that other nations possessed cultures with values, beliefs and standards quite different from his own. When, as Vice President, he encountered an impoverished African mother living in a mud hut he glibly assumed that the woman's ambitions for her children paralleled those of his mother forty years previously in the Texas hill country.

> To Johnson there were foreign customs, foreign religions, foreign governments, but there were no foreign cultures, only different ways of pursuing universal desires – in this case the transition from rags to riches. He knew about poor mothers with children – what else but determination could he see in her eyes? This defect, almost an inability to conceive of societies with basically different values, was the source of his greatest weakness as President.[29]

Johnson even managed to convince himself that if he could get foreign leaders into a room alone with him they would be able to resolve their differences. He assumed that despite appearances even Khrushchev broadly wanted what he wanted, shared his values and standards; if only he could get the Soviet leader on his own, speak to him man-to-man and, presumably, subject him to the 'treatment', all would be well.[30]

In early 1965, when he felt compelled to confront the problem of an impending communist takeover of South Vietnam, Johnson viewed the matter through the lens of a Senate majority leader. The difficulty, he seemed to believe, could be resolved by bargaining, by the careful deployment of sticks and carrots:

> I saw our bombs as my political resources for negotiating a peace. On the one hand, our planes and our bombs could be used as carrots for the South, strengthening the morale of the South and pushing them to clean up their corrupt house, by demonstrating the depth of our commitment to the war. On the other hand, our bombs could be

used as sticks against the North, pressuring North Vietnam to stop its aggression against the South.[31]

The assumption that everything was negotiable, that every leader had his price and desired for his people the same things that Johnson wanted for his, lies at the heart of the tragedy of Vietnam. It led Johnson to equate the war with a filibuster; it encouraged him to think of American know-how and resources turning the Mekong Delta into a Tennessee Valley project and caused him to ignore the fact, that far from being willing to bargain, Ho Chi Minh was an ideologue and an irreconcilable nationalist.

Johnson's outstanding record in domestic policy will never escape the shadow cast over it by the Vietnam War. Apart from the appalling suffering endured by the people of Vietnam itself, this conflict cost the United States more than $140 billion and 58,000 young Americans. In the long run the war also seriously weakened the American presidency, caused untold damage to national morale, wrecked Johnson's dream of a Great Society and forced him from office.

President Johnson's responsibility for the Vietnam débâcle is considerable, but too much of the blame tends to be heaped upon him. To a large extent he inherited from his predecessors the misguided policy that led to this disaster. Since the late 1940s both parties in the United States had believed in the need to resist communist expansion in South East and Eastern Asia. A rationale of sorts for that belief was provided in 1954 by President Eisenhower when he advanced his notorious 'domino theory'. According to this dubious doctrine, if the communist takeover of individual countries in Asia was not strongly resisted the same fate would befall neighbouring countries; one by one, like so many dominoes, they too would go communist. It was thinking such as this that lay behind the provision of economic and military aid to South Vietnam by both the Eisenhower and the Kennedy administrations. However, neither Eisenhower nor Kennedy was willing to send combat troops; they preferred to restrict the involvement of American personnel to military advisers. During the Kennedy years the number of advisers increased from 800 to approximately 17,000, but when Johnson entered office it was evident that the efforts to prop up the existing regime in South Vietnam were not succeeding. Within a short while it became clear 'that either the

United States would do something different or South Vietnam would fall. The problem could no longer be handled with hopeful in-between policies.'[32]

Eventually, after much agonizing and hesitation, Johnson decided to escalate the war. In Febuary 1965 he ordered continuous bombing of North Vietnam below the 20th parallel. Shortly afterwards, a small number of American troops was dispatched to Vietnam to protect the base from which the bombing raids were launched. By the end of April, the number of troops had increased to 50,000 and by June the function of such forces was no longer purely defensive. American troops in Vietnam increased relentlessly during the next few years totalling 184,000 by the end of 1965, 385,000 by the end of 1966, 475,000 by the end of 1967 and close to 550,000 by the time Johnson left the White House.[33]

What led Johnson to follow this disastrous policy? Escalation was, in many respects, the logical consequence of the policies pursued by his predecessors, although Johnson shared many of the assumptions upon which those policies had been based. As a young congressman he had been a fervent supporter of Roosevelt's militant responses to German aggression. For him, as for so many others, Munich and appeasement were dirty words; he subscribed fully to the widespread conviction that the free world's survival depended on standing firm against aggressors. As he saw it:

> whether by supplies, infiltration or regular troops, North Vietnam – with Red China behind it – was an aggressor, and the aggression was succeeding. American policy faced another 1930s, when Hitler went on the march, or another 1950, when North Korea backed by Red China invaded southward. The United States could either stop the new aggression with armed force or step aside and allow a Munich. And Lyndon Johnson was no President to preside over what he considered a Munich.[34]

But the decision to escalate was, by no means Johnson's alone. His National Security Advisor, McGeorge Bundy and his Secretary of Defense, Robert McNamara, both argued in January 1965 that the President's presently cautious policy would not suffice. These most senior advisers, both appointed by Kennedy, told Johnson that the existing situation placed the international prestige and influence of the United States at risk and reinforced 'a widespread belief that we do not have the will and force and patience and determination to take the necessary action'. Bundy and McNamara accordingly recommended a 'policy of sustained reprisal'.[35]

As Doris Kearns points out, the decision to embark on the bombing of Vietnam was supported by virtually all the relevant senior policy-makers in the Johnson administration, including the Secretaries of State and Defense, the Special Assistant for National Security Affairs, the Ambassador to Saigon and the Joint Chiefs of Staff.[36] In increasing troop levels in 1965, Johnson was acting on the recommendations of not only his own military and political advisers, but also of the so-called 'Wise Men' – elder members of the foreign policy establishment like Dean Acheson, Averell Harriman and Robert Lovett. Even as late as November 1967, with the war dragging on and dissent mounting in the country, another meeting of the 'wise' men urged Johnson to stay the course.[37]

For a long time there was in fact no opposition to speak of in Congress to Johnson's Vietnam policy. Only two senators and not a single member of the House voted against the infamous Gulf of Tonkin Resolution in 1964. When the war got fully under way in the following year, Congress consistently chose not to use the power of the purse to terminate the American action. The truth of the matter is that while Johnson was in the White House there was never more than a small handful of legislators who seriously dissented from his policy in Vietnam. Such limited resistance as did arise on Capitol Hill came entirely from the Democratic side, with the Republicans never criticizing the premises of the administration's policy. Similarly, Richard Nixon, in campaigning for the Republican presidential nomination in 1967 and 1968, hounded Johnson for not doing enough in Vietnam and would have crucified him if he had tried to withdraw. Meanwhile the aged Eisenhower, who had earlier declined to send troops to Vietnam was now remarkably hawkish, demanding that American forces be allowed to pursue the enemy into Laos and Cambodia.[38]

Conclusions

Why did the Johnson presidency end so disastrously? To a large extent the explanation lies in his pursuit of a misguided and ill-founded policy in South East Asia. Although overall responsibility for that policy lies with many American leaders rather than Johnson alone, the war nevertheless exposed major flaws in his approach to presidential leadership. If other leaders shared in the decision to escalate, it was the President who decided, against the advice of several senior colleagues, to do so by stealth, without taking the people or Congress into his confidence.[39] Having posed as a peace candidate in 1964, ('There can and will be, peace for all Americans as long as I am President'), Johnson, within a few months, began the bombing of North Vietnam. A short while later he moved from bombing to the deployment of troops, first on a small scale, but ultimately in enormous numbers until it eventually became apparent to all that, without a mandate to do so and without ever obtaining formal congressional approval, Johnson had committed his country to a full-scale military conflict.

In later years, in justifying his decision to escalate covertly, Johnson outlined his fear that an open approach would have destroyed his dream of a Great Society. In the summer of 1965 when the crucial decisions had to be taken, the President felt that he was on the verge of accomplishing his:

> youthful dream of improving life for more people and in more ways than any other political leader, including FDR. . . . I was determined to keep the war from shattering that dream, which meant that I simply had no choice but to keep my foreign policy in the wings. I knew the Congress as well as I know Lady Bird, and I knew that the day it exploded into a major debate on the war would be the beginning of the end of the Great Society.[40]

President Johnson's long-standing belief in the primacy of the chief executive's role in defence and foreign policy gave him further cause to conceal his purposes from both the people and Congress. As a senator he had consistently held to that view, supporting President Truman's decision to embark on the Korean War without a declaration of war and ready to give Eisenhower the same sort of support. In reminiscing on the period when Eisenhower was President, Johnson commented:

> People said to me, 'Why don't you get up and criticize?' I replied, 'We ought not to do anything that might be misunderstood by foreign countries. He is the only President we have, and I am going to support that President because if I make him weaker I make America weaker.'[41]

As President, Johnson expected Congress to treat him similarly; he regarded public dissent from his policies as unpatriotic and saw uninhibited debate on such sensitive matters as a luxury that the nation could not afford.

It should be borne in mind that in the 1960s the idea of a president taking upon himself the right to make major foreign policy decisions with scant reference to anyone else was widely accepted as proper, not least by many members of the legislature. As Chapter 5 showed, the view that Congress had relatively little to contribute in such matters was rooted in history and extensively supported by precedent. Only very recently, John Kennedy had almost completely ignored Congress in dealing with the Cuban missile crisis. Furthermore, Johnson had little time for the virtues of public debate on such matters:

> It was in the public's best interest – given its tendency every now and then 'to go off on a jag in one crazy direction or another' – to leave complicated questions of international affairs in the hands of the President. The public Johnson reasoned, would only hurt itself by knowing too much. Democracy demanded good results for the people, not big debates.'42

With the advantage of hindsight, Johnson's failure to 'level' with the American people over Vietnam appears to have been a crucial error on his part. If he had properly educated the public on the issues at stake, fully explaining what he was doing and the need for the great sacrifices that would be required – if, in other words, he had created a consensus behind his policy – he might have avoided the storms of bitter recrimination that finally engulfed him when the war began to go badly wrong.

Other presidents have, to put it bluntly, told lies and half-truths in the cause of national security, hoping thereby to protect their options and to conceal their plans from the nation's enemies. However, Johnson's deviousness was cruder and less subtle and, in the long run, the widespread conviction that he could not be trusted to tell the truth seriously undermined both his public prestige and his professional reputation – two resources indispensable to the exercise of presidential power.

The 'credibility gap' that afflicted Johnson's presidency first became apparent in 1965 and grew in significance the longer the war in Vietnam continued. He seemed to assume that presidential leadership and congressional leadership required more or less the same approach. He failed to understand 'the difference between the Hill and the White House . . . the tactics of a Senate majority leader automatically created a credibility gap as President'. As a brilliantly successful congressional leader, he had revelled in behind-the-scenes manoeuvring; secrecy and deviousness were essential to his exercise of control. 'That's the way you do business in the Senate; but when you're President, newspapermen start comparing different versions of what you say, and they check Source A against Source B against Source C.'[43]

Nor was the President's standing with the public helped by his lack of a sufficient sense of the dignity of his office. The president is, of course, both a prime minister and a head of state. In the latter role, he has important ceremonial and symbolic functions, but Johnson was not at his best in meeting these responsibilities. The image he conveyed of a somewhat unscrupulous wheeler-dealer was permissible in a congressional leader, but less acceptable in a president and eventually eroded his public support. Some Americans undoubtedly took offence at Johnson's notorious boorishness and were unimpressed by television pictures of their head of state lifting beagles by the ears or pulling up his shirt to display the scar from a recent gall bladder operation.

If impressive while it lasted, Johnson's command of Congress also proved to be short-lived, a development that can, by no means, be ascribed simply to Vietnam. Long before disenchantment with the war became a potent factor, the President's control over the legislature had faltered. After his landslide victory at the polls in 1964, Johnson had warned his staff of the danger of underestimating the capacity of Congress to derail the plans of the executive branch, saying 'I have watched the Congress from either the inside or the outside, man and boy, for more than forty years, and I've never seen a Congress that didn't eventually take the measure of the President it was dealing with.' Illustrating his argument by referring to incidents such as Wilson's humiliation at the hands of the Senate over the Treaty of Versailles and FDR's similar defeat over his plan to reshape the Supreme Court, Johnson noted that his present strong position would soon be eroded.[44]

This eventuality was made even more certain by the ambitious contours of Johnson's vision of a Great Society: 'The very existence of that voluminous programme was bound to accelerate the decline of presidential power following the election. No President could ask for so much and hope to maintain totally amicable relations with Congress.'[45] Intense presidential activism, in other words, would, as it had done before, eventually lead to negative reactions in Congress.

Congressional reassertion was inevitable in the long run, but Johnson appeared to neglect his own words of warning when he began treating the legislature like a rubber stamp, thereby building up resentment that would later cause him great difficulty. An example of this occurred when, in an attempt to save money to help finance Great Society programmes, Johnson authorized the Veterans Administration to close down a number of hospitals and regional offices. Members of Congress are well known to be obsessively concerned with their re-election. To further that end, they are constantly seeking to expand federal facilities in their district or state and members were bound to be outraged by this attempt to reduce, without prior consultation, the number of such facilities. After a bitter struggle Johnson was obliged to back down, 'Yet the wounds of this battle between President and Congress never quite healed. The President was stockpiling adversity.'[46]

Further damage to Johnson's relations with Congress arose from his intervention in the Dominican Republic in April 1965. Civil war had broken out in that country and Johnson, advised of the possibility of a communist coup and assured that American lives were at risk, had ordered US marines into action. Among liberals, the view developed that the President had acted precipitously on the basis of suspect advice and information, and moreover without any pretence of consulting with Congress. Congressional ire at this incident, particularly in the Senate Foreign Relations Committee, added to the deterioration in congressional/presidential relations.[47]

George Reedy, at one stage President Johnson's press secretary, has provided some insights into why Johnson lost his touch in dealing with Congress and saw his public support erode. According to Reedy, the court-like atmosphere of the White House has a corrupting influence on the psyche of even the most skilled and experienced of politicians. Incumbents are treated by their staff with the awe and reverence more appropriate to a monarch than to the leader of a democratic republic; they become surrounded by sycophantic mediocrities who pander to their every whim and are disinclined to tell them what they do not want to hear. Such treatment tends to cause presidents to become 'isolated from realities' reducing 'them to bungling amateurs in their basic craft – the art of politics'.[48]

Evidence of Johnson's political sensitivity being badly blunted while he was in the White House is to be seen in his personalization of his office. He became prone to talk about *my* boys and *my* bombers in Vietnam; he even spoke of *my* Congress and introduced a justice of the United States Supreme Court to a foreign visitor with the words: 'Mr Prime Minister, I want you to meet a member of *my* Supreme Court'.[49] On another occasion, when a marine sergeant helpfully said, 'Your helicopter is the next one, Mr President,' Johnson rejoined, 'They're all mine, son.'[50] Such language was more appropriate to a Shah of Iran than to a president of the United States and ran dangerously counter to the anti-authority traditions of the American political culture.

As we saw earlier, Fred Greenstein, in his work on Eisenhower, emphasized the importance of a president successfully marrying the two roles of prime minister and head of state. The former responsibility is inherently divisive and in pursuing it a president always runs the danger of undermining his position as the symbolic leader of the nation as a whole. If, as Greenstein suggests, Eisenhower was notably adept in reconciling the two roles, Johnson provides a classic instance of a president who failed to do so.

In preserving his standing in the public opinion polls and thereby his position as head of state, Eisenhower used a variety of strategies. In the first place, for ideological reasons, he had no ambition to make his office an engine of social change. In addition, he concealed whatever purposes he had by the 'instrumental use of language', distanced himself from the detail of policy-making and used senior staff as lightning rods to deflect criticism from himself. The subtleties of Eisenhower's 'hidden-hand' leadership were lost on a man like Johnson who came into office with a mission, with a determination to bring about change, to use his power resources in the cause of necessary reform: 'Some men want power,' he said later, 'simply to strut around the world and to hear the tune of "Hail to the Chief". Well, I wanted power to give things to people – all sorts of things to all sorts of people, especially the poor and the blacks.'[51]

In contradistinction to Eisenhower's view, Johnson believed that much could be achieved by moral leadership and the passing of laws, even in that most difficult of problem areas – race relations:

> Now I knew that as President I couldn't make people *want* to integrate their schools or open their doors to blacks, but I could make them feel guilty for not doing so and I believed it was my moral responsibility to do just that – to use the moral suasion of my office to make people feel that segregation was a curse they'd carry with them to their graves.[52]

In meeting his responsibilities as he saw them Johnson led loudly, aggressively and without subtlety from the front. His highly developed ego caused him to place himself constantly at the centre of the decision-making process whether in domestic or foreign policy. Suggestions from his staff that he should diffuse authority for policy-making as far as possible to the Cabinet and to agency heads went unheeded by Johnson.[53] He declined to make use of lightning rods and was often to be found addressing himself to policy minutiae, personally selecting bombing targets and monitoring with manic attention the casualty figures from Vietnam.

By placing himself at the centre of events in this way Johnson took much of the credit when things were going well, and, when the policies proved defective, the backlash fell with full force on him personally, critically damaging his public prestige and savagely undermining his position as head of state. Unhappiness about the war and the protestors, the blacks and the bigots, the young and their critics, attached itself to the man in the White House:

> When riots and demonstrations took place, as the people saw it, the President – the man at the nation's center – was to blame. Accordingly, the turbulent sixties became Lyndon Johnson's problem just as the depression had become Herbert Hoover's problem and the 'mess in Washington' had become Harry Truman's problem.[54]

Some later presidents appear to have learned from Johnson's experience; for example, Reagan's masterly avoidance of blame for the errors of his administration and Bush's meticulous refusal to become involved in the day-to-day conduct of the Gulf War.

Lyndon Johnson was surely one of the most extraordinary men to have become president of the United States. Half-educated, yet enormously intelligent, he strove ruthlessly to achieve political office and to attain the highest pinnacle of political power in his country. Once he had reached that peak, President Johnson sought to use the power he had gained to change the world. On the international scene, his efforts were tragically counterproductive whereas his record at home, while uneven, was at least partially successful.

Notes

1. Doris Kearns, *Lyndon Johnson and the American Dream*, New American Library, New York, 1976, p. 390.
2. Robert Caro, *The Years of Lyndon Johnson: The Path to Power*, Alfred Knopf, New York, 1982, part III, *passim*.
3. Kearns, *op. cit.*, pp. 97–8.
4. See Donald Matthews, *US Senators and their World*, Vintage Books, New York, 1960.
5. Kearns, *op. cit.*, p. 115.
6. Joseph Califano, *A Presidential Nation*, W. W. Norton, New York, 1975, p. 19.
7. Eric Goldman, *The Tragedy of Lyndon Johnson*, Dell Books, New York, 1969, p. 622.
8. Robert Caro, *Means of Ascent: The Years of Lyndon Johnson*, The Bodley Head, London, 1990, p. xxvii.
9. *ibid., passim.*
10. Fred Greenstein, *The Hidden-Hand Presidency: Eisenhower as Leader*, Basic Books, New York, 1982, p. 28.
11. Rowland Evans and Robert Novak, *Lyndon Johnson: The Exercise of Power*, Allen and Unwin, London, 1967, pp. 496–7.
12. *ibid.*, p. 4.
13. Robert Dahl and Charles Lindblom, *Politics, Economics and Welfare*, Harper and Row, New York, 1953, p. 333.
14. Evans and Novak, *op.cit.*, p. 104.
15. Kearns, *op. cit.*, p. 177.
16. George Edwards III, *Presidential Influence in Congress*, W. H. Freeman, San Francisco, 1980, p. 14.
17. *op. cit.*, pp. 67–8.
18. Goldman, *op. cit.*, pp. 70 and 73.
19. Evans and Novak, *op. cit.*, p. 378.
20. Barbara Kellerman, *The Political Presidency: The Practice of Leadership*, Oxford University Press, New York, 1984, p. 90.
21. *ibid.*, Ch. 7, *passim.*
22. Evans and Novak, *op. cit.*, p. 497.
23. *Revolution in Civil Rights*, Congressional Quarterly Press, 1965, p. 84.
24. Gerald David Jaynes and Robin M. Williams (eds), *A Common Destiny: Blacks in American Society*, National Academy Press, Washington DC, 1989, pp. 232–3.

25. Califano, *op. cit.*, p. 216.
26. *ibid.*, pp. 20–1.
27. See for example Malcolm Shaw (ed.), *Roosevelt to Reagan: The Development of the Modern Presidency*, C. Hurst, London, 1987, p. 83.
28. Kearns, *op. cit.*, 268.
29. *ibid.*, p. 202.
30. *ibid.*, p. 203.
31. *ibid.*, p. 277.
32. Goldman, *op. cit.*, p. 473.
33. Figures from *World Almanac and Book of Facts*, Scripps Howard, New York, 1991, p. 448.
34. Goldman, *op. cit.*, p. 475.
35. Kearns, *op. cit.*, pp. 273–4.
36. *ibid.*
37. Walter Isaacson and Evan Thomas, *The Wise Men*, Simon and Schuster, New York, 1987, pp. 676–80.
38. Stephen Ambrose, *Nixon: The Triumph of Politician 1962–72*, Simon and Schuster, New York, 1989, p. 129.
39. Kearns, *op. cit.*, p. 416.
40. *ibid.*, p. 296.
41. Goldman, *op. cit.*, pp. 489–90.
42. Kearns, *op. cit.*, p. 297.
43. Fred Greenstein, *Leadership in the Modern Presidency*, Harvard University Press, Cambridge, Mass., 1988, p.137.
44. Evans and Novak, *op. cit.*, p. 490.
45. *ibid.*, pp. 490–1.
46. *ibid.*, p. 499.
47. *ibid.*, Ch. 23.
48. *The Twilight of the Presidency*, New American Library, New York, 1970, p. 26.
49. Evans and Novak, *op. cit.*, p. 4.
50. Califano, *op. cit.*, p. 227.
51. Kearns, *op. cit.*, p. 57.
52. *ibid.*, p. 321.
53. Greenstein, *Leadership in the Modern Presidency, op. cit.*, p. 149.
54. Kearns, *op. cit.*, p. 353.

8

Ronald Reagan's Place in History[1]

The former Speaker of the House of Representatives, Tip O'Neill, has noted in his memoirs, 'I hate to say it about such an agreeable man, but it was sinful that Ronald Reagan ever became President. . . . I've known every president since Harry Truman and there's no question in my mind that [Reagan] was the worst.'[2] Many other observers have viewed the Reagan presidency in a negative light whereas it is my view that despite many limitations Ronald Reagan, far from being the 'worst' of modern presidents, was more effective in office than most who have held the position in the last fifty years.

Effectiveness in the White House, as I maintained earlier, is a rare commodity. Presidents come and go, but few of them really overcome those tendencies towards ungovernability in the political system discussed in the earlier chapters of this book.[3] In campaigning for office, candidates for the presidency espouse a range of policy ambitions; in effect they tell the voters, cast your ballots for me and I will pursue certain policy objectives. The odds, however, are heavily against any particular president being able to fufil his contract with the electorate, for the conversion of policy intentions into the realities of governmental action is infinitely problematical. Only a small minority of presidents are really effective in this sense whereas Reagan, I will argue, has some claim to be included in that elite. His record in office was undoubtedly mixed and he suffered more than a few defeats and disasters, but for all that, his overall performance was relatively impressive.

195

Not everyone takes easily to the idea of Reagan as an exceptionally effective president. The perceptions of some are coloured by their dislike of his policies and, looked at from abroad, there often seems to be more than a little truth in the media caricatures of him as an ageing, empty-headed, grade B movie actor who somehow stumbled into the White House. However, any reservations we may have regarding the content of Reagan's policies are irrelevant to this discussion. Our personal concerns about matters such as the treatment of poor people in the United States during the Reagan years, or the bullying of small countries in Central America must be set aside for the purposes of this consideration of presidential effectiveness. It is also necessary to take media caricatures for what they are and to be careful not to lose sight of the uniquely American nature of the office of president.

The latter point is of particular importance. All of us are products of a particular political culture and there is a natural inclination to see the politics of other countries in terms which are necessarily alien. It is, however, grossly inappropriate to evaluate an American president in accordance with criteria applicable to a British prime minister. The two roles are, of course, fundamentally different. The president must be not only prime minister but chief of state. He is not fortified by a disciplined party machine and does not operate in a system where the separation of powers between the legislative and the executive is virtually without meaning.

Success or failure in the White House

The assessment of presidential success or failure is fraught with many difficulties, but in this discussion I will endeavour to deal with this matter by using four criteria: (1) significant public policy change, (2) policy success, (3) party legacy and (4) the state of the presidency. I shall first briefly discuss these yardsticks before applying them to the case of Ronald Reagan.

Every modern president enters office bearing a policy agenda even if it is couched in broad generalities such as a determination to 'get the country moving again' or 'to get the government off the people's back'. To achieve these aims a president needs first of all a legislative strategy. *Significant public policy change* cannot occur without the agreement of the legislative branch, and the president who fails to establish a productive relationship with the Congress is doomed to failure.

Simply passing bills, however, is hardly sufficient. Presidential success cannot be adequately measured by *Congressional Quarterly* scores that do not differentiate between different sorts of bills. Some legislation is enormously consequential, and some is not. The really successful presidents get bills passed that do much more than merely tinker at the margin and go well beyond the sort of incremental change that most presidents are obliged to settle for. Such legislation involves a fundamental reordering of priorities and/or the reversal of long-standing policy directions.

A successful legislative strategy, however, will not, by itself, achieve significant public policy change. The legislative process, in the modern age, provides only for the enactment of policies in broad outlines leaving to federal bureaucrats the crucial work of fleshing out legislative frameworks with administrative detail.[4] This provides many opportunities for bureaucratic subversion of the president's intentions, an eventuality he must guard against by developing an adequate administrative strategy. This will require the careful selection of Cabinet members and other senior appointees, detailed supervision of the budgetary process and the manipulation of regulatory agencies. By these and other means gains made on the legislative front can be consolidated and built upon at the level of administration.

In considering the nature of presidential power in Chapter 4 reference was made to the policy-determining functions of the federal judiciary. This may present either opportunities or obstacles to a chief executive. In some circumstances he may, by working through the judiciary, accomplish objectives not achievable by other means. On the other hand, federal judges may prove resistant to his policy intentions. In either case his success in office may turn on his ability to develop an effective judicial strategy.

If a president has adequate legislative, administrative and judicial strategies he may accomplish significant public policy change of the sort seen in Woodrow Wilson's New Freedom, FDR's New Deal and Lyndon Johnson's Great Society. These presidents were successful in challenging long-held assumptions, in reordering priorities and in changing the terms of debate to a degree denied to other would-be activists in the White House like Harry Truman, John Kennedy, Richard Nixon, Gerald Ford and Jimmy Carter.

So far, in attempting to arrive at some suitable evaluative criteria I have been concerned with means rather than ends, with process rather than content, and there is much to be said for leaving the matter there.[5] Given the monumental difficulties of bringing order out of the chaos of the American political system, and getting it to produce any sort of policy outcomes, one is inclined to stand back and marvel at the accomplishment of those who manage to pull the trick off at all, irrespective of whether the policies are meritorious or actually achieve the desired results. Some, however, will regard this as an unduly narrow perspective and no doubt, in the long term, a president's reputation will rest not simply on whether he mastered the system, but also on whether his policies are perceived to have worked, whether he has achieved *policy success.*

Conclusive judgements in these matters are not possible until many years after a president has left office, and even then the historians are likely to disagree. In addition, there is always the danger, especially relevant in the case of presidents only recently in office, that the political preferences of the analyst will distort his or her conclusions.[6] Notwithstanding these important problems it is clear that the evaluation of any modern president, the determination of his place in history, will be greatly influenced by perceptions of his performance in two principal policy arenas – management of the economy and foreign policy. Ultimately, the historians will want to ask what was the state of the economy during and at the end of a particular president's term of office? Were his policies beneficial to the economic well-being of the nation? Similarly, in the realm of foreign policy general questions will, in the long run, be posed regarding a president's record in advancing and protecting the interests of the United States in the world. It will be asked, was the position of the country in international affairs strengthened or weakened during the course of the administration under consideration?

The third criterion of presidential success used here is *party legacy.* Presidents are party leaders and temporarily, at least, they represent what the party broadly stands for. As is well known, American parties are loosely structured, and in the modern age presidential coat tails are not what they were. Nevertheless the fates of presidents and their parties remain inextricably entwined. The party of a president who leaves office as a failure is bound to be diminished and damaged. Party candidates for lesser offices will have their political lives made more difficult and the fallout for presidential candidates may well prove fatal. This was the case for Hubert Humphrey in 1968, Gerald Ford in 1976 and Walter Mondale in 1984. By the same token, a phenomenally successful president like Franklin Roosevelt did wonders for the fortunes of his party at all levels of the political system.

Finally, in assessing a president it is also appropriate to take account of what a particular incumbent contributes to the institutional well-being of his high office – that is, *the state of the presidency*. Does he add to the credibility and stature of the office or does he diminish it? Is the position of the presidency in relation to its principal competitors in the struggle for power, most notably the Congress, strengthened or weakened during a particular administration? And what of public confidence and trust in the institution as evidenced by the public opinion polls? Thus Woodrow Wilson at the beginning of his first term considerably strengthened the position of the presidency, but he left it devastated in 1921. Franklin Roosevelt added enormous weight to the presidency as an institution, whereas Richard Nixon did it great damage. Jimmy Carter inherited a crippled office and arguably weakened it even further.

Reagan's record

The assessment of a particular president inevitably becomes at some stage a comparative exercise; that is to say, we are inexorably drawn into comparing one president with another. However, there are many difficulties in such comparative analysis if only because every president confronts a unique set of circumstantial variables. Some are blessed with large electoral mandates, whereas others are not; some are reinforced by large majorities in Congress, an important advantage that others lack. Before proceeding to an application to Ronald Reagan of the four criteria discussed in the previous section, it makes sense to summarize the circumstances that pertained as he took office.

Reagan was first elected to the White House by a large popular vote and a considerable margin of victory in the Electoral College, but for all that his mandate was distinctly fragile. Neither presidential candidate in 1980 excited the electorate greatly, many voters made up their minds in the closing weeks of the campaign and the result has been widely interpreted as a vote of no confidence in Carter's tenure rather than a positive vote for his opponent.[7]

In 1980, in addition to the presidency, the Republicans won control of the Senate for the first time for many years. This was a psychologically important victory, but the Republicans failed to win a majority in the House of Representatives. When the dust of the election settled Reagan's position *vis-à-vis* the Congress, although strong for a Republican, was far weaker than that of Lyndon Johnson, John Kennedy or even Jimmy Carter when those presidents took up office.

Reagan, moreover, came to the White House at a moment when Congress appeared to be in an even more recalcitrant mood than usual. The 1970s had been an era of congressional reform involving various changes that led to an even more fragmented and less manageable legislature than before. Furthermore, in 1980 public confidence in political institutions had slumped to a particularly low ebb, with the office of president particularly suffering from a large loss of credibility.[8]

Reagan's situation in 1981, in other words, was in no way comparable to that of, say, Roosevelt in 1933 or Johnson thirty years later, a fact that we need to bear in mind as we consider his record in the light of the four criteria discussed in the previous section. The first of those yardsticks was *significant public policy change*.

The revitalization of the US economy and a strengthening of the nation's defence capabilities were the immediate priorities of the administration taking office in 1981. Reagan and his advisers were convinced that the fulfilment of that agenda required a considerable increase in defence spending, reductions in domestic expenditure and a substantial tax cut. Initially at least, the Reaganites were spectacularly successful in reaching their goals; moving swiftly and effectively to take control of the legislative process they soon accomplished an unusual degree of significant public policy change.

Even the President's arch-critic, the Speaker of the US House of Representatives, was obliged to concede later that: 'In 1981 Ronald Reagan enjoyed a truly remarkable rookie year. He pushed through the greatest increase in defense spending in American history, together with the greatest cutbacks in domestic programs and the largest tax cuts this country had ever seen.'[9] The authoritative *Congressional Quarterly* similarly reported that Reagan in his first year in office signed 'into law the deepest and farthest–reaching package of budget cuts that Congress had ever appproved', while Richard Nathan in commenting on the significance of the 1981 budget act described it as 'the most important piece of domestic legislation since the Social Security Act of 1935 . . . [bringing about] a marked shift in the direction of social spending and fundamental changes in the substance of domestic policy and in American federalism.'[10]

The Reagan forces never managed to duplicate the heady successes of 1981 and Congress, in subsequent years, successfully resisted further cuts in domestic programmes, refused to sanction in full proposed increases in defence spending and imposed increases in taxation. Nevertheless there was no complete reversal of the new policy directions set in 1981.

Like all presidents Reagan was never able to achieve his ambitions in full, but for all that he did accomplish a significant reordering of national priorities over the eight years of his administration. Thus federal spending on defence was 5 per cent of GNP in 1980 whereas it rose to 6.4 per cent by 1985 and stood at 6.1 per cent in 1988; between 1980 and 1988 real expenditure on defence rose by 54 per cent.[11] A substantial cut in income tax was central to Reagan's economic policy and this was achieved in 1981 when Congress agreed to a succession of across-the-board cuts – 5 per cent in the first year and 10 per cent in each of the two years that followed. The top rate of marginal tax was reduced from 70 per cent when Reagan took office to 28 per cent when he left. Furthermore, despite various tax increases in later years, the burden of income tax on individuals was $201 billion less in 1988 compared with what it would would have been under pre-1981 tax law.[12]

In his memoirs Reagan admits that he failed to cut federal spending as much as he had hoped, although he took pride in having reduced the rate of growth of such spending.[13] This latter claim is confirmed by Office of Management and Budget figures that reveal a sharp reduction in the rate of growth of public spending in the 1980s (see Table 8.1).

Reagan's attempts to cut federal spending further were undermined by the need he felt to increase defence expenditures, the interest payments on the national debt arising from soaring budget deficits and congressional determination to resist more cuts in so-

Table 8.1   Percentage increase in real federal spending by decade

Decade	Percentage
1920s	−30.7
1930s	212.4
1940s	165
1950s	54.4
1960s	49.6
1970s	37.2
1980s	26.0

Source: From *Budget of the United States Government FY 1990*, US Government Printing Office, Washington DC, 1989, 2–2.

cial programmes. Furthermore, as every president discovers, large areas of federal expenditure for domestic purposes are virtually immune from cutting, and given the ageing of the population the cost of programmes such as Social Security and Medicare is bound to increase. Where it was possible to cut, however, the Reagan administration left its mark. Total outlays for 'non defense discretionary programs' as a proportion of GNP fell by a third from 5.8 per cent in 1980 to 3.8 per cent in 1988.[14] Real expenditures for such discretionary programmes were cut by 20 per cent during the Reagan years. Similarly, federal grants to state and local governments were sharply cut back. As a proportion of GNP such grants fell from 2.2 per cent in 1980 to 1.3 per cent in 1988 and in real terms dropped by more than a third, from $68 billion in 1980 to $43 billion in 1988.[15]

In short, Reagan and his staff did get closer to achieving their goals than most administrations are able to do:

> Even critics must admit that a determined President was able to accomplish many of his stated goals. Reagan gained the largest increase in peace time defense spending, a step he felt was necessary in order for the country to regain its position as the world's preeminent military power. Reagan cut tax rates sharply and dramatically altered the income tax system, policies to which his administration was also deeply committed. Reagan sheared back a great number of domestic programs, thus carrying out in good part his promises to reduce the scope of the domestic side of government.[16]

President Reagan, it seems, did accomplish significant public policy change and even an alteration in the terms of policy debate. According to one source:

> the basic domestic issue of the 1970s and indeed of the entire New Deal era has been superseded. The main issue is no longer how much the federal government's economic role – in taxing, spending, and regulating – will expand but where, when, and by how much it will be curtailed.[17]

The depth of the change that occurred was further reflected in the fact that Democrats in the 1980s were obliged to accept Reaganite assumptions about the virtues of tax cuts and the essential need to economize in domestic programmes. In other words, liberal Democrats had to suppress their natural inclination to initiate new grant programmes and were reduced to mounting rearguard actions in defence of those that already existed. As the *Congressional Quarterly* reported in 1986:

> Six years of retrenchment have forced liberal Democrats into a seemingly permanent defensive crouch. They have had to accommodate the widespread view that the government cannot afford major domestic expenditures and that public support is flagging for the kind of government programs that were a key tool of Great Society liberalism.[18]

As I noted earlier, fundamental change requires not only an effective legislative strategy but also an administrative strategy to buttress and expand upon whatever gains are made on the legislative front. This was especially necessary in the 1980s for a Republican president obliged to work with a federal bureaucracy manned largely by Democratic career civil servants. The Reagan forces immediately concentrated the appointments process in the White House and ensured that top-level appointments went only to men and women loyal to Ronald Reagan and to the goals he sought.[19] By cutting personnel in the regulatory agencies and the exercise of executive discretion, the Reagan forces also substantially undermined the system of regulating business built up over the years by successive Democratic regimes.

The high professionalism of the Reagan's staff could also be seen in their adoption of a notably successful judical strategy. As I argued in Chapter 4, by skilfully exploiting the judicial appointment system Edwin Meese, and others, ensured that the decisions of the federal courts at all levels would for years to come reflect Reagan's preferences in social policy.

Previous Republican administrations had failed to turn back the overall thrust of Democratic domestic policies, but Reagan's legislative, administrative and judicial strategies in combination were comparatively rather successful. The record is, of course, uneven, but after fifty years of proliferating government programmes and Keynesian economic policies, who can doubt that Reagan left a conservative mark on the political system? The virtues of limited government and market economics were reasserted, and many of the central values of the New Deal and the Great Society were successfully challenged. As Martin Anderson claimed:

> What Reagan and his comrades have done is to shape America's policy agenda well into the twenty-first century. The prospects are nil for sharply progressive tax rates and big, new social welfare programs, some of the former mainstays of the Democrats' domestic policy agenda. Everyone is for a strong national defense, differing only in the degree and quality of it.[20]

In foreign and national security policy, Reagan could also claim to have succeeded in bringing about significant policy change. He entered office believing that previous administrations had neglected the nation's defences and been too passive in the face of relentless Soviet expansionism. The long-standing US policy of containment needed to be replaced with a more positive and aggressive stance; Marxist regimes in the Third World were to be actively undermined by providing aid to rebel groups sympathetic to the West. In addition, as the Soviets understood only the language of strength, the United States needed to rearm, not as an end in itself, but as a means of bringing about serious arms reduction negotiations. Despite his bellicose rhetoric Reagan was appalled by the implications of the policy of 'mutually assured destruction' and was convinced of the need to rid the world of the menace of nuclear weapons, a concern that eventually led him to make 'Star Wars', otherwise known as the Strategic Defense Initiative, the centrepiece of his nuclear strategy. Many doubted the wisdom of these policy changes and not all of them were fully implemented, nevertheless substantial movement in the directions chosen by Reagan did occur. As I. M. Destler noted, Reagan 'may not have grasped, or cared about, the details: he may not have faced the contradictions; but *his* priorities, *his* values were being pursued'.[21]

The second criteria of presidential effectiveness discussed in the previous section was *policy success*; it was suggested that a president's reputation will ultimately be much dependent on his success or failure in two policy arenas – managing the economy and foreign policy. In assessing Reagan's record as manager of the economy, his critics have naturally fastened onto indicators such as the large budget and trade deficits, the weakening of the dollar, the enormous additions to the national debt and the heavy dependence on foreign investors, all of which arose during his tenure. These negatives are not, however, conclusive proof that Reagan's economic policy failed and there are other statistics that justify more favourable conclusions.

When Reagan took office inflation was *the* issue of economic policy, the matter that concerned the American public most.[22] By 1989 the problem of inflation had largely disappeared; during the last year of the Carter administration inflation rose to 13.5 per cent but was down to 4.7 per cent as Reagan's second term came to an end. Unemployment in 1980 was 7 per cent whereas it stood at 5.2 per cent at the end of 1988.[23] Administration spokesmen repeatedly pointed out, as Reagan prepared to leave office, that after the recession early in his first term the United States had experienced its longest ever period of economic growth in peacetime, making possible the creation of 19 million new jobs. According to the Office of Management and Budget 'the main macroeconomic indicators [showed] a picture of stability in 1988: robust growth, moderate inflation and low unemployment.'[24]

Conceivably at some point in the future it will be possible to say definitively whether Reaganomics failed. Ultimately, those many commentators who expect the worst over the long term may prove to be right. Arthur Schlesinger Jnr, for instance, may be vindicated in his speculation that 'Reagan's tax reduction act may be the most disastrous piece of legislation since the Second World War.'[25] For the moment, however, no conclusive assessments are possible, even if it is clear that, in 1988, Reagan's management of the economy was favourably perceived by the public at large. These positive perceptions, moreover, played a major part in securing Bush's victory in the presidential election.

A lapse of time will also be required before much of a conclusive nature can be said about the merits of Reagan's foreign policy. At this juncture the signing of a major arms control agreement (the INF treaty) and the inauguration of a new era of reasonably amicable relations with the Soviet Union would seem to represent large achievements for Ronald Reagan, far outweighing the accomplishments of most presidents in the foreign policy arena.

It is the case that these breakthroughs in foreign policy were much dependent on factors outside the President's control. However, it is possible to argue that Reagan was primarily responsible for bringing about the substantial redirection of foreign policy that ultimately proved beneficial to the United States. Under his leadership a large increase in armaments occurred and the United States adopted, initially, an uncompromising stance towards the Soviet Union and its satellites around the world. This new aggressive posture, so it could be claimed, was a major factor in bringing the Soviet Union to the arms control negotiating table and in curbing its expansionist inclinations abroad.

There were, of course, various foreign policy disasters, including incidents such as the ignominious and costly withdrawal from Lebanon, defeats by Congress over South Africa and the Philippines and, surpassing all else, the Iran–Contra débâcle. By any standard the latter was a massive set-back for the President personally and for American foreign policy. Reagan himself appeared to be grossly incompetent with little respect for the law, while the United States was made to look foolish and unreliable in the eyes of the outside world. Furthermore, the Reagan administration failed miserably to accomplish one of its principal foreign policy purposes, the unseating of the Sandinista regime in Nicaragua. As Reagan left office his policy in Central America had lost credibility and United States influence in the region was at its lowest ebb for many years. Overall, however, it seems likely that the historians will eventually give Reagan's foreign policy fairly high marks.

How does the Reagan presidency measure up to the standard of *party legacy*? Ronald Reagan won two landslide victories for his party and the Republicans also held the Senate for six out of eight years. These were large achievements and who can doubt that Reagan has contributed massively to the revival of Republican party fortunes? On the other hand, it is not possible to speak of an electoral realignment. Realignments involve seismic shifts in the electoral terrain that extend right down through the political system. The Democrats, however, remain firmly in control of the House of Representatives and have reasserted their supremacy in the Senate; they also continue to hold a majority of state governor-ships and, at the last count, controlled sixty-seven out of ninety-eight state legislative chambers. Reagan's electoral success, it would seem, was largely personal rather than party-based. He failed to carry significant numbers of his party's candidates into office with him and even when he campaigned extensively for fellow partisans in the mid-term elections of 1986 the effects of his intervention were slight.

Various extraneous factors help to account for the fact that presidential popularity is no longer easily transferable, and it may be that party realignments have become outdated historical phenomena. Reagan's legacy to his party was, for all that, a for-midable one. George Bush's election in 1988 was much dependent on Reagan. According to a Washington Post/ABC poll in October 1988 voters approving Reagan's presidency supported Bush rather than Dukakis by a margin of 4 to 1. Bush was strongest, further-more, in those areas of the country – the Midwest and the South – where Reagan was most popular.[26] Unlike many other retiring chief executives Reagan was no millstone around the neck of his party's candidate for the presidency. 1988 is not comparable to 1968, 1976 or 1984.

When Reagan assumed office many observers feared for the future of the American political system, including the *state of the presidency*. The polls showed that public confidence in political leaders had been substantially eroded; Congress appeared more fragmented than ever; political parties had been chronically weak-ened and special interests loomed large. The presidency mean-while appeared to have become a broken reed. Nixon had resigned in disgrace and his successor had proved to be pathetically ineffec-tual. Carter entered office with high hopes but was eventually reduced to agonizing in public over his inability to surmount the obstacles to presidential leadership.

As we have seen, Reagan and his staff transformed the situation during his first term. They demonstrated that notwithstanding all the gloom and doom of the late 1970s the political system could be made to work. Congress could be brought to order and the disad-vantages of weak parties overcome, given the right type of leader-ship by the White House. According to Harris polls, public confidence in governmental institutions grew sharply in the early Reagan years, increasing from 22 per cent to 38 per cent between November 1982 and November 1984.[27]

There seems little doubt that during the first six years of his administration Reagan did much to restore faith in the American political system and to repair the credibility of the presidency. What is less clear is how far these gains were negated by the Iran–Contra revelations. Not surprisingly, the public opinion polls after this scandal came to light showed an immediate and dramatic drop in public confidence in White House leadership. Again, according to Harris, 30 per cent of the American people had a great deal of confidence in White House leadership in the fall of 1985 whereas only 19 per cent had expressed similar sentiments in December 1986.[28] Confidence in the presidency was clearly damaged by Iran–Contra, but it seems that this decline by no means completely offset the important gains made in the earlier years. Irrespective of later disasters, Reagan and his team demonstrated then that the system could be made to work and that the presidency is even yet a viable institution. Very few incumbents pass on the presidency in strengthened and revitalized form to their successors, but Reagan, despite some setbacks, would appear to have joined this select group.

Why Reagan succeeded

So far I have considered some criteria that can be used in the assessment of presidents and then applied these to the Reagan case. That analysis supports my contention that Reagan has been one of the more effective of modern presidents. Any attempt to explain why he succeeded where so many others have failed requires more space than is available here, but I will conclude by reviewing briefly some of the more important reasons.

The first point to be made is that Reagan, despite some disadvantages and in marked contrast to his predecessor, enjoyed a considerable amount of luck.[29] Public disillusionment with big government and the thrust of New Deal and Great Society programmes began to set in well before Reagan took office. Keynesian economic policies fell out of favour in the 1970s, and during the same period the public became increasingly nervous about the possibility that the Soviet Union was gaining a military advantage over the United States. The Reagan administration, therefore, was able to exploit currents of elite and popular thinking that had begun their course well before 1981.

Developments within the Soviet Union also presented the Reagan administration with unusual opportunities. In the early 1980s an ageing and decrepit leadership and a weak Soviet economy provided a favourable context for the first, bellicose stage of Reagan's foreign policy. Later, the accession of Gorbachev and other factors facilitated arms agreements and détente and made possible a new era of accommodation with the USSR.

Luck, although important, does not however account for all that occurred during two four-year terms. One of Reagan's great strengths was his sense of vision and his tenacious hold on a few simple beliefs. For most of his life he has been convinced that the scope of government should be as restricted as possible; that taxation is inherently objectionable and that the evil of communism must be vigilantly resisted at every opportunity. Some regard these as excessively simplistic ideas, but they gave the Reagan administration a clear sense of direction, an important quality that other administrations have lacked.[30] Reagan's strength in this regard has been noted by one of his otherwise more trenchant critics, Arthur Schlesinger Jnr:

> Reagan is the triumph of a man who earnestly believed in something. And he believed in it in bad times as well as good. He went up and down the country expounding his gospel, and eventually the cycle turned from public purpose to private purpose, and it was his time. I don't think it was a triumph of packaging; I think it was a triumph of commitment. Substantive commitment. Reagan, whatever he did, got where he is by not compromising on his convictions whatever the polls said. I think that Reagan is proof of the power of conviction politics.[31]

As this quotation suggests, Reagan was one of the most intensely ideological of presidents. On the other hand, he displayed a capacity to give way, to compromise when it became necessary to do so. As another commentator put it, Reagan:

> demonstrated an unerring sense of just how far to go. This is an invaluable, indeed an essential, political skill. A leader in a democracy must present himself as a person of firm principles. He or she must, however compromise those principles in order to govern.

A leader without any guiding principles is spineless and aimless; one who will never bend them is a fanatic. The successful statesman is the one who can navigate between the two extremes, earning a reputation for being principled but not bull-headed. Mr. Reagan has that reputation. His predecessor did not.[32]

Reagan's firm but flexible stances in conjunction with some attractive personal qualities combined to make him exceptionally formidable in the crucial role of dealing with members of the legislature. Paranoid and self-important congressmen and senators who remembered being bullied by Lyndon Johnson, glowered at by Richard Nixon and intellectually upstaged by Jimmy Carter responded more positively to Reagan's style. His relaxed, non-specific, congenial, light-hearted and unassuming manner put visitors to the Oval Office at their ease and made him an unusually effective negotiator on behalf of his policies.[33]

The importance of Reagan's modesty in explaining his popularity both with the public and the political elite should not be underestimated. George Reedy has written convincingly about the corrupting, court-like atmosphere of the White House, where a president is treated like a quasi-monarch and is surrounded by sycophants only too willing to flatter their master's ego.[34] Unlike many of his predecessors, however, Reagan appeared to be relatively immune to such blandishments. Even after some years in the White House his feet remained on the ground; as Jeane Kirkpatrick said, 'He doesn't treat himself like a statue of himself.'[35] Reagan's benign, non-threatening, modest manner was particularly appropriate to an anti-authority political culture and a political system where the chief executive can rarely command other political leaders but must constantly negotiate with them.

Since the beginning of the twentieth century presidents have sought to overcome resistance to their wishes in Congress by direct appeals to the people. They have used their office, in the words of Theodore Roosevelt, as a 'bully pulpit'. For those who can master it television has much enhanced these possibilities. In fact, few presidents have been effective on television, but Reagan was a notable exception; in set-piece situations at least, he displayed outstanding ability in this role. He was rightly dubbed the 'Great Communicator' and his exceptional talents in this area enabled him to mobilize popular support behind his policies and successfully pressure recalcitrant members of Congress into cooperation. Testimony to President Reagan's ability to use television to bring Congress into line has been provided by former Senator Laxalt: 'While Reagan very often could not convince [members of the legislature] on given major policy issues,' he said, 'they'd better not cross him because he'd get on television and appeal to their constituencies and build up enormous constituent pressure. . . On issue after issue, I saw Reagan change the complexion of Congress on key votes because he had that capability.'[36]

In the past it has been assumed that presidential leadership required a chief executive to immerse himself in the detail of policy-making in the manner of a Wilson, a Roosevelt or a Johnson. The example of Eisenhower, and the subsequent research into his presidency, suggested otherwise and pointed to the advantages of a president acting as a chairman of the board – that is to say, setting the general directions of policy but then delegating the details to his staff. Standing back from the detail has important advantages: it protects the president from the odium that may arise when policies fail, enabling him to preserve his personal popularity and to retain his position as symbolic leader of the nation.[37]

Ronald Reagan provided further support for such a strategy. In the media he came to be known as the Teflon President, and his readiness to delegate extensively to his staff was one of the strengths of his presidency, although also ultimately a weakness. Cynics might argue that Reagan was always obliged to rely heavily on staff, given his intellectual limitations and a slothful lifestyle. Lou Cannon, however, views the matter more charitably, seeing the inclination to delegate as:

> a reflection of his belief in the virtues of cabinet government and of his confidence that he could select the managers to carry out his policies. By temperament and training, Reagan was simply not a detail man. Even on issues where he was well informed, Reagan chose conspicuously to focus on the broad goals of what he intended to accomplish and leave the details to others.[38]

Given the profound complexity of modern government, the case for delegation stands on its own merits, and there is no doubt that it helps to explain the achievements of Reagan's first term in particular. The success of such an approach, however, is heavily dependent on the calibre of a president's staff. In the early years

Reagan was served by some outstanding senior staff, but, as noted earlier, the possible hazards of delegating were dramatically high-lighted by the Iran–Contra affair.

Reagan's record as President was uneven, of course. Many ob-jectives were not achieved; compromises were often necessary and in the latter days of his presidency he sometimes appeared on our television screens to have become a rather pathetic, marginal, al-most irrelevant figure. For all that, when his record is taken as a whole and set against that of almost anyone else who has held the office in modern times, he emerges as one of the more competent of recent presidents. He and his aides, particularly at the begin-ning, achieved an unusual degree of mastery over the political system and used it to move the country in significantly new dir-ections in both domestic and foreign policy. Reagan, furthermore, gave new life to the presidency as an institution and contributed much to the revitalization of a battered Republican Party. None of this analysis, needless to say, should be interpreted as implying approval of the substance of Reagan's policies; our views on such matters have been treated as irrelevant for the purposes of this exercise.

Those who remain unconvinced of the thesis advanced here should consider the claims of the other contenders for the title of the most effective president since FDR.[39] Presumably Nixon, Ford and Carter can be disposed of without discussion, but what of the others? Truman's stature rests largely on his position as an archi-tect of the policy of containment, but, on the home front, his relations with Congress were appalling and his domestic policy achievements negligible. There may have been more to Eisenhower than we thought and, unlike the others, he had no aspirations towards activism in the realm of domestic policy; however, whatever the reasons, conservative Republicans seeking to roll back the New Deal derived little solace from the Eisenhower era. John Kennedy was not in office long enough to fulfil the promise that some believed he possessed, but his positive achievements were very few. Lyndon Johnson mastered the policy-making apparatus for a while and brought about some im-portant changes; however his dominance was remarkably brief, and eventually he was driven from office, leaving both the presi-dency and his party seriously weakened. The American presidency may well have become an impossible office denying anything more than very limited success to all incumbents; nevertheless, according to the criteria elaborated above, Ronald Reagan has been rather more effective than most.

Notes

1. This chapter is a modified version of my 'Ronald Reagan's Place in History', *Journal of American Studies*, vol. 23, no. 2, August 1989, pp. 269–86.
2. *Man of the House*, Random House, New York, 1987, p. 360.
3. See especially Ch. 4 above.
4. Richard Nathan, 'Institutional Change under Reagan' in John Palmer (ed.), *Perspectives on the Reagan Years*, The Urban Institute Press, Washington DC, 1986, p. 128.
5. Especially for students of politics. According to Frederick M. Watkins political science should be 'concerned not with the potentially infinite content of all public decisions, but with the process by which those decisions are reached'. James C. Charlesworth (ed.), *A Design For Political Science: Scope, Objectives and Methods*, The American Academy of Political and Social Science, Philadelphia, 1966, p. 28.
6. For evidence of such dangers see Walter B. Roettger and Hugh Winebrenner, 'Politics and Political Scientists', *Public Opinion*, September/October 1986, pp. 41–4.
7. Everett Ladd, 'The Brittle Mandate; Electoral Dealignment and the 1980 Election', *Political Science Quarterly*, vol. 96, Spring 1981.
8. John Chubb and Paul Peterson (eds), *The New Directions in American Politics*. Brookings, Washington DC, 1985, p. 21.
9. O'Neill, *Man of the House, op. cit.*, p. 341.
10. *Congressional Quarterly Almanac 1981*, CQ Press, Washington DC, 1982, p. 245; Nathan, *op. cit.*, p. 127.
11. *Budget of the United States Government FY 1990*, US Government Printing Office, Washington DC, 1989, pp. 2–4.
12. *ibid.* pp. 4–4.
13. Ronald Reagan, *An American Life*. Hutchinson, London, 1990. p. 335.
14. *Budget . . .. FY 1990, op. cit.*, pp. 2–9.
15. *ibid.*, pp. 2–14.
16. Paul Peterson and Mark Rom, 'Lower Taxes, More Spending and Budget Deficits' in Charles O. Jones (ed.), *The Reagan Legacy*, Chatham House, New Jersey, 1988, pp. 213–40.
17. Chubb and Peterson, *op. cit.*, p. 25.
18. Weekly Report, 9 August, vol. 44, no. 2, 1797–1801.
19. Harold Seidman and Robert Gilmour, *Politics, Position and Power* (4th edition), Oxford University Press, New York, 1986, p. 127. NB For a fuller discussion of the steps taken by the Reagan Administration see Ch. 4 above.

20. *Revolution*. Harcourt Brace Jovanovich, New York, 1988, p. 438. Anderson was himself one of the 'comrades', although also an academic. In any case his judgement stands on its own merits.

21. 'Reagan and the World: An Awesome Stubborness' in Jones, *op. cit.*, pp. 241–61.

22. *The Sunday Times*, 28 December 1988.

23. *ibid.*

24. *Budget . . .. FY 1990, op. cit.*, pp. 3–9.

25. 'Reagan: Failed Revolutionary', *The Times*, 17 January 1989.

26. *The Washington Post* National Weekly Edition, 17–23 October 1988, p. 36.

27. Seymour Martin Lipset and William Schneider, 'The Confidence Gap During the Reagan Years', *Political Science Quarterly*, vol. 102, Spring 1987, pp. 1–23.

28. *ibid.*

29. See especially Michael Mandelbaum, 'The Luck of the President' in William G. Hyland (ed.), *The Reagan Foreign Policy*, New American Library, New York, 1987, pp. 127–46.

30. David Osborne argues that vision is an essential presidential requirement found in Franklin Roosevelt and Ronald Reagan, but missing from Jimmy Carter and Michael Dukakis. 'On A Clear Day He Can See Massachusetts', *The Washington Post* National Weekly Edition, 25 April–1 May 1988, pp. 24–5.

31. Interview 'Seeing Daylight', *Playboy*, March 1988.

32. Mandelbaum, *op. cit.*

33. See Allen Schick, 'How the Budget Was Won and Lost' in Norman Ornstein (ed.), *President and Congress: Assessing Reagan's First Year*, American Enterprise Institute, Washington DC, 1982.

34. *The Twilight of the Presidency*, New American Library, New York, 1970.

35. Quoted in Lou Cannon, *Reagan*, G. P. Putnam's Sons, New York, 1982, p. 306.

36. Miller Center Report, vol. 6, no. 4, Winter 1990.

37. See Fred Greenstein, *The Hidden-Hand Presidency: Eisenhower as Leader*, Basic Books, New York, 1982.

38. *op. cit.*, p. 375.

39. Sceptics might also refer to Aaron Wildavsky, 'President Reagan as Political Strategist', *Society*, May/June 1987, pp. 56–62. The essence of Wildavsky's argument is that Reagan was a 'superb political strategist'.

9

Conclusions:
The Bush Example

By way of conclusion it will be useful to consider how successful George Bush has been in meeting the challenges of the modern presidency discussed in earlier chapters. To what extent has he been able to overcome the constraints that all presidents face in domestic affairs, and how far has he succeeded in taking advantage of the relatively stronger position of his office in the making of foreign policy? Is Bush best seen as a latter-day Eisenhower? How does his presidential style compare with that of presidents such as Johnson and what are the main differences between his approach and that of his immediate predecessor?

In terms of their background and pre-presidential experience Ronald Reagan and George Bush could hardly have been more different. The former, the child of working-class parents grew up in a succession of small towns in the Midwest. Educated at an obscure, small, church-related college, Reagan's prior political experience was limited to some years as a film industry, trade union leader and two four-year terms as Governor of California. George Bush, by contrast, was the product of a wealthy, Eastern establishment family. His father, Prescott Bush, was an investment banker and a US senator from Connecticut. Bush himself was educated at Phillips Academy, the equivalent of an up-market English public school, and at Yale University. After an abortive attempt to win one of the Texas seats in the US Senate in 1964, Bush's political career began two years later with his election to the US House of Representatives. After two terms in the House, he was successively US Ambassador to the United Nations, chief of the United States Liaison Office in China, Chairman of the Republican National Committee and Director of the CIA before becoming Reagan's Vice President in 1981.[1]   Reagan entered the White House as an outsider totally lacking in national political experience whereas Bush, in running for the presidency in his own right in 1988, could claim lengthy and wide-ranging experience of both Washington politics and international affairs. After a bitter campaign against the Democratic candidate, Michael Dukakis, Bush was elected by a comfortable majority of the popular vote. However, in the 1988 elections to Congress the Republicans lost ground in the Senate and the House making Bush's position *vis-à-vis* the legislature one of the weakest of any new president in the twentieth century.

Despite this major disadvantage Bush initially made a favourably impression on two crucial audiences – the general public and the 'Washington community'. His predecessor had enjoyed great popularity for much of his two terms, but his detached managerial style, particularly after the Iran–Contra debacle, had been the subject of widespread concern. Bush offered an apparently reassuring contrast; he had extensive Washington experience to draw on and this seemed to be reflected in his 'hands-on', professional approach to presidential governance. At the beginning Bush also impressed Democratic leaders in Congress by his low-key, consensual, non-ideological posture, by his willingness to disavow confrontation and to seek a dialogue with the opposition.[2] At this stage at least, a reasonably productive relationship between the White House and Capitol Hill appeared to be in prospect. Furthermore, throughout 1989 Bush stood impressively high in the public opinion polls.[3] The following year, however, was to provide two defining events for the Bush presidency – the budget crisis and the Iraqi invasion of Kuwait – occurrences that brought to the fore the strengths and weaknesses of George Bush's approach to presidential leadership.

The 1990 budget crisis

I noted in Chapter 4 the enormous difficulties that presidents face in the realm of economic policy. The country holds the chief executive primarily responsible for the conduct of economic affairs, but he is denied control of the means whereby policy is made. Monetary and credit policy is determined by an independent regulatory agency, the Federal Reserve System, whereas fiscal policy, with its crucial decisions on taxes and appropriations, is ultimately decided by the legislature. However, even allowing for this impossible situation George Bush was found notably wanting in 1990.

At the Republican National Convention in 1988 the future president, in reflecting on how he would deal with economic policy when he was in the White House had said, 'The Congress will push me to raise taxes, and I'll say no, and they'll push me again, and I'll say to them, "Read my lips; no new taxes."' In line with this famous pledge, constantly repeated throughout the 1988 campaign, Bush, in January 1990, submitted a budget to Congress that contained no significant increases in taxes and indeed provided for a cut in the tax rate on capital gains. By May, however, the President, aware of the fact that Congress would not approve his budget as it stood, was allowing it to become known that he might be prepared to abandon his electoral pledge regarding taxes.[4] Several months later, after protracted and often acrimonious negotiations with congressional leaders of both parties, the administration announced that a package of tax increases and expenditure cuts had been agreed.

The President and his staff now lobbied members of Congress hard and he made a nationally televised address to the people to urge support for the package. He described the notoriously massive budget deficit as, 'a cancer gnawing away at our nation's economic health' and warned, 'if we fail to enact this agreement our economy will falter, markets may tumble and recession will follow.' In a clear attempt to appeal over the heads of congressmen to their constituents Bush said, 'This is the first time in my presidency that I have made an appeal like this to you, tell your congressmen and senators you support this agreement.'[5]

Despite these dire warnings and exhortations the House of Representatives refused by a large margin to ratify the budget compromise that had been worked out between the White House and congressional leaders. The House as a whole voted it down on 5 October by 254–179; the Democrats opposed it 149–108 while the Republicans voted against 105–71.[6] Many Democrats opposed the agreement because they could not accept proposed cuts in welfare programmes and did not believe that the suggested tax increases hit better-off Americans sufficiently hard. Conservative Republicans on the other hand were mortified by the President's willingness to renege on his repeated pledge not to increase taxes.

In the days immediately following this humiliating set-back President Bush, in an abortive effort to frighten Congress into submission, vetoed a continuing resolution designed to prevent the shutting down of essential government services now that authority for spending money had elapsed. In addition, Bush, as presidents are inclined to do in such circumstances, strove to place all the blame for the situation on Congress. He said, 'I think it's very important that our able team, in who I have total confidence, stay in touch' (with House and Senate negotiators trying to put together a new agreement), 'But we're not going to force our way in. This is the business of the Congress. The American people know that. They know that the president doesn't pass the budget, and doesn't vote on all this stuff. It's the Congress that does it.'[7] While, of course, factually correct this statement ignored the President's clear obligation to provide effective leadership in the making of economic policy.

As the crisis rumbled on and negotiators struggled to reach agreement Bush further damaged his credibility by vacillating wildly on a major issue, changing his mind four times within a few days on whether he would accept an increase in income taxes for the affluent in exchange for his high-priority aim of a reduction in capital gains tax.[8] Eventually, after more acrimony and much re-crimination a budget was cobbled together that provided for an increase in taxes over the next five years of $140 billion coupled with various cuts in domestic and defence expenditures. This second set of proposals passed the House by 228–200 and the Senate by 54–45 on 27 October 1990.[9]

The budget battle of 1990 appeared to reveal a president badly lacking in the skills and inclinations required to bring an extraordinarily fractious political system to order. There were several dimensions to this presidential disaster. In order to get negotiations underway with Congress in the first place the President had abandoned the central plank of his 1988 campaign, thereby seriously undermining his credibility with the public at large and badly splitting the Republican Party. The negotiations with congressional leaders were made needlessly acrimonious by the heavy-handed, insensitive tactics of senior members of the Bush administration – John Sununu, the Chief of Staff and Richard Darman, the Director of the Office of Management and Budget.[10]

The President's attempt to use his office as a 'bully pulpit' in the manner of a Theodore Roosevelt or a Ronald Reagan backfired badly. Thus, after Bush's televised appeal to Americans asking them to phone or write to their law-makers in support of the original package it was reported that an overwhelming majority of those voters who contacted their members of Congress advised them to vote against, rather than for, the President on this issue.[11]

It is evident that Bush's authority was seriously weakened both in the country and in the 'Washington community' by the failure of the House of Representatives on 5 October 1990 to pass the package that he had so clearly placed the full weight of his office behind. The House was, of course, controlled by the opposition, but what was especially damaging was the heavy vote against the package by members of the President's own party. An impression was created during this critical test of presidential leadership of a chief executive who was chronically indecisive and bereft of serious convictions

In addition to reams of severely critical comment in the media Bush, after the reverse on 5 October 1990, suffered a sharp drop in his public opinion poll rankings and leading members of the Washington community began to speculate on the dire consequences of these events for his presidency. Robert Strauss, a former chairman of the Democratic National Committee, said to the press, 'You know and I know that when they smell blood in the water, they go in this town.' Meanwhile Jody Powell, who, as President Carter's press secretary, had first-hand experience of the weakening of a presidency said, 'Any time you get beat, it makes people inclined to think they can beat you again.'[12] As Powell and Strauss knew only too well, presidents are inherently vulnerable political leaders and any sign of weakness will excite and encourage that host of potential enemies lurking in the bureaucracy, the pressure groups, Congress and elsewhere, thereby increasing the chief executive's vulnerability even further.

Early in his presidency Bush had demonstrated certain strengths, but the budget crisis exposed two serious weaknesses. First, the ignominious failure of his attempt to appeal for support through a televised address to the nation demonstrated George Bush's inability to master *the* medium of political communication of the present age. This is a crippling disadvantage for any modern president who, if he is to govern effectively, must constantly resort to television as a means of garnering popular support for his policies. Second, Bush revealed on this occasion his lack of the guiding beliefs and convictions needed to give his presidency a sense of direction; he almost casually abandoned his pledge on taxes leaving himself open to the allegation that he was an opportunist rather than a real leader; a politician lacking in courage and substance.

The Gulf crisis

The budget imbroglio of 1990 was a presidential leadership disaster whereas George Bush's response to the crisis in the Persian Gulf that began in August of the same year came to be widely perceived as a leadership triumph. As the war came to an end with Iraq's ejection from Kuwait, pollsters established that nine out of ten Americans approved of President Bush's conduct of his office and he was received rapturously when he addressed a joint session of Congress on 6 March 1991.

Over a period of seven fraught, difficult months Bush provided what many observers clearly regarded as an impressive demonstration of foreign policy crisis leadership comparable to that of John Kennedy in the Cuban missile crisis.[13] The crisis began on 2 August 1990 with the Iraqi invasion of Kuwait. President Bush immediately condemned the invasion as 'naked aggression' and demanded 'immediate and unconditional withdrawal'.[14] In addition he issued an executive order banning all trade with Iraq and freezing Iraqi and Kuwaiti assets and sought support at the United Nations. With the United States taking the lead, the Security Council voted 14–0 in favour of Resolution 660 which condemned Iraq, urged a cease-fire and demanded the withdrawal of Iraqi troops from Kuwait. Most significantly those voting for the resolution included the Soviet Union, formerly a close ally and supplier of arms to Iraq. A few days later a second Security Council resolution was passed by a vote of 13–0 imposing wide-ranging sanctions against Iraq.

For several days after the Iraqi invasion President Bush considered his options. At the forefront of his concern was not only the invasion of Kuwait, but the real possibility that Saddam would now turn his attention to the militarily weak but massively oil-rich Saudi Arabia. General Colin Powell, the chairman of the Joint Chiefs of Staff, advised the President that if US forces were to be deployed it would need to be on a massive scale, but, on the other hand, there were many potential difficulties to be considered. The United States had no military bases in the area and it was doubtful whether Saudi Arabia, a rigidly conservative and devoutly Muslim state, would welcome the presence of American troops on its soil. Even if that obstacle could be overcome, US service personnel would encounter harsh, totally unfamiliar, desert conditions and would face an enormous, battle-hardened Iraqi army. It was entirely possible that the Iraqis would resort to chemical warfare and early contingents of American troops would be desperately vulnerable prior to the inevitably later arrival of tanks and other heavy weaponry. Finally, above all else, there was good reason to believe that the people of the United States would soon lose the political will for what might well be a protracted and difficult war with many American casualties.[15]

Despite the tremendous risks involved President Bush decided that a substantial deployment of American forces, as suggested by Powell, was required. Egged on at a crucial moment by the British Prime Minister, Mrs Thatcher, the President convinced himself that there could be no question of sitting still while Iraq incorporated Kuwait as a first step towards becoming the dominant power in the Middle East with control over 56 per cent of the world's oil supplies. As Bush saw it, Saddam Hussein was a nasty tyrant comparable to Hitler and allowing his aggression to go unpunished would be tantamount to appeasement and an encouragement to others with similar ambitions; the United States not only had a responsibility to lead the free world in this crisis, it was also the only power with the military resources required to force Saddam to relinquish his hold on Kuwait.[16] Having decided how to proceed, the President moved first to gain the cooperation of Saudi Arabia as a preliminary to arranging for the dispatch of what would soon become a force of 210,000 troops to that country. In tandem with these steps Bush and his staff worked tirelessly to isolate Saddam Hussein in the international community. To that end they continued to seek favourable votes in the United Nations and brought together a vast, unprecedented coalition that embraced a host of unlikely collaborators including not only the Soviet Union, but also Syria, Iran and Israel.

In this first phase of the Gulf crisis Bush had given an undeniably impressive display of leadership. In circumstances of great difficulty he had been bold and decisive and his past experience and his inclination for telephone diplomacy proved to be formidable assets in the process of coalition building:

> The intimate knowledge of world leaders and world politics that he had acquired during his years as ambassador to the UN, envoy to Beijing and CIA director helped him forge an unprecedented international alliance. Throughout, Bush . . . displayed an exquisite sensitivity to diplomatic nuance and the need for subtle compromise – and sometimes outright bribes – required to bring together such mutually suspicious bedfellows as Syria, Israel, Iran and the Soviet Union. His performance went beyond competence to sheer mastery.[17]

For three months after the invasion of Kuwait the Bush administration remained ostensibly committed to a defensive strategy – a programme of sanctions combined with the deployment of substantial military force as a guard against further aggression. By the end of October, however, a fundamental change of strategy had taken place. At some point Bush and his closest advisers decided that sanctions would take too long to have the required effect, making it necessary to prepare for a possible war. In accordance with this decision, on 8 November Bush announced that he had 'directed the Secretary of Defense to increase the size of US forces committed to Desert Shield to ensure that the coalition has an adequate offensive military option should that be necessary to achieve our common goal.'[18]

In other words, without consulting with the UN, with the allies or with Congress, the President gave the order for a doubling of the number of US troops in Saudi Arabia to a figure in excess of 400,000. Given this level of commitment war now became virtually certain short of a most unlikely total Iraqi withdrawal. Who could doubt at this moment that the President was a leader of great power and what price the constitutional rights of Congress in committing the United States to war?

This pattern of events is relevant to the discussion in Chapter 5 where I argued that, whatever the Constitution says, presidential paramountcy in national security crisis situations was not only inevitable, but was also supported by a large body of precedent. Like Lincoln, FDR and many other presidents Bush in 1990 believed that he had the right to act as he saw fit in defence of the national security without waiting for congressional approval.

Thomas Foley, the Speaker of the US House of Representatives, has confirmed that the executive branch made no attempt to ascertain the legislature's view on the momentous matter of doubling US forces in the Gulf; he later mournfully recounted on television how he had been informed of the President's intention:

> There was a call from Secretary Cheney in the morning – not very elaborate, just an announcement – the Administration was doubling the forces – this, of course, had never been discussed with the congressional leadership group that had been visiting the White House in recent weeks.[19]

Furthermore, as the Bush administration moved towards war against Iraq, supporting resolutions from the House and the Senate were sought for political rather than constitutional reasons. These were agreed on 12 January 1991 by votes of 250–183 in the House and 52–47 in the Senate. However, in seeking congressional authorization the executive was doing no more than going through the motions as Richard Cheney, the Secretary of Defense, has made clear: 'We always believed that the President had the constitutional authority to go forward and to send the troops into combat and liberate Kuwait and that we did not need an additional vote from Congress.'[20] Similarly, the President himself said after the war, 'It was argued I can't go to war without the Congress. And I was saying, I have the authority to do this.'[21]

In short in 1990–91, as on so many occasions in the past, a president took the United States into war with little regard for the formal constitutional rights of the legislature. Moreover, leaving aside a few isolated rumblings of discontent from individual members of Congress, there was no significant objection to the administration's actions on *constitutional* grounds from the legislature, the Courts or the American people. It seems that irrespective of the ruminations of constitutional scholars and the occasional, ritual protests of legislators, Americans, in general, have come to accept that the president must be accorded the freedom to commit US forces to military action in response to his perceptions of threats to the national security.

On 29 November 1990 the UN Security Council passed a resolution authorizing the use of force against Iraq if it had not removed its forces from Kuwait by 15 January 1991. The war began on 16 January 1991 with the launch of massive bombing raids against Iraq and Kuwait. Five weeks later coalition troops began a ground offensive and the war came to an end a few days later. Not surprisingly, the swift and comprehensive routing of Saddam Hussein was rapturously received in the United States. It appeared to confirm American military and technological superiority and to provide evidence of President Bush's outstanding skill as a leader – those approving of his presidency soared to 92 per cent in one poll, the highest figure ever recorded.[22]

The contrasts with the last occasion when the United States had despatched massive military force abroad – the war in Vietnam – could hardly have been more striking. As we saw in Chapter 7, Lyndon Johnson's lack of experience in international affairs had been a grave disadvantage and the Vietnam conflict turned into a long-drawn-out affair bedevilled by uncertain objectives, bringing heavy US casualties and conducted in the face of widespread international opprobrium. Rather than immediately committing large forces to Vietnam, Johnson had begun by sending relatively small numbers which were subsequently surreptitiously escalated over several years until they reached half a million plus. Johnson had also erred in concentrating the key decisions on the war in his own hands and immersing himself in the detail of military planning. Consequently, when the war began to go badly wrong the President was held personally responsible and his public prestige collapsed.

George Bush and his advisers were keenly aware of Johnson's mistakes as well as those made by President Carter during the Iranian hostage crisis of 1979–81. They also assumed that, particularly after the trauma of Vietnam, the American people lacked the stomach for a long-drawn-out conflict. If there was to be a war it needed to be short and sharp and, to accomplish that, a wholehearted commitment of troops on a massive scale was required. Saddam Hussein made a most plausible enemy and, as a short-term objective, the intention of ejecting him from Kuwait was undeniably clear cut. The UN threw its support behind the United States from the start and President Bush was able to draw on his experience in putting together a vast, disparate anti-Saddam alliance. The President made no attempt to micro-manage the war, which, in any case, lasted for only a few weeks and incurred few American casualties – 148 dead, of whom 38 were killed by friendly fire.[23]

In taking the measure of Bush's achievement in leading his country during the Gulf crisis account needs to be taken of the large element of luck that he enjoyed. As I have argued in previous chapters, good fortune is often an essential ingredient of presidential accomplishment – the successes of Franklin Roosevelt and Ronald Reagan were, for example, heavily dependent on luck. In the case of Bush he was very fortunate, on the international scene at least, in 1990–91.

The UN for instance was, at this point, in a position to play a central role in pressurizing Saddam Hussein and in cementing the international coalition that made possible his ejection from Kuwait. But it had only recently become possible for the UN to take on such a role. For the previous four decades it had been racked by ideological division, with the Soviet Union routinely using its veto in the Security Council to defeat Western initiatives, and vice versa. The General Assembly, meanwhile, became by the 1970s a bastion of Third-World and other powers generally hostile to the United States. As a consequence, many Americans, particularly conservatives, were deeply sceptical of the value of the United Nations. One such was Vice President George Bush, who wrote in his autobiography in 1987: 'Clearly, the United Nations has much to be said for it, but it still has a long way to go before it can ever achieve its early promise as "the world's best hope for peace".'[24]

By 1990, however, the Cold War was at an end, the Warsaw Pact had disintegrated and Soviet–American relations had never been more amicable. In these new circumstances the Bush administration was able to make the maximum use of the UN in its efforts to drive Iraq out of Kuwait. During the course of the Gulf crisis the Security Council passed a dozen resolutions hostile to Iraq, ranging from Resolution 660 on 2 August 1990 demanding immediate withdrawal, to 678 on 29 November 1990 authorizing the use of force, if that should be necessary.[25]

In the past the Middle East had been a region of intense superpower rivalry and any move made by presidents from Truman to Reagan had to take careful account of how the USSR might respond. No such difficulty attended the Gulf crisis. Notwithstanding the Soviet Union's earlier support for Iraq it now gave US policy-makers a free hand. This new posture can hardly be explained as a result of Bush's diplomacy – it arose in large part from the for-tuitous accession of Gorbachev and the internal and external weakness of the Soviet Union, all developments which predated the Bush presidency.

President Bush was also fortunate to face a crass and incompe-tent foe in Saddam Hussein. The Iraqi invasion was instantly the subject of condemnation throughout the world and there must be doubts about the competence of a national leader who causes his country to become such a pariah in the international community. Even Nazi Germany was never as isolated as Iraq became in 1990–1 with overwhelming votes against it, not only in the Security Council but also in the General Assembly where, for example, it was condemned by a vote of 132–1 on 3 December 1990 and by 144–1 on 18 December 1990.[26]

For reasons already mentioned, it was important that the United States did not become bogged down in a long Vietnam-type war with heavy casualties. However, contrary to the pre-war hype re-garding the might and prowess of the Iraqi army, it soon became apparent that Bush and his allies had the good fortune to be facing military forces much smaller than anticipated and singularly lack-ing in the will to fight. Various sources have suggested that far from 'a million man army', as Secretary of Defense Cheney and others maintained, Saddam may have had less than 200,000 troops in the field facing coalition forces in excess of 550,000 and in pos-session of vast technological superiority. When the war got under way the ill-equipped, demoralized, ramshackle army of an im-poverished Third World country was, not surprisingly, no match for the overwhelming weight of the American-led coalition.[27]

It is evident from the above that President Bush enjoyed a con-siderable amount of luck during this crisis. In addition, any com-plete assessment of his leadership must go beyond the sequence of events that extended from the invasion at the beginning of August to the cessation of hostilities at the end of the following February. It has, for instance, been argued that the Bush administration failed to heed many warning signs of a crisis developing throughout the first half of 1990 and even gave Saddam Hussein reason to believe that the United States would not intervene if he attacked Kuwait.[28]

Such an attack had been a possibility for some time. Although the two countries were temporarily allied during the Iraq/Iran war, there were long-standing areas of dispute between them. The mutual border was arbitrarily, and none too precisely, drawn by the British in the 1920s and, in particular, two islands, Warba and Bubiyan, controlling Iraq's access to the sea, had been given to Kuwait. For years this had rankled with the Iraqis and after the Iraq/Iran war ended relations with Kuwait deteriorated even further. In May 1990, Saddam Hussein complained bitterly that by grossly exceeding its OPEC oil production quota, Kuwait had severely depressed the price of oil, with disastrous consequences for Iraq. 'You are wrecking our means of sustenance,' Saddam told the Kuwaitis, 'and if you cut people's means of sustenance, it is equivalent to cutting their neck and killing them.'[29]

Aggrieved by long-standing border disputes and the violation of OPEC rules, Saddam, in 1990, made numerous belligerent statements, but the Bush administration, preoccupied with events elsewhere in the world, gave mixed signals in response. Thus, eight days before the Iraqi invasion Ambassador April Glaspie, in a meeting with Saddam, assured him that the United States wanted better relations with Iraq and went on 'we have no opinion on the Arab–Arab conflicts, like your border disagreement with Kuwait.'[30] Ms Glaspie later claimed that she also said that the United States would protect its interests in the area and that Saddam had asked her to assure President Bush that he had no intention of attacking Kuwait.[31] Neverthelesss the comments of Glaspie and other administration spokespeople at this time suggested that the United States would not interfere if Iraq seized Kuwait.[32]

It is arguable, in other words, that a more alert administration might have taken steps to prevent the invasion before it occurred, thereby preventing a conflict which may have done wonders for American national pride, but had disastrous consequences for Kuwait and for the Iraqi people, including an enormous loss of life. No one knows just how many Iraqi soldiers and civilians were killed, but it seems that the figure probably lies somewhere between 100,000 and 200,000.

There are also reasons for questioning whether the United States and its allies resorted to the use of force prematurely. Many of those members of Congress who voted on 12 January 1991 against the resolutions authorizing the President to take military action were of the view that more time should have been allowed for sanctions, diplomatic pressure and the *threat* of military action to take effect – a strategy that might have avoided an appalling loss of life and much other devastation. One leading congressman who took this view was Lee Hamilton, a member of the US House Foreign Affairs Committee and Chairman of its Sub Committee on Europe and the Middle East who, immediately after the war, also drew attention to the need for a long-term perspective on these matters:

> Victory should better be judged in the longer term. . . . Our military success will be of little lasting value if we do not fare well with postwar political and economic challenges: containing Iraq, rebuilding Kuwait, dampening calls for revenge and retribution, promoting a fairer distribution of wealth, and encouraging democracy and more openness in the closed societies of the Gulf. We need to work with regional states on a security structure to begin controlling arms and to reduce the flow of advanced arms, weapons of mass destruction and ballistic missiles to the Middle East. We must also return to the search for peace between Israelis and Arabs. Without progress on these issues, our military victory will be tarnished.[33]

As this is written a year later it is clear that Hamilton's hopes, which were widely shared, are far from realization in full. Iraq is contained by sheer weakness, but Saddam Hussein remains in office and continues to torment the Kurds. Kuwait is being rebuilt, but revenge and retribution has been visited on the hapless Palestinians living in that country. Despite various assurances no discernible progress has been made towards the democratization of Kuwait or in the opening up of other closed societies in the region. Arms continue to flow into the area and peace between Israel and the Arabs is hardly any closer now than it was a year ago.

There can be no doubt that George Bush displayed leadership of a high order during the Gulf crisis. With the advantage of hindsight it is easy to be critical, to emphasize the elements of good fortune and to downplay the hazards that had to be negotiated and the desperately difficult choices that the President alone was ultimately responsible for. Under fire Bush appears to have remained calm, resolute and decisive. He stated his objective in August, 'this aggression will not stand' and drove unflinchingly towards it, declining to be deflected by those who looked for compromise, wanted more time for sanctions to work, or shrank from the probability of large-scale bloodshed.

Having said that, it is the case that this was a narrowly focused demonstration of effective leadership that, to be seen in its best light, has to be isolated from what went before and what has happened since. Without question, Bush succeeded brilliantly in getting from point A to point B; he began by denouncing Saddam's aggression and then seven months later presided over his expulsion from Kuwait. This was an important achievement, discouraging would-be aggressors around the world, doing much to revive American national self-confidence and allowing the President to claim with some apparent justification: 'By God, we've kicked the Vietnam syndrome once and for all.'[34] Nevertheless this one, important, yet limited, success has to be set against Bush's distinctly unimpressive record as a leader when taken as a whole.

Presidential leadership

As previous chapters have shown, given the nature of the American political system, effective presidential leadership is extremely difficult to accomplish and is especially problematical in domestic affairs. Effectiveness in a chief executive in the sense used here means his ability to get Congress, the bureaucracy and other leaders to accept his policies. As we have seen, a few twentieth-century presidents have performed relatively well in this regard, including Theodore Roosevelt, Woodrow Wilson, Franklin Roosevelt, Lyndon Johnson and Ronald Reagan. At this juncture there would seem to be little chance of Bush joining this select group.

Every new president enjoys a 'honeymoon' period at the beginning and Bush was no exception even though he faced a Congress where the Democrats were in a majority in both houses. Bush, however, failed to exploit the opportunities available at the outset of his presidency. His administration was accused of 'hitting the ground crawling' and his first year was bereft of significant legislative breakthroughs. Indeed, according to the *Congressional Quarterly* in 1989 'George Bush fared worse in Congress than any other first-year president elected in the post war era.'[35]

Earlier in this chapter I discussed Bush's faltering and unimpressive leadership during the budget crisis of 1990, but in the spring of

1991 his success in the Gulf war appeared to offer a new 'window of opportunity' for achievement on the domestic front. Shortly after the war ended Richard Fenno, an eminent American political scientist, noted that the President had:

> an historic opportunity to define his goals. We've had six weeks in which he set very clear objectives and exercised very strong leadership. Now is the time for him to expend some of the popularity he has gained in pursuit of a comparably large cause at home.'[36]

Three months later commentators were bemoaning the fact that once again Bush had missed the chance to make domestic policy gains. Such criticisms were to be expected from the opposition, but similar complaints were voiced by Republicans. Kevin Phillips, for example, said, 'The moment when Bush could have done something existed in March. A lot of possibility slipped away after that. . . He can try to promote a set of domestic policies now . . . but we all know that is not his speciality.' Even Jack Kemp, the Secretary of Housing and Urban Development, obliquely criticized the President's lack of activity in domestic policy when he said: 'The White House is the epicenter of national policy. There are problems of poverty and despair and economic decline in many people's neighborhoods which the president has both a moral and political obligation to address.'[37]

Elsewhere in this book I have stressed the importance of avoiding the tendency prevalent among so many American political scientists of evaluating presidents according to criteria that will inevitably find conservative incumbents wanting. Presidents are entitled to be judged on their own terms. Eisenhower, for instance, doubted the value of attempting to solve the problems of society by passing laws; he was deeply sceptical of the New Deal and all its works and believed he had a responsibility to hold the line against further change in that direction.

Bush clearly shares some common ground with Eisenhower. He similarly prefers to work behind the scenes; he is also a Republican facing a largely Democratic Congress and one would not expect him to be a reforming president in the mould of FDR or Lyndon Johnson. Nevertheless there is no evidence that Bush shares Eisenhower's minimalist attitude towards legislation. He has not equated the present condition of the United States with the 1950s and is aware of the existence of many problem areas at the present time – the economy, crime, education, drugs, the environment, health care and poverty. Periodically, the President touches on these matters in his speeches and expresses an interest in remedial legislation, yet he has consistently failed to provide the sort of sustained and skilful leadership in domestic affairs that he demonstrated in removing Saddam from Kuwait.

How is this dichotomy to be explained? At a superficial level we have Bush's often expressed preference for dealing with foreign policy rather than domestic matters, but the reasons surely go deeper than that.[38] At the root of the matter is a major weakness in George Bush's style of leadership – his chronic lack of consistently held beliefs and convictions.

In the previous chapter I highlighted as one of Reagan's strengths his tenacious hold on a few simple beliefs. Throughout his political career he remained firmly convinced of the need to minimize the scope of government wherever possible; he never lost his conviction that taxation was inherently objectionable or that communism was an irredeemable evil. These rather simplistic beliefs, coupled with Reagan's insufficiently recognized toughness of purpose, had the effect of providing him with a compass, with a sense of direction, or, to put it another way, with the vision required for effective presidential leadership. Other presidents and presidential contenders have notably lacked this quality, including Jimmy Carter, Michael Dukakis and George Bush.[39]

Throughout Bush's career he has been criticized for lacking vision; he has at times denied the charge and on other occasions insisted that vision was, in any case, not necessary.[40] As he began his attempt to win the presidency in 1988 Bush insisted, 'I am a practical man. I like what's real. I'm not much for the airy and the abstract. I like what works. I am not a mystic, and I do not yearn to lead a crusade.'[41] It is evident that Bush's approach to his job is that of a pragmatic problem-solver who likes to deal with each question as it arises on an *ad hoc* basis rather than trying to fit it into an overarching vision of how the world should be. There is clearly a positive side to such an approach; in the right circumstances Bush can appear to be a thoughtful statesman rather than a mindless ideologue.

Nevertheless the lack of firm beliefs and convictions and of some sense of where he is attempting to lead his country would seem to be a crippling liability in a president. Given the mind-boggling complexity of the American political system, a president without some guiding principles, who is an entirely reactive leader, is unlikely to be able to bring that system to order.

Complaints about George Bush's lack of vision while in the White House have by no means been restricted to his political opponents. Republican congressman Dick Armey from Bush's own state of Texas complained in 1991: 'This administration hasn't developed a coherent and, more important, consistent message. The American people don't believe the Bush administration is guided by a set of sincere, deeply felt beliefs that will never be compromised. Everything seems negotiable.' An unidentified administration official meanwhile was quoted as saying, 'Reagan was a man of conviction and everyone knew where he stood. Right now you can't say that about George.'[42] In early 1992 the conservative columnist George F. Will remarked caustically: 'The administration is sharply defined as an administration without definition. . . Because Bush on the stump expresses synthetic sentiments in garbled syntax Americans often wonder what he means. The answer may be that he doesn't mean anything very much.'[43] Even Bush's mentor Ronald Reagan was widely reported in March 1992 to have remarked privately that President Bush 'doesn't seem to stand for anything'.[44]

A political leader who appears to have no convictions, who treats every issue as negotiable, runs the danger of being perceived as an opportunist, as a man prepared to say anything to get elected. George Bush's willingness to take that risk was made remarkably clear during the 1992 primary season. In a radio broadcast the President went so far as to say that his abandonment of his 'no new taxes' pledge in the budget crisis of 1990 was the worst mistake of his presidency: 'Listen. If I had to do that over, I wouldn't do it. Look at all the flak its taking.' Bush admitted that Republican voters were 'just overwhelmed by the fact that I went for a tax increase' and were giving him 'political grief' as a consequence.[45] This astonishing second U-turn on economic policy, apparently primarily motivated by electoral concerns, seriously damaged the President's credibility as he began his quest for re-election in 1992.

On a range of other issues the President has, throughout his career, appeared to change his views for reasons of political expediency. In 1964 he contested a Texas seat in the US Senate as a Goldwater conservative; he virulently denounced the 1964 Civil

Rights Act and adopted other positions hostile to civil rights.[46] Two years later Bush ran for the US House of Representatives and modified his views to take account of a rather different constituency. Now, in reference to his 1964 campaign, he admitted to a church minister: 'You know, John, I took some of the far right positions to get elected. I hope I never do it again. I regret it.'[47]

Elected to the House in 1966 with an estimated 60–70 per cent of the black vote Bush shed the conservative positions he had taken earlier to join the moderate wing of the Republican party. Having opposed open housing during the 1966 election Bush broke with the Republican leadership in the House to vote for the 1968 open housing bill. In 1970 Bush campaigned for racial quotas and when he ran for the Republican nomination in 1980 he continued to project himself as a moderate, expressing regret at having opposed the 1964 Civil Rights Act. Once he had been selected as Reagan's running mate however, 'Bush tied his fortunes to the conservative wing of the [Republican] party, and to its racial politics.' This swing back to the right on racial questions reached its climax in 1988 with Bush, in campaigning for the presidency, crudely exploiting racial prejudice with the infamous Willie Horton television commercial.[48]

Bush's weaving back and forth on the civil rights issue as electoral considerations require is neatly summarized by Jefferson Morley:

> The George Bush of 1964, 1988, and 1990 campaigned against federal civil rights legislation, evoked the specter of black violence against whites and criticized racial quotas. Between 1966 and 1980, on the other hand, George Bush refused to appeal to the white backlash, supported federal civil rights legislation, and favored using federal power to promote black economic empowerment.[49]

George Bush's position on abortion has been similarly inconsistent over the years. As a congressman in the the late 1960s he became very enthusiastic about the virtues of family planning, was appointed chairman of a House task force on the subject, and appeared to support the liberalization of abortion laws.[50] In the 1980 primary campaign Bush, as a moderate, opposed the idea of introducing an anti-abortion clause into the Constitution, but abandoned this position when he became Reagan's running mate. By 1988 Bush had become a fervent opponent of *Roe* v. *Wade*, the US Supreme Court decision legalizing abortion.[51]

Complaints about George Bush's lack of clear-cut convictions are by no means restricted to domestic issues. Even in foreign policy, supposedly the President's strongest suit, he has been repeatedly charged with lacking consistent beliefs and having no vision. During the Gulf crisis he appeared to have a narrowly defined objective, the removal of the Iraqis from Kuwait, but many critics berated him for failing to place that purpose in a wider framework of long-term goals.[52]

Many of those critics were also unimpressed by President Bush's lurching away from his preoccupation with foreign affairs in late 1991 and early 1992 in response to public opinion poll findings and the imminence of a campaign for re-election.[53] Richard Nixon, for example, in a document entitled 'How to lose the Cold War' accused the President of abysmally failing to respond adequately to the challenges faced by the collapse of the Soviet Union.[54] In the same vein and in reference to the same problem area *Time* magazine questioned the President's foreign policy leadership accusing him of being 'unwilling to use his position of authority to explain the historic moment to Americans and persuade them to act accordingly. Under the pressure of election politics, Bush has led from the rear.'[55]

Bush's lack of convictions coupled with his notorious inability to express himself intelligibly in public has made him a poor communicator and weakened his presidency accordingly. President Bush's tendency towards garbled syntax was spectacularly revealed in his reply to a high school student who had asked whether the President would seek ideas overseas to improve American education:

> Well, I'm going to kick that one right into the end zone of the Secretary of Education. But, yes, we have all – he travels a great deal, goes abroad. We have a lot of people in the department that does that. We're having an international – this is not as much education as dealing with the environment – a big international conference coming up. And we get it all the time – exchanges of ideas. But I think we've got – we set out there – and I want to give credit to your Governor McWherter and to your former Governor Lamar Alexander – we've gotten great ideas for a national goals program from – in this country – from the governors who were responding to, maybe, the principal of your high school for heaven's sake.[56]

Bush has made many such peculiar, ungrammatical and incomprehensible remarks on public occasions, but there is nothing especially new about garbled comments falling from the presidential mouth. I referred in Chapter 6 to President Eisenhower's propensity for mangled syntax and the earlier belief that this damaged his reputation among the all-important Washington community. But as we saw, revisionists have argued that Eisenhower's evasive and confused answers at press conferences were conceivably part of a sophisticated leadership strategy designed to protect his options. It may be that Bush has sometimes similarly used language instrumentally, but that hardly explains the incessant stream of unintelligible comments.

Elsewhere in this book I have argued that communication skills are essential if a president is to gain mastery over the American political system. Chief executives gifted with the ability to communicate can develop a rapport with the people, which can become a major presidential resource invaluable for pressurizing Congress and others into cooperation with the White House. Some presidents have been devastatingly effective in using their office as a 'bully pulpit' and since the 1950s the possibilities inherent in such tactics have been immeasurably enhanced by the advent of television.

President Bush would have been a poor communicator in any age, but he is a notably inept performer before the television cameras. When Reagan was in office his staff understood the unavoidable importance of television to governance and ruthlessly manipulated the medium to the President's advantage:

> In the television age, the battle between the president and the media has become a kind of proxy for governing. Ronald Reagan regularly won this combat and was able to set his own agenda; and, in part for that reason he was seen as a strong president.[57]

Lacking the skills of his predecessor George Bush has been unable to use television in the same way and his presidency has suffered badly as a consequence.

Notes

1. See George Bush (with Victor Gold), *Looking Forward*, The Bodley Head, London, 1988, *passim*.
2. See for example David Hoffman, 'Bush is saying to Congress: Let's make a deal', *The Washington Post* National Weekly Edition, 3–9 April 1989, p. 12.
3. See Gallup figures in *The American Enterprise*, Jan/Feb 1990, vol. 1, no. 1.
4. *Time*, 21 May 1990, p. 44.
5. Quotations from *The Sunday Times* 7 October 1990, p. 18 and *The Times*, 4 October, p. 15.
6. *Time* 15 October 1990, p. 24.
7. Thomas Edsall, 'The Gridlock of Government' *The Washington Post* National Weekly Edition, 15–21 October 1990, p. 6.
8. *Time* 22 October 1990, p. 54.
9. *ibid.*, 9 November 1990, p. 30.
10. Dan Balz and Ann Devroy, 'Sununu and Darman Give the Hill the Screaming Meanies', *The Washington Post* National Weekly Edition, 15–21 October 1990, pp. 7–8.
11. *Time*, 22 October 1990, p. 56.
12. Edsall, *op. cit.*
13. Dan Balz and Ann Devroy, 'Bush Became a Leader When It Mattered Most', *The Washington Post* National Weekly Edition, 11–17 March 1991, p. 9.
14. *The Gulf Crisis: A Chronology, July 1990–July 1991*, USIS, US Embassy, London, 1991.
15. Bob Woodward and Rick Atkinson, 'Launching Operation Desert Shield', *The Washington Post* National Weekly Edition, 3–9 September, 1990, pp. 8–9.
16. Dan Goodgame, 'What If We Do Nothing?', *Time* 7 January 1991, pp. 14–15.
17. *ibid.*
18. Rick Atkinson and Bob Woodward, 'The Doctrine of Invincible Force', *The Washington Post*, National Weekly Edition, 10–16 December 1990, pp. 6–7.
19. Television programme, *The Washington Version*, AEI/BBC 1991.
20. *ibid.*
21. Quoted in Theodore Draper, 'The True History of the Gulf War', *New York Review of Books*, 30 January 1992, pp. 38–45.
22. Richard Marin, 'George Bush Could Set A Record', *The Washington Post* National Weekly Edition, 16–22 March 1992, p. 37.
23. Draper, *op. cit.*, p. 42.
24. *op. cit.*, p. 120.
25. *The Gulf Crisis . . .*, *op. cit.*
26. *ibid.*
27. Draper, *op. cit.*, pp. 41–2.

28. Don Oberdorfer, 'The War No One Saw Coming', *The Washington Post* National Weekly Edition, 18–24 March 1991, pp. 6–10
29. *ibid.*, p. 9.
30. Theodore Draper, 'The Gulf War Reconsidered', *New York Review of Books*, 16 January 1992, pp. 46–53.
31. Oberdorfer, *op. cit.*
32. Martin Walker, 'Congress Confronts Bush on Gulf Policy', *The Guardian*, 9 September 1990, p. 8.
33. Lee H. Hamilton, 'Who Voted Wrong?', *The Washington Post* National Weekly Edition, 18–24 March 1991, p. 30.
34. E. J. Dionne, 'We Don't Have Ourselves to Kick Around Anymore', *ibid.*, 11–17 March 1991, pp. 8–9.
35. *Congressional Quarterly Weekly Report*, 30 December 1989, p. 3540.
36. Quoted in David Broder and Richard Marin, 'Sure, That Was Good, But What Have You Done For Me Lately?', *The Washington Post* National Weekly Edition, 11–17 March 1991, p. 38.
37. Quoted in Ann Devroy, 'There's No Homecoming For Bush', *ibid.*, 17–23 June 1991, p. 12.
38. See interview with Bush, *Time*, 7 January 1991.
39. See David Mervin, *Ronald Reagan and the American Presidency*, Longman, London, 1990, p. 195.
40. Bush, *op. cit.*, pp. 203–4.
41. Quoted in John Yang, 'Who Is George Bush?', *The Washington Post* National Weekly Edition, 24 February–1 March 1991, pp. 9–10.
42. James Adams, 'Bush at Bay . . .', *The Sunday Times*, 1 December 1991, p. 21.
43. 'The President's Own Worst Enemy', *The Washington Post* National Weekly Edition, 3–9 Febuary 1992.
44. Martin Walker, 'Elder Statesmen Gain Wealth of Experience', *The Guardian*, 16 March 1992, p. 7.
45. Martin Walker and Simon Tisdall, 'Bush Says Sorry for Tax U–turn', *ibid.*, 4 March 1992, p. 1.
46. Jefferson Morley, 'Bush and the Blacks: An Unknown Story', *New York Review of Books,* 16 January 1992, pp. 19–26.
47. Robert Shogan, *The Riddle of Power: Presidential Leadership From Truman to Bush*, Dutton, New York, 1991, p. 264.
48. Morley, *op. cit.*, p. 26.
49. *ibid.*
50. *ibid.*
51. Bush, *op. cit.*, p. 207.
52. See Daniel Pipes, 'What Kind of Peace?', *The National Interest*, Spring 1991, pp. 8–12.
53. In October 1991 a Washington Post/ABC News Poll found that 70 per cent agreed that Bush 'spends too much time on foreign policy and not enough on problems in this country'. *The Washington Post* National Weekly Edition, 23–29 December 1991, p. 13.
54. Martin Walker, *op. cit.*, *The Guardian*, 16 March 1992.
55. 16 March 1992, p. 32.

56. Maureen Dowd, 'The Language Thing', *The New York Times Magazine*, 29 July 1990, p. 32.
57. David Ignatius, 'After Reagan the Media Miss Being Manipulated', *The Washington Post* National Weekly Edition, 15–21 May 1989, p. 23.

Appendix A

Presidents and presidential elections 1789–1992

Term	President		Main Opponent		PopV	EcV
1789–1793	George Washington	(F)	None		a	
1793–1797	George Washington	(F)	None			
1797–1801	John Adams	(F)	Thomas Jefferson	(DR)		71–68
1801–1805	Thomas Jefferson[b]	(DR)	Aaron Burr	(DR)		73–73
1805–1809	Thomas Jefferson	(DR)	Charles Pinckney	(F)		162–14
1809–1813	James Madison	(DR)	Charles Pinckney	(F)		122–47
1813–1817	James Madison	(DR)	DeWitt Clinton	(F)		128–89
1817–1821	James Monroe	(DR)	Rufus King	(F)		183–34
1821–1825	James Monroe	(DR)	John Quincy Adams	(DR)		231–1
1825–1829	John Quincy Adams[c]	(DR)	Andrew Jackson	(DR)	31%–41%	84–99
1829–1833	Andrew Jackson	(D)	John Quincy Adams	(NR)	56%–44%	178–83
1833–1837	Andrew Jackson	(D)	Henry Clay	(NR)	54%–37%	219–49
1837–1841	Martin Van Buren	(D)	William H.Harrison	(W)	51%–37%	170–73
1841	William H Harrison[+]	(W)	Martin Van Buren	(D)	53%–47%	234–60
1841–1845	John Tyler	(W)				
1845–1849	James Polk	(D)	Henry Clay	(W)	49%–48%	170–105
1849–1850	Zachary Taylor[+]	(W)	Lewis Cass	(D)	47%–43%	163–127
1850–1853	Millard Fillmore	(W)				
1853–1857	Franklin Pierce	(D)	Winfield Scott	(W)	51%–44%	254–42
1857–1861	James Buchanan	(D)	John C. Fremont	(R)	45%–33%	174–114
1861–1865	Abraham Lincoln[d]	(R)	Stephen A. Douglas	(D)	40%–30%	180–12
1865	Abraham Lincoln[+]	(R)	George B. McClellan	(D)	55%–45%	211–21
1865–1869	Andrew Johnson	(R)				

239

Term	President		Main Opponent		PopV	EcV
1869–1873	Ulysses Grant	(R)	Horatio Seymour	(D)	53%–47%	214–80
1873–1877	Ulysses Grant[e]	(R)	Horace Greeley	(D)	56%–44%	286–**
1877–1881	Rutherford Hayes[f]	(R)	Samuel J. Tilden	(D)	48%–51%	185–184
1881	James Garfield[+]	(R)	Winfield S. Hancock	(D)	48%–48%	214–155
1881–1885	Chester Arthur	(R)				
1885–1889	Grover Cleveland	(D)	James Blaine	(R)	48%–48%	219–182
1889–1893	Benjamin Harrison	(R)	Grover Cleveland	(D)	48%–48%	233–168
1893–1897	Grover Cleveland	(D)	Benjamin Harrison	(R)	46%–43%	277–145
1897–1901	William McKinley	(R)	William J. Bryan	(D)	51%–47%	271–176
1901	William McKinley[+]	(R)	William J. Bryan	(D)	52%–45%	292–155
1901–1905	Theodore Roosevelt	(R)				
1905–1909	Theodore Roosevelt	(R)	Alton Parker	(D)	56%–38%	336–140
1909–1913	William H. Taft	(R)	William J. Bryan	(D)	52%–43%	321–162
1913–1917	Woodrow Wilson[g]	(D)	William H. Taft	(R)	42%–23%	435–8
1917–1921	Woodrow Wilson	(D)	Charles Evan Hughes	(R)	49%–46%	277–254
1921–1923	Warren Harding[+]	(R)	James Cox	(D)	60%–34%	404–127
1923–1925	Calvin Coolidge	(R)				
1925–1929	Calvin Coolidge	(R)	John Davis	(D)	54%–29%	382–136
1929–1933	Herbert Hoover	(R)	Alfred Smith	(D)	58%–41%	444–87
1933–1937	Franklin Roosevelt	(D)	Herbert Hoover	(R)	57%–40%	472–59
1937–1941	Franklin Roosevelt	(D)	Alfred Landon	(R)	61%–36%	523–8
1941–1945	Franklin Roosevelt	(D)	Wendell Wilkie	(R)	55%–45%	449–82
1945	Franklin Roosevelt[+]	(D)	Thomas Dewey	(R)	53%–46%	432–99
1945–1949	Harry Truman	(D)				
1949–1953	Harry Truman	(D)	Thomas Dewey	(R)	49%–45%	303–189
1953–1957	Dwight Eisenhower	(R)	Adlai Stevenson	(D)	55%–44%	442–89
1957–1961	Dwight Eisenhower	(R)	Adlai Stevenson	(D)	57%–42%	457–73
1961–1963	John Kennedy+	(D)	Richard Nixon	(R)	50%–49%	303–219
1963–1965	Lyndon Johnson	(D)				
1965–1969	Lyndon Johnson	(D)	Barry Goldwater	(R)	61%–38%	486–52
1969–1973	Richard Nixon	(R)	Hubert Humphrey	(D)	43%–43%	301–191
1973–1974	Richard Nixon[++]	(R)	George McGovern	(D)	61%–37%	520–17
1974–1977	Gerald Ford	(R)				
1977–1981	Jimmy Carter	(D)	Gerald Ford	(R)	50%–48%	297–240
1981–1985	Ronald Reagan	(R)	Jimmy Carter	(D)	51%–41%	489–49
1985–1989	Ronald Reagan	(R)	Walter Mondale	(D)	59%–41%	525–13
1989–1993	George Bush	(R)	Michael Dukakis	(D)	53%–46%	426–111

Notes:

PopV Popular vote percentages; EcV Electoral College vote.

(F) Federalist; (DR) Democrat Republican; (NR) National Republican; (W) Whig; (D) Democrat; (R) Republican.

+ Died in office; ++ Resigned.

a. Reliable popular vote totals not available before 1824.

b. Tie in Electoral College – election decided by US House of Representatives.

c. Henry Clay received 37 votes in the Electoral College and W.H. Crawford 41 – each of the four candidates represented factions of Democrat Republicans. Election decided in favour of Adams by the US House of Representatives.

d. John Breckinridge, Southern Democrat, received 72 votes in the Electoral College and John Bell, Constitutional Union, obtained 39.

e. Greeley died between the popular election and the calculation of Electoral College Votes.

f. Results in four states disputed. Congress in joint session elected Hayes.

g. Theodore Roosevelt, Progressive, received 88 Electoral College votes.

Sources: Sidney Milkis and Michael Nelson, *The American Presidency: Origins and Development*, Congressional Quarterly Press, Washington DC, 1990 and *The World Almanac and Book of Facts 1991*, Scripps Howard, New York, 1990.

Appendix B

Party control of the Presidency, Senate and House in the twentieth century

Congress	Years	President	Senate			House		
			D	R	O	D	R	O
57th	1901–1903	**McKinley** **T. Roosevelt**	**31**	**55**	**4**	**151**	**197**	**9**
58th	1903–1905	**T. Roosevelt**	**33**	**57**	–	**178**	**208**	–
59th	1905–1907	**T. Roosevelt**	**33**	**57**	–	**136**	**250**	–
60th	1907–1909	**T. Roosevelt**	**31**	**61**	–	**164**	**222**	–
61st	1909–1911	**Taft**	**32**	**61**	–	**172**	**219**	–
62nd	1911–1913	**Taft**	**41**	**51**	–	228	161	1
63rd	1913–1915	Wilson	51	44	1	291	127	17
64th	1915–1917	Wilson	56	40	–	230	196	9
65th	1917–1919	Wilson	53	42	–	216	210	6
66th	1919–1921	Wilson	**47**	**49**	–	**190**	**240**	**3**
67th	1921–1923	**Harding**	**37**	**59**	–	**131**	**301**	**1**
68th	1923–1925	**Coolidge**	**43**	**51**	**2**	**203**	**225**	**5**
69th	1925–1927	**Coolidge**	**39**	**56**	**1**	**183**	**247**	**4**
70th	1927–1929	**Coolidge**	**46**	**49**	**1**	**195**	**237**	**3**
71st	1929–1931	**Hoover**	**39**	**56**	**1**	**167**	**267**	**1**
72nd	1931–1933	**Hoover**	**47**	**48**	**1**	220	214	1
73rd	1933–1935	F.Roosevelt	60	35	1	319	117	5
74th	1935–1937	F.Roosevelt	69	25	2	319	103	10
75th	1937–1939	F.Roosevelt	76	16	4	331	89	13
76th	1939–1941	F.Roosevelt	69	23	4	261	164	4

Congress	Years	President	Senate			House		
			D	R	O	D	R	O
77th	1941–1943	F.Roosevelt	66	28	2	268	162	5
78th	1943–1945	F.Roosevelt	58	37	1	218	208	4
79th	1945–1947	Truman	56	38	1	242	190	2
80th	1947–1949	Truman	**45**	**51**	–	**188**	**245**	**2**
81st	1949–1951	Truman	54	42	–	263	171	1
82nd	1951–1953	Truman	49	47	–	234	199	1
83rd	1953–1955	**Eisenhower**	**47**	**48**	1	**211**	**221**	**1**
84th	1955–1957	**Eisenhower**	48	47	1	232	203	–
85th	1957–1959	**Eisenhower**	49	47	–	233	200	–
86th	1959–1961	**Eisenhower**	65	35	–	284	153	–
87th	1961–1963	Kennedy	65	35	–	263	174	–
88th	1963–1965	Kennedy Johnson	67	33	–	258	177	
89th	1965–1967	Johnson	68	32	–	295	140	–
90th	1967–1969	Johnson	64	36	–	247	187	–
91st	1969–1971	**Nixon**	57	43	–	243	192	–
92nd	1971–1973	**Nixon**	54	44	2	254	180	–
93rd	1973–1975	**Nixon Ford**	56	42	2	239	192	1
94th	1975–1977	**Ford**	60	37	2	291	144	–
95th	1977–1979	Carter	61	38	1	292	143	–
96th	1979–1981	Carter	58	41	1	276	157	–
97th	1981–1983	**Reagan**	**46**	**53**	1	243	192	–
98th	1983–1985	**Reagan**	**45**	**55**	–	267	168	–
99th	1985–1987	**Reagan**	**47**	**53**	–	252	183	–
100th	1987–1989	**Reagan**	54	46	–	258	177	–
101st	1989–1991	**Bush**	57	43	–	262	173	–
102nd	1991–1993	**Bush**	56	44	–	267	167	1

Notes:
Republican control
Democratic control
This table excludes vacancies at the beginning of each session.
Sources: Roger Davidson and Walter Oleszek, *Congress and Its Members* (2nd edition), Congressional Quarterly Press, Washington DC, 1985 and *The World Almanac and Book of Facts 1991*, Scripps Howard, 1990.

Appendix C

The Presidency in the Constitution

(A selection of clauses particularly relevant to the presidency. Author's additions in italics.)

Article I

Section 7

2. Every bill which shall have passed the House of Representatives and the Senate, shall, before it becomes a law, be presented to the President of the United States: If he approve he shall sign it, but if not he shall return it, with his objections to that House in which it shall have originated, who shall enter the objections at large on their journal and proceed to reconsider it. If after such reconsideration two thirds of that House shall agree to pass the bill, it shall be sent, together with the objections, to the other House, by which it shall likewise be reconsidered, and if approved by two thirds of that House it shall become a law . . . If any bill shall not be returned by the President within ten days (Sundays excepted) after it shall have been presented to him, the same shall be a law, in like manner as if he had signed it, unless the Congress by their adjournment prevent its return, in which case it shall not be a law.

Article II

Section 1

1. The executive power shall be vested in a President of the United

States of America. He shall hold his office during the term of four years, and together with the Vice President, chosen for the same term, be elected as follows:

2. Each State shall appoint, in such manner as the legislature thereof may direct, a number of electors, equal to the whole number of Senators and Representatives to which the State may be entitled in the Congress: but no senator or representative, or person holding an office of trust or profit under the United States, shall be appointed an elector.

The next paragraph in the original Constitution was replaced in 1804, in accordance with the Twelfth Amendment.

(The Electors shall meet in their respective States, and vote by ballot for President and Vice President . . . in distinct ballots. . . [*the results shall be*] directed to the President of the Senate [*who*] . . . shall, in the presence of the Senate and the House of Representatives, open all the certificates and the votes shall then be counted. The person having the greatest number of votes for President, shall be the President, if such number be a majority of the whole number of Electors appointed; and if no person have such a majority, from the persons having the highest number not exceeding three on the list of those voted for as President, the House of Representatives shall choose immediately, by ballot, the President. But in choosing the President, the votes shall be taken by States, the representation from each State having one vote . . .)

5. *In the original, this paragraph details the arrangements for replacing the President following death, resignation or inability to perform the powers and duties of the office. It was superseded in 1967 by the Twenty–fifth Amendment.*

(Section 1. In case of the removal of the President from office or of his death or resignation, the Vice President shall become President.

Section 2. Whenever there is a vacancy in the office of the Vice President, the President shall nominate a Vice President who shall take the office upon confirmation by a majority vote of both Houses of Congress.

Section 3. Whenever the President transmits to the President pro tempore of the Senate and the Speaker of the House of Representatives his written declaration that he is unable to discharge the powers and duties of his office, and until he transmits to them a written declaration to the contrary, such powers and duties shall be discharged by the Vice President as Acting President.

Section 4. Whenever the Vice President and a majority of either the principal officers of the executive department, or of such other body as Congress may by law provide, transmit to the President pro tempore of the Senate and the Speaker of the House of Representatives their written declaration that the President is unable to discharge the powers and duties of his office, the Vice President shall immediately assume the powers and duties of the office of Acting President . . ..)

7. Before he enter on the execution of his office . . . [*the President*] shall take the following oath or affirmation: 'I do solemnly swear (or affirm) that I will faithfully execute the office of the President of the United States, and will to the best of my ability, preserve, protect and defend the Constitution of the United States.'

Section 2

1. The President shall be commander in chief of the army and navy of the United States, and of the militia of the several states, when called into the actual service of the United States . . . he shall have power to grant reprieves and pardons for offenses against the United States, except in cases of impeachment.

2. He shall have power, by and with the advice and consent of the Senate, to make treaties provided two thirds of the Senators present concur; and he shall nominate, and by and with the advice and consent of the Senate, shall appoint ambassadors, other public ministers and consuls, judges of the Supreme Court, and all other officers of the United States, whose appointments are not herein provided for, and which shall be established by law. . .

Section 3

[*The President*] shall from time to time give to the Congress infor-

mation of the state of the Union, and recommend to their consideration such measures as he shall judge necessary and expedient;
he may on extraordinary occasions, convene both Houses. or
either of them. . . he shall receive ambassadors and other public
ministers; he shall take care that the laws are faithfully executed,
and shall commission all the officers of the United States.

Section 4

The President, Vice President, and all civil officers of the United
States, shall be removed from office on impeachment for and conviction of, treason, bribery, or other high crimes and
misdemeanours.

Amendment XXII [*1951*]

No person shall be elected to the office of President more than
twice, and no person who has held the office of President, or acted
as President for more than two years of a term to which some other
person was elected to the office of President more than once. . .

Bibliography

Aberbach, Joel and Rockman, Bert, 'Clashing Beliefs in the Executive Branch: The Nixon Administration Bureaucracy', *American Political Science Review*, vol. LXX, no. 2, June 1976.

Abraham, Henry, *Justices and Presidents*, Oxford University Press, New York, 1985.

Adams, James, 'Bush at Bay . . .' *Sunday Times*, 1 December 1991, p. 21.

Ambrose, Stephen, *Nixon: The Triumph of a Politician 1962–72*, Simon and Schuster, New York, 1989.

Ambrose, Stephen, 'The Ike Age', *The New Republic*, 9 May 1981.

Anderson, Martin, *Revolution*, Harcourt Brace Jovanovich, New York, 1988.

Andrews, Wayne (ed.), *The Autobiography of Theodore Roosevelt*, Charles Scribner's Sons, New York, 1958.

Atkinson, Rick and Woodward, Bob, 'The Doctrine of Invincible Force', *The Washington Post*, National Weekly Edition, 10–16 December 1990, pp. 6–7.

Bailey, Thomas, *Woodrow Wilson and the Great Betrayal*, The Macmillan Company, New York, 1945.

Bailey, Thomas, *Presidential Greatness*, Appleton Century Crofts, New York, 1966.

Bailyn, Bernard, *The Ideological Origins of the American Revolution*, Harvard University Press, Cambridge, Mass., 1967.

Baker, Ray Stannard, *Woodrow Wilson; Life and Letters*, vol. 4, William Heinemann, London, 1932.

Balz, Dan and Devroy, Ann, 'Sununu and Darman Give the Screaming Meanies', *The Washington Post*, National Weekly Edition, 15–21 October 1990, pp. 7–8.

Balz, Dan and Devroy, Ann, 'Bush Became a Leader When It Mattered Most', *The Washington Post*, National Weekly Edition, 11–17 March 1991, p. 9.

Berns, Walter, 'Constitutional Power and the Defense of Free Government', in B. Netanyahu (ed.), *Terrorism; How the West Can Win*, Farrar, Strauss, Giroux, New York, 1986, pp. 149–54.

Broder, David and Marin, Richard, 'Sure, That Was Good, But What Have You Done For Me Lately?', *The Washington Post*, National Weekly Edition, 11–17 March 1991, p. 38.

Brummer, Alex, 'How to Buy Friends and Influence History', *The Guardian*, 16 April 1985, p. 21.

Budget of the United States Government FY 1990, US Government Printing Office, Washington DC, 1989.

Burns, James MacGregor, *Roosevelt: The Lion and the Fox*, Harcourt Brace, New York, 1956.

Burns, James MacGregor, *The Power to Lead: The Crisis of the American Presidency*, Simon and Schuster, New York, 1984.

Burns, James MacGregor and Beschloss, Michael, 'The Forgotten FDR', *The New Republic*, 7 April 1982, pp. 19–22.

Bush, George (with Gold, Victor), *Looking Forward*, The Bodley Head, London, 1988.

Califano, Joseph, *A Presidential Nation*, W. W. Norton, New York, 1975.

Cannon, Lou, *Reagan*, G. P. Putnam's Sons, New York, 1982.

Caro, Robert, *The Years of Lyndon Johnson: The Path to Power*, Alfred Knopf, New York, 1982.

Caro, Robert, *Means of Ascent: The Years of Lyndon Johnson*, The Bodley Head, London, 1990.

Carter, Jimmy, *Keeping Faith*, Collins, London, 1982.

Chambers, William Nisbet, *Political Parties in a New Nation*, Oxford University Press, Oxford, 1963,

Charlesworth, James C. (ed.), *A Design For Political Science: Scope, Objectives and Methods*, The American Academy of Political Science, Philadelphia, 1966.

Chubb, John and Peterson, Paul (eds), *The New Directions in American Politics*, Brookings, Washington DC, 1985.

Coit, Margaret (ed.), *John C. Calhoun*, Prentice Hall, New Jersey, 1970.

Corwin, Edward S., *The President: Office and Powers*, New York University Press, New York, 1957.

Crabb, Cecil and Holt, Pat, *Invitation to Struggle: Congress, the President and Foreign Policy*, Congressional Quarterly Press, Washington DC, 1984.

Cronin, Thomas, *The State of the Presidency*, Little, Brown, Boston, 1980.

Cunliffe, Marcus, *American Presidents and the Presidency*, Fontana/Collins, London, 1972.

Dahl, Robert, *Congress and Foreign Policy*, W. W. Norton, New York, 1950.

Dahl, Robert, *Pluralist Democracy in the United States*, Rand McNally, Chicago, 1967.

Dahl, Robert, 'The Myth of the Presidential Mandate', *Political Science Quarterly*, 104 (Fall 1990), pp. 355–72.

Dahl, Robert and Lindblom, Charles, *Politics, Economics and Welfare*, Harper and Row, New York, 1953.

Davidson, Roger and Oleszek, Walter, *Congress and Its Members*, Congressional Quarterly Press, Washington DC, 1985.

Degler, Carl, *Out of Our Past*, Harper and Row, New York, 1970.

Destler, I. M., 'Reagan and the World: An Awesome Stubborness', in Jones, Charles O. (ed.), *The Reagan Legacy*, Chatham House, New Jersey, 1988.

Devroy, Ann, 'There's No Homecoming For Bush', *The Washington Post*, National Weekly Edition, 17–23 June 1991, p. 38.

Dionne, E. J., 'We Don't Have Ourselves to Kick Around Anymore', *The Washington Post*, National Weekly Edition, 11–17 March, 1991, pp. 8–9.

Divine, Robert, *Eisenhower and the Cold War*, Oxford University Press, Oxford 1981.

Dodd, Lawrence and Oppenheimer, Bruce, *Congress Reconsidered*, Congressional Quarterly Press, Washington DC, 1985.

Donovan, Robert, *Eisenhower: The Inside Story*, Harper, New York, 1956.

Dowd, Maureen, 'The Language Thing', *The New York Times Magazine*, 29 July 1990, p. 32.

Draper, Theodore, 'The Constitution in Danger', *New York Review of Books*, 1 March 1990.

Draper, Theodore, 'The Gulf War Reconsidered', *New York Review of Books*, 16 January 1992, pp. 46–53.

Draper, Theodore, 'The True History of the Gulf War', *New York Review of Books*, 30 January 1992, pp. 38–45.

Edsall, Thomas, 'The Gridlock of Government', *The Washington Post*, National Weekly Edition, 15–21 October 1990, p. 6.

Edwards, George III, *Presidential Influence in Congress*, W. H. Freeman, San Francisco, 1980.

Eisenhower, Dwight, *Waging Peace: White House Years*, Doubleday, New York, 1965.

Evans, Rowland and Novak, Robert, *Lyndon Johnson: The Exercise of Power*, Allen and Unwin, London, 1967.

Farrand, Max (ed.), *The Records of the Federal Convention of 1787*, 4 volumes, Yale University Press, New Haven, 1937.

Fenno, Richard, *The President's Cabinet*, Harvard University Press, Cambridge, Mass., 1963.

Ferrell, Robert (ed.), *The Eisenhower Diaries*, W. W. Norton, New York, 1981.

Fisher, Louis, *Constitutional Conflicts Between Congress and the President*, Princeton University Press, Princeton, 1985.

Freeman, Douglas Southall, *George Washington: A Biography*, Charles Scribner's Sons, New York, 1954.

Fulbright, J. William, 'The Fatal Arrogance of Power', *New York Times Magazine*, 15 May 1966, p. 104.

Gallagher, Hugh, 'Presidents, Congress and the Legislative Functions', in Tugwell, Rex and Cronin, Thomas (eds), *The Presidency Reappraised*, Praeger, New York, 1974.

George, Alexander and George, Juliette, *Woodrow Wilson and Colonel House*, Dover Publications, New York, 1964.

Goldman, Eric, *The Tragedy of Lyndon Johnson*, Dell Books, New York, 1969.

Goldwater, Barry, *Goldwater*, St. Martin's Press, New York, 1988.

Goodgame, Dan, 'What If We Do Nothing?' *Time*, 7 January 1991, pp. 14–15.

Greenstein, Fred, *The Hidden–Hand Presidency: Eisenhower as Leader*, Basic Books, New York, 1982.

Greenstein, Fred (ed.), *Leadership in the Modern Presidency*, Harvard University Press, Cambridge, Mass., 1988, p. 137.

Greenstein, Fred, 'Eisenhower as an Activist President: A Look at New Evidence', *Political Science Quarterly*, vol. 94, Winter 1979–80, pp. 575–99.

Grove, Lloyd, 'Israel's Force in Washington', *The Washington Post*, National Weekly Edition, June 24–30, 1991.

The Gulf Crisis: A Chronology, July 1990 – July 1991, USIS, U.S. Embassy, London, 1991.

Hagedorn, Hermann (ed.), *The Theodore Roosevelt Treasury*, G.P. Putnam's Sons, New York 1957.

Hamilton, Lee H., 'Who Voted Wrong?', *The Washington Post*, National Weeekly Edition, 18–24 March 1991, pp. 8–9.

Hart, John, *The Presidential Branch*, Pergamon Press, New York, 1987.

Henderson, Phillip, 'Organising the Presidency for Effective Leadership: Lessons from the Eisenhower Years', *Presidential Studies Quarterly*, Winter 1987, pp. 43–69.

Hess, Stephen, *Organizing the Presidency*, Brookings, Washington DC, 1988.

Hinckley, Barbara, *The Seniority System in Congress*, Indiana University Press, Bloomington, 1971.

Hodder-Williams, Richard, 'The President and the Constitution', in Shaw, Malcolm (ed.), *Roosevelt to Reagan*, C. Hurst, London, 1987.

Hodder-Williams, Richard, 'Ronald Reagan and the Supreme Court', in Hogan, Joseph (ed.), *The Reagan Years*, Manchester University Press, Manchester, 1990.

Hoffman, David, 'Bush is Saying to Congress: Let's Make a Deal', *The Washington Post*, National Weekly Edition, 3–9 April 1989, p. 12.

Hofstadter, Richard, *The American Political Tradition*, Vintage Books, New York, 1948.

Hughes, Emmet, *The Ordeal of Power*, Macmillan, London, 1963.

Huntington, Samuel, *American Politics: The Promise of Disharmony*, Harvard University Press, Cambridge, Mass., 1981.

Ignatius, David, 'After Reagan the Media Miss Being Manipulated', *The Washington Post*, National Weekly Edition, 15–21 May 1989, p. 23.

Isaacson, Walter and Thomas, Evan, *The Wise Men*, Simon and Schuster, New York, 1987.

James, Marquis, *Andrew Jackson*, Grosset and Dunlap, New York, 1937.

Jaynes, Gerald David and Williams, Robin M. (eds), *A Common Destiny: Blacks in American Society*, National Academy Press, Washington DC, 1989.

Jones, Charles O., 'Congress and the Presidency', in Mann, Thomas and Ornstein, Norman (eds), *The New Congress*, American Enterprise Institute, Washington DC, 1981.

Kearns, Doris, *Lyndon Johnson and the American Dream*, New American Library, New York, 1976.

Kellerman, Barbara, *The Political Presidency: The Practice of Leadership*, Oxford University Press, New York, 1984.

Ketcham, Ralph, 'Concepts of Presidential Leadership, Citizenship and Good Government. . .', in Wellenreuther, Herman (ed.), *German and American Constitutional Thought*, Berg, New York, 1990.

Koenig, Louis, *The Chief Executive* (5th edition), Harcourt Brace Jovanovich, New York, 1986.

Ladd, Everett, 'The Brittle Mandate: Electoral Dealignment and the 1980 Election', *Political Science Quarterly*, vol. 96, Spring 1981.

Leuchtenberg, William, *In The Shadow Of FDR*, Cornell University Press, Ithaca, 1983.

Leuchtenberg, William, 'Franklin Roosevelt: The First Modern President', in Greenstein, Fred (ed.), *Leadership in the Modern Presidency*, Harvard University Press, Cambridge, Mass., 1988.

Light, Paul, *The President's Agenda*, Johns Hopkins University Press, Baltimore, 1982.

Link, Arthur, *Wilson: The Road to the White House*, Princeton University Press, Princeton, 1947.

Link, Arthur, *Wilson: The New Freedom*, Princeton University Press, Princeton, 1956.

Link, Arthur, *Wilson the Diplomatist*, Johns Hopkins University Press, Baltimore, 1957.

Link, Arthur, *et al.* (eds), *The Papers of Woodrow Wilson*, Princeton University Press, Princeton, 1966– .

Lipset, Seymour Martin, *The First New Nation*, Basic Books, New York, 1963.

Lipset, Seymour Martin and Schneider, William, 'The Confidence Gap During the Reagan Years', *Political Science Quarterly*, vol. 102, Spring 1987, pp. 1–23.

Locke, John, *The Second Treatise of Government,* Thomas Pearden (ed.), The Liberal Arts Press, New York, 1952.

Lodge, Henry Cabot, 'The Treaty Making Powers of the Senate', *Scribners Magazine*, vol. 31, no. 1, January 1902.

Lowi, Theodore, *The Personal President*, Cornell University Press, Ithaca, 1985.

Mandelbaum, Michael, 'The Luck of the President', in Hyland, William (ed.), *The Reagan Foreign Policy*, New American Library, New York, 1987.

Manley, John and Dolbeare, Kenneth (eds), *The Case Against the Constitution*, M. E. Sharpe, New York, 1987.

Marin, Richard, 'George Bush Could Set A Record', *The Washington Post*, National Weekly Edition, 16–22 March 1992, p. 37.

Mathias, Charles, 'Ethnic Groups and Foreign Policy', *Foreign Affairs*, no. 5, Summer 1981, pp. 975–98.

Matthews, Donald, *US Senators and Their World*, Vintage Books, New York, 1960.

McClosky, Herbert and Zaller, John, *The American Ethos*, Harvard University Press, Cambridge, Mass., 1984.

Mervin, David, *Ronald Reagan and the American Presidency*, Longman, London and New York, 1990.

Mervin, David, 'Henry Cabot Lodge and the League of Nations', *Journal of American Studies*, vol. 4, no. 2, February 1971.

Mervin, David, 'Ronald Reagan's Place in History', *Journal of American Studies*, vol. 23, no. 2, August 1989, pp. 269–86

Milkis, Sidney and Nelson, Michael, *The American Presidency: Origins and Development*, Congressional Quarterly Press, Washington DC, 1990.

Morison, Samuel Eliot and Commager, Henry Steele, *The Growth of the American Republic*, 2 volumes, Oxford University Press, New York, 1942.

Morley, Jefferson, 'Bush and the Blacks: An Unknown Story', *New York Review of Books*, 16 January 1992, pp. 19–26.

Nathan, Richard 'Institutional Change Under Reagan', in Palmer, John (ed.), *Perspectives on the Reagan Years*, The Urban Institute Press, Washington DC, 1986.

Neustadt, Richard, *Presidential Power*, John Wiley and Sons, New York, 1960 and 1976.

Neustadt, Richard, *Presidential Power and the Modern Presidents*, The Free Press, New York, 1990.

Neustadt, Richard, 'Presidency and Legislation: The Growth of Central Clearance', *American Political Science Review*, vol. 48, no. 3, September 1954.

Nicholas, H. G., *The Nature of American Politics*, Oxford University Press, Oxford, 1986.

Oberdorfer, Don, 'The War No One Saw Coming', *The Washington Post*, National Weekly Edition, March 18–24, 1991, pp. 6–10.

O'Brien, David, *Storm Center: The Supreme Court in American Politics*, W. W. Norton, New York, 1986.

O'Brien, David, 'The Reagan Judges: His Most Enduring Legacy?', in Jones, Charles O. (ed.), *The Reagan Legacy*, Chatham House, New Jersey, 1988.

O'Neill, Tip, *Man of the House*, Random House, New York, 1987.

Osborne, David, 'On A Clear Day He Can See Massachusetts', *The Washington Post*, National Weekly Edition, 25 April–1 May, 1988.

Oudes, Bruce (ed.), *From The President: Richard Nixon's Secret Files*, André Deutsch, London, 1989.

Peterson, Merrill, *The Jefferson Image in the American Mind*, Oxford University Press, New York, 1962.

Peterson, Paul and Rom, Mark, 'Lower Taxes, More Spending and Budget Deficits', in Jones, Charles O. (ed.), *The Reagan Legacy*, Chatham House, New Jersey, 1988.

Pious, Richard, *The American Presidency*, Basic Books, New York, 1979.

Pipes, Daniel, 'What Kind of Peace?', *The National Interest*, Spring 1991, pp. 8–12.

Plano, Jack and Greenberg, Milton, *The American Political Dictionary* (6th edition), Holt, Rinehart and Winston, New York, 1982.

Pringle, Henry, *Theodore Roosevelt: A Biography*, Harcourt Brace and Company, 1956.

Randall, J. G., *Constitutional Problems Under Lincoln*, Peter Smith, Gloucester, Mass., 1963.

Ranelagh, John, *The Agency: The Rise and Decline of the CIA*, Hodder and Stoughton, London, 1987.

Ranney, Austin, *Channels of Power: The Impact of Television on American Politics*, Basic Books, New York, 1982.

Reagan, Ronald, *An American Life*, Hutchinson, London, 1990.

Reedy, George, *The Twilight of the Presidency*, New American Library, New York, 1970.

Reeves, Thomas C., *The Life and times of Joe McCarthy*, Blond and Briggs, London 1982.

Revolution in Civil Rights, Congresssional Quarterly Press, Washington DC, 1965.

Robinson, Donald, *To The Best of My Ability: The Presidency and the Constitution*, W. W. Norton, New York, 1987.

Roettger, Walter and Winebrenner, Hugh, 'Politics and Political Scientists', *Public Opinion*, September/October 1986, pp. 41–4.

Rose Richard, *The Postmodern President*, Chatham House, New Jersey, 1988.

Rossiter, Clinton, *Conservatism in America*, Vintage Books, New York, 1962.

Rossiter, Clinton, *The American Presidency*, Harcourt Brace, New York, 1956.

Rossiter, Clinton, *Alexander Hamilton and the Constitution*, Harcourt Brace and World, New York, 1964.

Rossiter, Clinton (ed.), *The Federalist Papers*, The New American Library, New York, 1961.

Schick, Allen, 'How the Budget Was Won and Lost', in Ornstein, Norman (ed.), *President and Congress: Assessing Reagan's First Year*, American Enterprise Institute, Washington DC, 1982.

Schlesinger, Arthur Snr., 'Our Presidents: A Rating by 74 Historians', *New York Times Magazine*, Sunday, July 29 1962, p. 12.

Schlesinger, Arthur Jnr., *The Coming of the New Deal*, Houghton Mifflin, Boston, 1959.

Schlesinger, Arthur Jnr., *The Imperial Presidency*, André Deutsch, London, 1974.

Schlesinger, Arthur Jnr., *The Cycles of American History*, André Deutsch, London, 1986.

Schlesinger, Arthur Jnr., 'Congress and the Making of American Foreign Policy', in Tugwell, Rexford and Cronin, Thomas (eds), *The Presidency Reappraised*, Praeger, New York, 1974.

Schlesinger, Arthur Jnr., 'Seeing Daylight', *Playboy*, March 1988.

Seidman, Harold and Gilmour, Robert, *Politics Position and Power*, Oxford University Press, New York, 1986.

Seymour, Charles (ed.), *The Intimate Papers of Colonel House*, Ernest Benn, London, 1926.

Shaw, Malcolm (ed.), *Roosevelt to Reagan: The Development of the Modern Presidency*, C. Hurst, London, 1987.

Shepsle, Kenneth, 'The Changing Textbook Congress', in Chubb, John and Peterson, Paul (eds), *Can the Government Govern?*, Brookings, Washington DC, 1989.

Shogan, Robert, *The Riddle of Power: Presidential Leadership From Truman to Bush*, Dutton, New York, 1991.

Silbey, Joel, Bogue, Allan and Flanigan, William (eds), *The History of American Electoral Behavior*, Princeton University Press, Princeton, 1978.

Smith, Hedrick, *The Power Game*, Random House, New York, 1988.

Solberg, Winton (ed.), *The Federal Convention and the Formation of the Union of the American States*, Bobbs Merrill, Indianapolis, 1958.

Sundquist, James, *The Decline and Resurgence of Congress*, Brookings, Washington DC, 1981.

Syrett, Harold, *Andrew Jackson*, Greenwood Press, Westport, Conn., 1953.

Tatalovich, Raymond and Daynes, Byron, *Presidential Power in the United States*, Brooks/Cole, Monterey, 1984.

Thomas, Benjamin, *Abraham Lincoln: A Biography*, Alfred Knopf, New York, 1952.

Tindall, George B. and Shi, David. E., *America*, (brief 2nd edition), W. W. Norton, New York, 1989.

Tower, John, 'Congress Versus The President: The Formulation and Implementation of American Foreign Policy', *Foreign Affairs*, Winter 1981/1982, pp. 239–46.

Tulis, Jeffrey, *The Rhetorical Presidency*, Princeton University Press, Princeton, 1987.

Van Doren, Carl, *The Great Rehearsal*, The Viking Press, New York, 1948.

Walker, Martin, 'Congress Confronts Bush on Gulf Policy', *The Guardian*, 9 September 1990, p. 8.

Walker, Martin, 'Elder Statesmen Gain Wealth of Experience', *The Guardian*, 16 March 1992, p. 7.

Walker, Martin and Tisdall, Simon, 'Bush Says Sorry for Tax U–turn', *The Guardian*, 16 March 1992, p. 1.

The Washington Version, AEI/BBC Television programme, 1991.

Wayne, Stephen, *The Legislative Presidency*, Harper and Row, New York, 1978.

Weinberger, Caspar, *Fighting For Peace*, Warner Books, New York, 1990.

Wildavsky, Aaron, 'President Reagan as Political Strategist', *Society*, May/June 1987, pp. 56–62.

Will, George F., 'The President's Own Worst Enemy', *The Washington Post*, National Weekly Edition, 3–9 February 1992.

Wilson, Woodrow, *Constitutional Government in the United States*, Columbia University Press, New York, 1908.

Wilson, Woodrow, *Congressional Government*, Houghton Mifflin, Boston, 1925, (first published 1885).

Woodward, Bob and Atkinson, Rick, 'Launching Operation Desert Shield', *The Washington Post*, National Weekly Edition, 3–9 September 1990, pp. 8–9.

Yang, John, 'Who is George Bush?', *The Washington Post*, National
Weekly Edition, 24 February–1 March 1991, pp. 9–10.
Yoffie, David, 'American Trade Policy: An Obsolete Bargain?', in Chubb,
John and Peterson, Paul (eds), *The New Directions in American Politics*,
Brookings, Washington DC, 1985.

Index